THE POLICE AND THE
UNDERPROTECTED CHILD

THE POLICE AND THE UNDERPROTECTED CHILD

By

C. J. FLAMMANG

Police Science Instructor, Fresno City College
Formerly, Detective Sergeant, Juvenile Bureau
Fresno County Sheriff's Department
Fresno, California
Former Chairman, Fresno County Battered Child Committee
Instructor, Delinquency Control Institute
Indiana University of Pennsylvania
Indiana, Pennsylvania

CHARLES C THOMAS • PUBLISHER
Springfield • Illinois • U.S.A.

Published and Distributed Throughout the World by

CHARLES C THOMAS • PUBLISHER

Bannerstone House

301-327 East Lawrence Avenue, Springfield, Illinois, U.S.A.

Natchez Plantation House

735 North Atlantic Boulevard, Fort Lauderdale, Florida, U.S.A.

©1970, *by* CHARLES C THOMAS • PUBLISHER

Library of Congress Catalog Card Number: 71-975 24

With THOMAS BOOKS careful attention is given to all details of
manufacturing and design. It is the Publisher's desire to present books that are
satisfactory as to their physical qualities and artistic possibilities and
appropriate for their particular use. THOMAS BOOKS will be true to those
laws of quality that assure a good name and good will.

Printed in the United States of America
RN-10

Dedicated with sincere affection to
Christie, Suzie, Mary, John, Anne, and Clare

PREFACE

LAW enforcement effort in the sensitive area of the juvenile tends toward the traditional role of the police in criminal matters. The identification and apprehension of a juvenile suspected of violating an ordinance or statute receives major emphasis within a police juvenile-control program. Consequently, efforts in the area of child protection have been left to the jurisdiction of other disciplines. The rightful role of the police in the performance of this function is now being raised. If the police are not performing this task, it is because of default rather than inability.

The proper protection of children is within the scope of the police mission. The fact that certain police officials, as well as those in other disciplines, do not give credence to this concept, is due to their short-sightedness. For many police personnel, any departure from the traditional views of police work is an intolerable inconsistancy. Child protection is not new to the police function. It is a part of the obligation of law enforcement to protect persons and property. As such, there is a need for understanding of this mission, and for the development of practices and procedures to insure its effective and efficient completion.

It is the intent of this book to give to the police the most current and sophisticated information relating to child protection. It is hoped that from the insight gained herein, law enforcement will bring to the community the leadership and service necessary to the adequate protection of children. The capability of performing this function is there. This book merely coordinates the information and knowledge that will cause the function to be operable.

Because of the nature of the problem of underprotected children, other disciplines, professions and agencies also have roles and functions to perform. It is a community challenge, touching many areas of society. It has been necessary in the writing of this book to consider various aspects of the numerous disciplines and professions involved. Not only has the role of law enforcement been presented, but also that of the entire judicial process, the medical profession, social welfare and education. The interrelationships that exist, or should exist, between the police and other practioners and agencies have been explored throughout the text. Methods of improving these relationships and attendant services have received attention. The total of society's answer to the problem of neglect and abuse has been addressed.

This has given rise to certain criticisms of the present system; yet these have been tempered with suggested modification and innovation directed toward the improvement of the community effort in child protection. The book is based on the philosophy that the underprotected child is a community problem, and as such requires a community response. The interrelationship of the police to this societal involvement is stressed throughout the text. The discerning reader is offered the opportunity to increase his knowledge and understanding of the problems of child protection, while at the same time gaining an overview of the system of social intervention. Not only police officers, but all practioners should benefit from the information related herein.

No author stands alone, but instead owes so many for what appears as his singular accomplishment. It is now that I take the opportunity to thank my colleagues and associates who have aided in providing me with the necessary experience and insight to undertake the writing of this book. As in any experience, one person stands out clearly. In this case, the man is William Ziering, M.D., former Chief of Pediatrics, Fresno General Hospital, Fresno, California; who unselfishly gave of himself for the benefit of the children of Fresno County. His leadership and devotion to an ideal sustained many of us through trying periods, and brought a community to life.

To Melvin A. Wilmirth, Sheriff-Coroner, Fresno County, my thanks for the opportunities extended during my tenure as a member of his department, and for his cooperation during the preparation of this text.

And, to my wife, Donna, for her support and encouragement, and the many hours spent preparing the manuscript for publication.

C. J. F.

CONTENTS

xi

THE POLICE AND THE
UNDERPROTECTED CHILD

Chapter I

INTRODUCTION

AFTER World War II, a new and complex area of law enforcement came as an outgrowth of a changing society, and with it came the advent of a specialized police unit charged with juvenile enforcement. Since that time the police have become, in many jurisdictions, sophisticated in the handling of juvenile matters. Juvenile specialization has many facets, most of them being in the area of the detection and apprehension of delinquents. But the police mission in juvenile work also includes the protection of the juvenile. This means protection from adults, other juveniles, himself and, in some cases, his own parents. It is the purpose of this book to deal with the problem of the underprotected child; the child suffering the effects of neglect or abuse. To do so, it will be necessary to provide some background in areas of police procedure that will tend to demonstrate not only police capabilities, but also deficiencies. For some readers, the findings outlined herein will be of significant value; and for others there will be found departures from traditional police orientation. In either case, it is hoped that the work will stimulate thought among police officials for better recognition of a problem, while at the same time causing new methods and practices to be implemented that will improve the ability of the police to deal with the underprotected child.

Police Decision-making

Before addressing oneself to the problem of the underprotected child, it is well to assess the general police practice of discretionary decision-making. In doing so, some of the inherent problems of the police role in the disposition of cases of child neglect and abuse may be brought into focus. Decision-making is the constant

3

partner of the police officer. No situation coming to the attention of the police can be handled without its utilization. All police action involves people in some manner. It is important for the police to make the right decision at the right time, to bring about the right purpose. The role of the police is united to decision-making; and this is borne out by police administrators who, while making personnel selections, look for the man who can properly exercise good common sense.

Nowhere in the field of law enforcement is decision-making more important than in the area of juvenile specialization. This is true for several reasons. First, it is well accepted that the best time for altering antisocial behavior patterns is during the early, formative years when the individual is still capable of and receptive to change. Second, the problems juveniles encounter are of such complex nature that easy decisions cannot be made. Third, the decisions that are made must be viewed from the perspective of possible long-range effects, not only in the life of the individual but also in the lives of many other people. Juvenile personnel are selected for specialization partly on the basis of demonstrated decision-making in other areas of police work, along with other considerations regarding qualifications. Once specialization in the juvenile unit begins for the new officer, he is closely supervised in the area of his decisional judgements. Of all police branches, juvenile enforcement can least afford an officer who is incapable of making solid decisions that can stand the test of time.

With decision-making being as important as it is to functional law enforcement, it is significant that few studies have been made into the basis of police discretionary power. This is an area where research is badly needed. It is needed not only for the academicians, who would seize the chance of discovery in an unknown area; but most importantly, research is needed for the benefit of the police themselves. Many departments have no established policy guidelines for the officers to follow in the application of police discretionary power. The officer is sent forth to analyze the situation, and only after he has taken action will the "second guessing" begin. This may be by the police supervisor or administrator, it may be done by the district attorney, the probation department, a social agency, the court, the public or any combination of these. The "hindsight" completed, the fact remains that the officer still has no guidelines to follow. If, as most professionals argue, such policies cannot be set down in writing because of the individuality of each case; then it must be conversely stated that the officer, when making a bad decision on an individual case cannot be expected to learn from his own experience, as the case is individual and unique. Thus, the officer shall never be faced with a similar case. The truth is, no policy is written because there is not enough knowledge and understanding of the basis of police decision-making at this time to form a foundation for the establishment of adequate policy.

If policy cannot be established adequately, or if it is not set down at all, then what can be expected of the police officer in the field? The most logical expectation is that the officer will function in the use of his discretionary power, but he will not know why. The most frequent answer when the question is asked, reverts back to the common-sense concept. This, in essence, indicates that the officer who acts in a prudent manner will somehow arrive at the proper decision. The same police officials, holding to this simplified version of the decision-making process, have themselves experienced years of dealing with numerous persons from the general public who continually demonstrate a formidable lack of common sense. This should indicate that common sense is a term applied to an intangible act of the intellect to describe the manner of reaching a conclusion without being able to give a factual explanation of the process. It would be as if one could present the correct answer to a mathematical problem without knowing the mechanics of arriving at the answer. If this were to occur, we would hold that the person had arrived at the answer by chance, or the person had guessed correctly, or perhaps the person was endowed with a special skill that remained unexplained. We would not attribute mathematical exactness or competence to that individual.

For the police to hold to the common-sense concept is to suggest that only the police receive persons, on a wholesale basis, into service who are capable of utilizing common sense to a high degree of skillful application. At the same time, our law is full of precedent decisions made to overrule improper use of police discretion that strongly document poor common sense on the part of the officer involved. Why, in this one isolated field of endeavor, common sense plays such an important role in the minds of those who lead the field, is a question in the face of the fact every other vocation is one in which decisions are based on factual and established knowledge and practice. The answer lies in the use of common sense to explain away the unknown. The unknown is the basis of police decisions that have not been adequately studied. Without knowing the basis of these decisions we cannot know their correctness. The basis of police decisions will not be fully understood until adequate research has been accomplished that will bring forth more than just correlative factors.

Research into Police Decision-making

It must be understood that the police are incapable of undertaking real research. The police do not have the time, the budgets or the trained personnel to perform this task. The police mission is one of service, and police research is directly limited to the efficient performance of that function. The needed research would have to be performed by practitioners of another discipline, most probably from the field of sociology. Here is the first obstacle: Gibbons(1) points out that such a study would involve research into the internal workings of the police, and, for the most part, that is a closed society. Furthermore, there has been a variance in philosophies between the police and the social scientist, restricting the latter's free access to the research scene. In order for this area of research to be fully covered, it will be necessary for barriers between the police and the researchers to be removed. For this to happen will necessitate concession on both sides, a unification of effort which will occur only when the police learn that they suffer from a void in the most important part of their functional existence.

For the purpose of this text, discussion will be limited to the use of police discretionary power in juvenile enforcement. The reader is cautioned to bear in mind that the research material is quite limited, and at the present time no fruitful study has been made regarding police decisions pursuant to the underprotected child. It is felt important to indicate the findings of studies relating to delinquency and police decisions, to point out the variations and subjectivity encountered in that area of juvenile work. From this base, the inference may be drawn that police decisions regarding the underprotected child are more unclear and hazy for a number of reasons. The police do not fully understand their role in relation to the underprotected child. The police role in such cases is not agreed upon by other disciplines. The police role varies greatly from community to community and state to state, depending on community services and state statutes. There are also many factors affecting the individual officer, such as training, interest, skill and knowledge. These will be covered in depth in subsequent chapters.

The National Research and Information Center of the National Council on Crime and Delinquency published a research work authored by Nathan Goldman(2) in 1963. This work intended to indicate the selection process for police referrals to juvenile court. The study was conducted in Allegheny County, Pennsylvania near the city of Pittsburg. Four communities were used for this study: a small mill town, an industrial community, a trade community and an upper-class residential area. Importantly, Goldman discovered wide variations in police juvenile enforcement from community to community. These variations appeared in the arrest rates, ranging from 12.4 to 49.7 arrests per thousand population aged ten to seventeen. The average rate of arrest in the four communities was 32.6 per thousand. These arrest-rate variations were found to be based mainly on the arrests for minor offenses, with arrests made for serious offenses remaining fairly constant. In those communities where serious offenses occurred, both adult and juvenile, the minor offenses were handled unofficially with limited arrests. In the upper-class residential area where serious offenses were less frequent, the minor acts resulted in more police action. This variance stemmed from two sources. First, police activity in areas of serious offenses, of necessity, was expended on those offenses; and secondly, the community concept of the minor offense varied from area to area, the police acting in accordance with the prevailing outlook of the particular community.

It was further found that not all children contacted by the police are recorded as a contact; only about half of those encountered reach the police station, the remainder being released in the field to the parents, or otherwise dismissed unofficially.

A significant finding indicates that the police decision to process is based in part on the seriousness of the offense. Goldman found that the more serious offenders were referred to court. Within the communities studied, an average of 80.2 percent were referred to court for serious acts as compared to a minor offense referral average of 20.3 percent. This placed an importance on the seriousness of the offense as a factor in police decision making. This same factor will influence the officer's decision in the field at the point of contact. The seriousness of the offense not only affects the court referral rate, but also the arrest rate.

It may easily be argued that this approach is correct; however, the seriousness of the offense is based on several factors. Obviously, it is based on statute; and if this were the only basis for knowing when an act is serious, then the decision based on this factor would have some reliability. But seriousness may also be established, as indicated in the study, through community reaction to otherwise lesser offenses; at which time the seriousness of the offense has immediately become a subjective criterion. Also, what is known to be a technical violation of a severe statute may in its reality be a minor offense. As an example, in California burglary is committed whenever a person enters a building with the intent to commit a felony or grand or petty theft (larceny). By statute, burglary is a serious crime. However, if the youth enters his friend's house and removes a toy or some small amount of money from the friend's bank, should this be considered a burglary and a serious offense? The question at this point becomes academic, and the arguments pro and con will all have validity. It would be difficult to find officers agreeing in entirety in such a situation, though few would do more than disagree. In other words, the disagreement might exist, but not as to the disposition of the matter even though such opinion differed greatly. The reason for the willingness to understand the disposition would result from the seeming validity of the arguments that could be advanced to support almost any course chosen. In this example is found a police decision based on the seriousness of the offense, but the decision has been arrived at by subjective judgement, not statutory definition. The experience of the officer may also affect this subjective appraisal regarding the seriousness of the offense. In the example, an officer who has worked many check cases in the past may not view this offense as a true burglary, and, in fact, might handle the case as a petty theft. At the same time, a burglary investigation background may cause the officer to view all burglars as serious offenders. To further confuse the situation, depending upon the officer, the backgrounds described may tend to reverse the outcome of the decision relating to the seriousness involved. It is evident that seriousness of offense as a criterion for police action may be a matter of highly personal and subjective judgement on the part of the officer.

The opinion of the officer's supervisor or the policy of the department in relation to selective enforcement may have the most important influence on the officer's decision as to seriousness. For these reasons, seriousness of offense cannot be assigned too much importance in decision making. Yet Goldman's study, as well as other studies, indicates this to be one of the strongest reasons for police action.

Another factor found by Goldman to affect the police in juvenile enforcement relates to the officer's concept of the family situation. This seems very true in cases where there is depravity on the part of the mother, or where the parents are uncommitted or uncooperative. In these encounters, the police often feel compelled to take official action by means of court or other agency referral. Keeping in mind that no officer has the opportunity for an extensive exposure to the family situation, this criterion again falls readily into the subjective judgment classification. It may be based on the officer's attitudes developed in early childhood, or on those developed from his professional experience. In any case, his judgement of the family may differ widely from the judgment of another officer on that or another occasion.

The attitude and demeanor of the juvenile is another highly important element in the police decision to take action. A polite, well-mannered youth who appears sincere is less likely to be exposed to the full extent of police action; while the youth who is defiant, belligerent or otherwise displays negative aggression may find himself in court on a charge which is lesser in nature than that committed by the more polite youth. Appearance is a part of this observation by the officer, and the fad type clothing, the characteristic swagger and expression held to be that of the "hood" may lead to aggressive enforcement. This has been found to be a judgment based on a steryotyped impression of the delinquent on the part of the officer. The utilization of this criterion as a basis of police discretionary power tends quite rapidly to become subjective. This subjectivity is further complicated by the officer's own reaction to the defiance he has encountered. This becomes a direct assault on the authority of the officer and his department, as well as a lack of personal respect. Accordingly, during the confrontation the attitude and demeanor of the youth will become an important factor upon which the officer will make his decision.

Similarly, the findings of Piliavin and Briar,(3) resulting from their study of police contacts with juveniles in a large California city, also indicated the police use of discretionary power in dealing with juveniles. They state, "the disposition decisions made by police officers have potentially profound consequences for apprehended juveniles"(3). They proceed to discuss role expectation leading to criminal careers, a recognized concept in dealing with delinquency and seen as having an influence on deviant behavior through reinforcement; and the police identification of the individual as a delinquent serving as a cohesive factor in starting the delinquent career(4). These authorities see the police decision as an important factor in the control and prevention of delinquency and recognize the need for further empirical study in this area.

Piliavin and Briar found two significant criteria utilized by the police in deciding whether to take official or unofficial action. These were: the record of prior offenses, and the attitude and demeanor of the youth. There were other bases for action, but these were the strongest indicators to the officers observed and interviewed during the course of the nine month study. Beyond the individual officer, it was found that the department tended to sanction the discretionary use of police power. Officers were found to hold broad alternatives regarding police action in juvenile matters. These findings are consistant with the author's experience as a juvenile officer. Police action may take the form of immediate release, or it can run the scale of action to the point of incarceration, with several alternate actions in between. In this respect the police depart from traditional police methods and, in effect, remove their attention from the offense itself, to an offender-oriented "what's best for the juvenile?"(3)

When looking at the reliability of the record of prior offenses, it may appear that the official record of a youth's wrongdoing would be a valid indicator. This is not so simple. The variations between the different communities will affect the rate of arrest, as found by Goldman. This means that an offender whose record is lengthy may have been unfortunate enough to have resided in a community where police action toward juveniles was aggressive. In another community, the subject's actions may have warranted police warnings and reprimands, or possibly may have been viewed as boyish pranks and not reported to the police. Another youth, with a less serious appearing record, may have been handled many times by the police in an unofficial capacity before the first action was taken on an official basis. In the event that the decision-making process leading to arrest, which in turn causes the formation of a record, is affected by the officer's recognition of the seriousness of the offense, the official record may be but a reflection of police subjectivity. The record is not, per se, a reliable measurement in juvenile matters. This is due to the sanctioned use of discretionary power in police decision-making, leading to the arrest of the juvenile and, in turn, to the initiation of the record.

It is interesting to note the correlation between the findings of the two studies that have been presented. First, there is a relationship between basing decisions on the seriousness of the offense and the youth's prior record, as the latter tends to reflect the officer's judgment of whether a situation was serious or not. Further, it is generally held that a majority of the offenses are minor. Therefore, the record is a manner by which the officer may discover the seriousness of the youth's past activities. Second, both studies revealed the attitude and demeanor of the subject to be a strong influence on the officer's decision. As previously pointed out, this calls for a subjective interpretation.

Add to these factors the sanction of the department for the use of discretion in decision-making, and what appears to be a solid procedure for arriving at a course of action quickly degenerates into a personal opinion from which the officer makes a decision. This decision can be based on only two explainable factors. One, the decision was based on the officer's experience; and the other, the decision was based on the officer's observation of the situation. In the event the officer is properly experienced in relation to both quantity and quality, there may be some credence given this factor. On the other hand, in the area of supervision and administration, law enforcement has discovered too often that experience is merely one or two years of poor police methods multiplied many times. Most police officers now judge experience in relation to where it was gained and to what extent it was varied and successful. From these facts, there is some question as to the reliability of experience as a measurement of the officer's competence in making anything but a subjective judgement. It follows that the officer can only be as observant as his experience, training and skill. If the officer is one whose experience is in doubt, his objective observation prior to a decision must also be in doubt. In the face of this evidence, police agencies continue to sanction the individual's discretionary actions with little or no review. In the area of juvenile enforcement, this review would most often be handled by the commander of the juvenile unit, as too few police administrators have an actual grasp of the purpose and function of juvenile enforcement.

The foregoing discussion has been related to the police and delinquency. The primary studies of the police decision-making process in the performance of that mission have been presented. How does this relate to the underprotected child? First, there have been no worthwhile studies of the basis of the police decision in the area of child neglect or abuse. The concentration of effort has been toward delinquency. This indicates the lack of attention given to the area of the underprotected child, not only by the police, but by other agencies and disciplines. If these types of cases were included in the studies, they have been lumped into the total context, and the ramifications of any findings have been lost. If no attention has been given this area of enforcement, it may point to a lack of recognition of the existence of a problem in this respect. In any event, the facts are not there. No adequate study has been performed. Notwithstanding, the police are daily faced with situations involving severely underprotected children. Upon what should their decisions be based? There is strong evidence obtained through observation of police in action that officers do not know on what to base their decisions. This text will attempt to set forth guides to police decision-making in cases of neglect or abuse, but first it will be necessary to define the underprotected child.

The Underprotected Child Defined

Much of our attention has been given to the problems arising from the situation of overprotection(5). This is the child who has everything done for him by usually sincere parents who are often acting without the full realization of the consequences of the action. This child is placed in a position where the development of the personality is retarded due to the enveloping cocoon of protection. While there are cases where this protection is an attempt to conceal their own parental rejection of an unwanted child, more often it is the result of parental possessiveness and anxiety toward the child. Persons coming in contact with such situations easily recognize the parental attitude and can foresee future adjustment problems on the part of the child. Many delinquent careers have found their origin in this approach to child rearing.

Closely related to overprotection, and often mistaken for it, is the problem of overindulgence(5). This is the child the police find quite difficult to deal with. It is the child who has been given everything, usually getting these items at an earlier age than other children. This child's personality traits usually include aggression, negative reactions and infantile behavior(6).

The problem under discussion in this text is that of the underprotected child. This child is the center of a whole segment of police juvenile enforcement, and the core of a social phenomenon just now being studied and concerning which we woefully lack adequate data. It encompasses both the neglected child and the abused child. The term "underprotected" is utilized to denote that child who lacks the proper protection to insure his safety, health and well-being while in the confines of his home and under the care and supervision of his parent or guardian. This term denotes lack of a physical as well as an emotional state of safety. It alludes to cognizance on the part of the child that he is not receiving consistency of love and affection from his family environment and that the supervising parent is not seeing to his needs, withholding love either by means of rejection or displeasure.

One may be quick to realize that many children are emotionally underprotected. While this may be a social concern, the physical protection of the child must be accomplished first to insure his survival to the age of full emotional development. What we are concerned with is the failure of the social community to adequately protect a child who is neglected, abused or otherwise mistreated in his own home. It must become a point of social recognition and concern to provide for the protection of endangered children.

Society's Right of Intervention

This protection suggests intervention in the parent-child relationship by society in some manner. Does society have a right to come between a parent and his child, or does the parent have an absolute right to the custody and control of a child? We know from civil legal actions that parents do not have such an absolute authority, and in many instances the courts have intervened in the lives of the children and their relationship with parents. But these are civil actions and, as such, are more of a contest between parents in which the court is acting as an arbiter of a dispute, rather than the court or some other agency intervening in the family unit without the request of one or more of the parties concerned. This is not the intervention of which we speak. Does society have the right to arbitrarily initiate an action that may end in the severance of parent and child? If so, who should have the power to make that decision? Where should the power come from? All of these questions must be answered before proceeding into the area of the problem itself.

The parental right to custody of the legitimate offspring was well entranched in common law(7). No law was needed to establish this right. It was inherent to parenthood. As late as the nineteenth century in England, the father was granted close to absolute custodial rights over his child. In the United States it was 1874 before the state court ruled to protect a child(8). In this case, a church worker coming upon a situation deemed to be child maltreatment appealed to the police and the district attorney of New York City but found the appeals useless. There appeared to be no statute or ordinance covering such a situation. The only laws that could be quoted existed in reference to the care and treatment of animals. The worker, in desperation, appealed to the Society for the Prevention of Cruelty to Animals. The action of this organization led to a court decision resulting in the subsequent removal of the child from the home environment and the abusing parents(8).

With the advent of the concept of *parens patriae,* it was held in English law that the king was the father of his country or, better stated, the father of all. As such, the king had the right, through his governmental administration, to intervene in the lives of the subjects. This principle was brought to America and became incorporated in early American common law where it developed the form of *in loco parentis,* wherein the state may stand in the place of the parent. In other words, in the development of our society there has been a recognition of the need for the state to act for the well-being of the citizenry *in toto,* and this at times has caused the state to intervene in the lives of some of the citizens. An example of *parens patriae* experienced by most of us is the right of the state to legislate compulsory school attendance. This is because the state has the right to demand that all persons who are capable receive educational benefits within the state's recognition of this need for productive citizenship and the perpetuation of the state, the latter being a right of the state also. The fact that the school official has control over the actions and behavior of the students and may · demand obedience to reasonable rules and regulations places the official in the position of acting in the place of the parent during the period that the child is in the school. This is a means of the state exercising the principle of *in loco parentis.*

Both concepts, *parens patriae* and *in loco parentis,* have become the basis of the juvenile court law as it now exists throughout the country. It was on the basis of the state's right to intervene in the lives of its citizens to insure the welfare of the state that the first juvenile court law was established in Illinois in 1899. In the application of that law, the concept *in loco parentis* has been consistently applied by the courts in acting in behalf of the child. This has been true in both dependent child and delinquency cases. Anytime the juvenile court adjudicates a juvenile to be a ward of the court, the court acts *in loco parentis.* Our juvenile court system has provided for society to intervene in the parent-child relationship, including at least a temporary severence of that relationship. At the present time, all states have a juvenile court law, and the two principles heretofor discussed are the foundation of the right of the court to intervene on the part of the state or society. In so doing, the court may utilize any assistance or agencies that have been provided by law. The court may take any action provided by law that will tend to remedy or alleviate the present situation for the betterment of the child or his condition. Therefore, the power of the court comes to the court from the constitution of the state and through legislative enactment. It is the responsibility of the court to carry out the intent of the legislature in accordance with the constitution. To what extent the court carries out these functions is dependent upon numerous factors.

It must be recognized that society not only has the right to intervene in the lives of others for the protection of children, but it has the duty and obligation to offer protection. It is not enough to have laws which give protection. It is just as important to provide the means of implementing the laws in order to insure the protection of all the children of the state when needed. This means that the state must provide adequate laws; competent courts; social agencies with the potential of intensive casework to strengthen the family unit; supportive services such as health, education, and welfare to produce a reduction of incidence of neglect and abuse; fully armed mental health programs and counseling services; and the means and methods by which the identification of such cases may readily be accomplished. This requires a full-scale societal approach to a problem. It means the reexamination of existing procedures; the evaluation of goals and objectives; unified planning; the establishment of policies and procedures understood and agreed upon by all concerned; a departure from unsatisfactory panaceas; and the direction of the efforts of society toward rational solutions.

References

1. Gibbons, Don C.: Society, Crime and Criminal Careers — An Introduction to Criminology. Englewood Cliffs, Prentice-Hall, 1968, p. 48.
2. Goldman, Nathan: The Differential Selection of Juvenile Offenders for Court Appearance. New York, Nat. Council Crime Delinq., 1963, pp. 125-132.
3. Piliavin, Irwing, and Briar Scott: Police Encounters With Juveniles, Survey Research Center and Center for the Study of Law and Society, Berkeley, U. of Calif., 1964, pp. 1-5.
4. Becker, Howard S.: Outsiders: Studies in the Sociology of Deviance. New York, Macmillan, 1963, Chap. I and II.
5. Kaplan, Louis: Foundations of Human Behavior. New York, Harper, 1965, pp. 79-82.
6. Schmideberg, M.: Tolerance in upbringing and its abuses. Int J Soc Psychiat, 5:123-130, 1959.
7. Armstrong, Barbara: California Family Law. San Francisco, Bancroft, 1954, Vol. II, p. 953.
8. Fontana, Vincent J.: The Maltreated Child. Springfield, Thomas, 1964, p. 8.

Chapter II

THE NEGLECTED CHILD

THE problem of neglect is one of much larger proportions than is generally believed. The neglected comprise the largest number of children being victimized than any offense. Neglect is seen daily by many representatives of various agencies and governmental institutions, but often no action is forthcoming, because recognition does not equal action. Many of those coming in contact with neglect cases attempt to explain away their existence, while others are unfamiliar with any method of remedy. This latter is not a failure of the individual to respond, but a failure of the community and of society to establish practical methodology for the proper and expedient handling of such cases. Many times, professionals in various fields are concerned, but recognize that they have nowhere to go, nowhere to turn. It is as if time had transported them back to 1874 in New York City, and they were the church worker seeking assistance with a sordid social situation. This confusion, this ignorance, is the fault of a society that has too long closed its eyes to the events about it; the sores on its own thick skin.

One of the first groups to come into contact with neglect on a large scale were the police. Today, no police officer can work for long on any assignment without coming into contact with such a case. For the majority of these officers, the procedures are as unknown, as confused, as hidden or as foreign as they are to workers from other disciplines. The difference is that the police have nowhere to go. They must either face the situation and do the best they can, or leave; and in so doing, know that a child or ten children have been left in jeopardy. In many instances of neglect, the police cannot leave without action being taken; such as in a situation where children have been left unattended at night for long hours. In these cases the police must act, sometimes without proper understanding of what they are attempting to accomplish.

The Problem

What is a neglected child? Any child who has willfully been placed by any person having care, custody and control of said minor, in a position where the child's health, safety or general welfare is endangered is a neglected child. Immediately we can visualize numerous situations where the position of the child might involve some risk, but in which it would be difficult to assume the child were being neglected. The foregoing definition is merely a guideline to a social problem that has many ramifications and which is seen in many different disguises. The variation in the manifestations of neglect are part of the complexities with which it is necessary to cope. By definition, one could visualize a father entering his young son in a baseball league where the boy will play catcher. At that point a critic could state that the father willfully placed his son in a position where the youth's safety was endangered. This is not the type of risk with which we are concerned. A quote from the California Report of the Assembly Interim Committee on Social Welfare will tend to clarify risk: "Living requires some exposure to risks. The more serious the risk, the longer and more repeatedly the child is exposed to it, the greater the neglect"(1). We are dealing with situations involving serious danger existing within the child's environment and from which the child is not capable of retreating. We are concerned with time, and as we continue it will be discovered how crucial time is in neglect situations. We are faced with parents or guardians who are willfully allowing certain conditions to continue to exist in the face of warnings and admonishments from other persons, both private citizens and public agency representatives. To adequately encounter such situations it is necessary to have a good conception of what neglect is, how it appears and what remedies are available.

Neglect is the lot of the underprotected child. It tends to be concentrated within the lower socioeconomic group, but it is by no means restricted to that group. There is a considerable amount of neglect occurring in the upper-lower and lower-middle class;

however, because of family and social pressure, the higher into the class strata, the less the length of time the neglect will exist without some action. This action may be private or personal, or within the larger sphere of relatives and the influences they exert. It may be remedied by means of business or social pressure. There are occasions when it is changed by the violent dissection of the marriage through separation and divorce. In the higher income groupings, neglect cannot long survive, for the pressures, as mentioned, will be brought to bear; and if these pressures fail to bring about change and the situation continues, someone will report it to a public agency.

In the higher income group, neglect stands out in contrast to the surrounding environment. The undernourished child appears more undernourished at a school when his is the only pale, thin face in a room full of plenty. Dirty and soiled clothing will be in stark contrast to bright and colorful clothes on a playground. Requests for free lunches are few in such schools, and continual absence will result in home visits at a more rapid rate. This is because the neglected child here is the unusual, and agencies such as the schools respond more quickly to the unusual.

The neighbor who is maintaining his yard and property through hired service will not condone the house next door entering a state of disrepute. This will reflect badly upon his home, so the neighbor complains about the uncut lawn, the bottles, papers and mixture of junk and garbage collecting on the property. He may contact the offenders himself or go among the other neighbors and discuss action. He may find assistance through a public-figure contact or he may resort to calling in the authorities. The point is that action will occur, because this area of the community is attuned to better-kept property and better-kept children.

In the lower-income groups the opposite is true. In any large city ghetto, it would be difficult to assess neglect from the outside appearance of a home. No classroom would be without its pale, thin and listless children. Few clothes would be so new and bright as to cause the older, more worn clothing to appear out of place. The fact of absences from school becomes a worry because of the average daily attendance requirement; but, in itself, the absence list becomes a routine. Many children are at home during much of the winter months for many reasons; including babysitting while a parent is ill, or the lack of proper clothing to brave the elements. Neighbors come and go, and often a family lives in semi or complete isolation in a crowded world. Many do not wish to get involved and others are unconcerned, numbed by years of living an existence. Consequently, many cases of neglect can bloom in this bed of family disorientation, and these cases can exist for long periods of time partially unnoticed. Pertinent to these inherent facts of ghetto or lower-income life is the influx of public agencies into such an area. It is in the lower class that the work must be done, and there the need, all types of need, is greatest. There are more welfare clients, more health and sanitation problems, more bill collections and more police action than in any other area. The lower-class neighborhood is invaded daily by case workers, parole officers, probation officers, police, health workers, utilities, special school personnel and numerous other public and private representatives. Because of this, eventually neglect will be uncovered and reported. This is not to say that the relatives and other private persons in the area never make a report of such activity, for they do; but in many instances only after a situation has existed for a considerable time.

The situation in the lower middle-class presents a greater problem of identification. Here there is isolation, especially in the larger communities where migration is still a part of the culture, if it is no more than moving about in the same community. There is a quasi-suspicion of each other existing in such areas. It is not often recognized, but it rises to the surface on occasions wherein public apathy is displayed; this tends to reduce the reporting of neglect in these areas. The schools are a cross section of lower and middle-class children; and teachers often hate to chance hurting the feelings of a sensitive child in order to pursue questions of a personal nature relating to the child's family and home environment. It is quite easy to be mistaken in judging outward appearances. Official public and private ventures into such areas produce quick contacts and often good results. These visits do not lessen the number of persons entering the area each day, but they do lessen the amount of actual contact each has with the residents; this in turn reduces opportunity for identification. The partially kept yard is not unusual, nor is the house that needs painting or the fence that is falling over. At the same time, the well-kept property is not without its presence, and so the area is a combination of both the lower and middle class. For the most part, they tend to live with each other, keeping faith with an unwritten code to "mind my own business." Often, in these hybrid communities, relatives are the reporters. When this occurs it is usually in desparation, after some time and effort has been expended at attempting to influence a change.

Types of Neglect

Neglect can be classified as moral, civil or criminal(2). Police officers and other public employees are constantly contacted regarding all three. For the police, the only one in which they can be of service is in the area of criminal neglect. There are other public agencies and services that may be able to assist in situations falling under the first two classes. This determination would have to be made in keeping with the policies and procedures of each agency. It should be noted at this time that the police should be familiar with all services that are rendered within their jurisdiction. Without this knowledge, the police cannot perform one of the most important functions of juvenile enforcement, the act of referral. More will be covered later on this subject as it relates to the underprotected child.

By "moral neglect" is meant those situations where the child is apparently being wronged, but in which no regulatory rule or law exists to alleviate what may be a problem. This is a value-judgment situation that leaves room for doubt as to the validity of the claim. It often refers back to the upbringing of and the values held by the complainant. In most moral neglect problems no certain agreement can be arrived at; for as a value judgment, the wrong deed is actually the opinion of another about a value held by the parent or custodian of the child. Some examples of moral neglect follow:

1. A neighbor complains because a father is using foul language in the presence of the children.

   On the face it appears a bad situation, but investigation will often reveal that the parent is in all ways but this, a good or exceptional parent. This may be the person's only fault. It may turn out to be nothing more than an evesdropping into the family fight that is bound to occur. An overly self-righteous neighbor may see this as a very severe case of neglect.

2. A grandparent complains that the grandchildren are being forced to drink skim milk, and everyone knows that a certain other type is necessary for children.

   Such actions on the part of the child's parents may be very disturbing to grandparents who have their own set ideas regarding nutrition, and the grandparents may even be right. However, many children have been raised successfully on such a beverage. To deal with this as a police neglect problem would be erroneous, but it may remain neglect in a moral sense.

3. A relative states that the children always went to Sunday school with them; but now that the parents have begun fishing, the children are accompanying them on Sundays for fishing excursions.

   There is no doubt of the need for religious education and exposure. Studies have indicated a correlation between the lack of religious involvement and delinquency(3,4,5). It is impossible to assume that a situation as stated in this example would be of detrimental harm to the children. Certainly, if there were no interference with church attendance the complaint would not have originated. Few people would condemn parents who were involved with their children in such a recreational activity. The act is not neglect, but the question of which is the most important of the two activities is a value judgment. This may be a case of moral neglect, but a report of such to the police would result in little or no action. Probably, the most productive move would be the referral of such a problem to the clergyman involved.

4. A complaint is made of a mother allowing her young child to go into the deep end of the family swimming pool.

   This complaint may require some police follow-up merely to determine if the act goes beyond moral neglect. It may well be that no neglect is involved at all. Many persons having private pools find that little children take to the water like tadpoles. A determination should be made of the safety precautions that have been taken, the age of the child, the child's competency in the water and the swimming ability and experience of the parent. Most of this information could be gleaned without a contact at the family home, with much of it from the complainant.

5. There is a complaint regarding the way the parent allows the

children to play outside in the various elements without proper clothing.

This type of problem usually calls for a value judgment, and the complaint often follows such a judgment. For the healthy, normal child who is actively engaged in outdoor activity without an undue length of exposure, the weather has little ill effect. In fact, the exposure of the body in such cases may be the best foundation for a future healthy life of outdoor activity during the adult years.

There are many examples of moral neglect. Each have several things in common. First, the activity, per se, is seldom one of an antisocial nature; and, usually, when viewed in an isolated manner, no wrong can be attached to it. Secondly, the complainants are often upset because of the failure to be able to force their views upon the parent. These people are rigid personalities with strict standards and values that may not be universally accepted. Many times they are anxious personalities, especially in relation to children. Most have very definite thoughts on child rearing and become easily upset when they see a variation from what they hold to be correct. Third, the complaining person is most often voicing his value judgment regarding an observed situation. While there is nothing immoral about a value judgment, and while it may, in reality, be more correct than the values held by the parents, a value judgment is little more than a subjective analysis of a situation. It does not set standards of conduct and does not measure such standards; therefore it cannot be used as the criteria for social intervention in a parent-child relationship, as it does not represent the values of the society, but, rather, is representative of the values of the reporting individual.

As a further example of moral neglect situations, the author had occasion several years back to be approached by two sets of grandparents, both the maternal and paternal. They were very upset and were on the verge of demanding police action. Their children had been married about seven years previous to this contact. From that union there were two children, a boy and a girl. The grandparents were caucasions of southern heritage, and both of their children had been born and raised in the south. About two years before the contact, the parents of the grandchildren had divorced. Subsequent to that action, the mother, who had custody of the children, began dating a Negro man. On the occasion of the contact, the mother had just married this man. The grandparents wanted action to remove the children from the mother and her new husband's custody. In the state in which this occurred, there were no laws forbidding such a union, and such laws have since been declared unconstitutional by the United States Supreme Court. As the mother was an adult, and the only complaint the grandparents could allege regarding the care of the children was racially oriented, there was no cause for a police action. These grandparents were sincere. They were faced with a situation that was against their value system, and had reacted by making the value judgment which led to their contacting the police. The interesting part of this case was the fact these grandparents had entered the office with the full expectation that the officer would share their values. When this did not occur, they were quite upset. There may or may not be moral neglect in such a situation, but it remains that such an evaluation is a value judgment and it is quite beyond the scope of the police to place any limitations on the legally executed actions of the members of the community.

Many cases of civil neglect are referred to the police. Civil neglect constitutes activity of such a nature as to give rise to a civil court action being brought by a party to remove a child from the custody of a second party. In most of these situations, the matter is the aftermath of a separation or divorce action. In these cases, quite often there are serious residues of hostility on the part of one or both parties. This hostility is, many times, passed on to become an emotional part of grandparents and other relatives. In most jurisdictions, the mother is awarded custody at the time of the action, unless the father can show in court a serious cause why such custody should not be granted. People are subject to change, and as this is a growth process of life and cannot be avoided, numerous problems continue to occur between the two parties subsequent to the court action. In many instances the children become pawns to be moved in accordance with the desire to hurt or carry out one parent's hostility toward the other. In doing so, situations are created that cause various reactions. Some of these include the father's refusal to support "that woman," while he maintains he would not mind supporting the children if he knew they would benefit from the payments. The mother may seek to severly restrict the father's visitation rights. This, in turn, causes him to take such action that will allow his visitation. All of this in order to be handled in court, requires continued payment for professional service to attorneys; and the crowded court calendars tend to keep this subsequent court action slowed to a time-consuming pace. The usual reactive behavior in many of these family problems, is to attempt to circumvent the legal process. This is done because of frustration, lack of money and impatience with the court process.

The father, if pressured to make adequate support payments, will attempt to retaliate by bringing various complaints regarding the incompetence or depravity of the mother to the attention of the police. Such complaints range from listing accounts of moral neglect to relating various actions of the mother only. As an example, the mother may have a boyfriend. They hire a capable babysitter or leave the children with the maternal grandparents or other relatives and leave town or just go to a motel. The father views this as child neglect. In a civil sense it may be neglect, in a moral sense it may be neglect, but it does not justify a police action. This is because the actions of any adult out of the view of the children cannot harm the safety, health or welfare of the children in any tangible way. This situation cannot even constitute contributing to the delinquency of a minor. Furthermore, if the child were very young, such as an infant, and this activity occurred in the home, the cohabitation would not constitute neglect in the criminal sense. It may not be an acceptable situation, but it is not criminal neglect; rather, it is civil neglect. In numerous situations of this type the complainant is requesting of the police an action that should be taken by a private investigation agency, or the investigator employed by a private attorney to gather such evidence for a civil court custody suit.

Criminal neglect is the type of neglect to be fully considered in this text. It is a problem that stems from the principle that the biological fact of conception and birth causation does not bring about adequate parenthood. With all the childless couples, it is paradoxical that such should be the case. The fact is, many children are born each year into home environments that offer little love and affection, and only minor amounts of care and supervision. These children are placed in surroundings from which they have no escape. They are raised to the age of puberty with little knowledge of the fact that their environment is improper. They know no other way of life, until age takes them further beyond the confines of the home and maturity allows them a better judgment of what standards do prevail. This childhood ignorance serves in two opposite ways. First, because the child has no notion of what a proper home should be, he will hesitate to complain about some of the discomforts faced daily. This tends to prolong a neglect case for years beyond the date of entering school. This is important to students of this problem, for the school represents the first true break from the confines of the home. It further represents a public agency that can be of help in alleviating the sufferings of the child. But very often the child enters school and progresses through several years of class work before becoming willing to engage in a criticism of the family situation. By this time, many neglecting parents will have already coached the child in a number of ways in order to overcome his impulse to seek outside assistance.

All children need love. All are eager to be loved and to respond to a love situation. Long before entering school the child has recognized the parental image, even if it is not fulfilling and is somewhat confused in the mind of the child. There is a notion that this person is an important being in the life of the child. The child does not wish to conceive of the parent as inadequate. The child desires to hold the parent in the same esteem as other children do. If the parent is not performing the tasks of parenthood, the child will begin feeling a rejection. In order to overcome the rejection of the parent at this early age, the child will often attempt to please the parent more. At the same time, most neglecting parents are defensive regarding their shortcomings. These factors combine to place the child in a position of being readily susceptible to parental conditioning.

Consequently, these children will often excuse the actions of the parent, because the parent has told them, "Mommie doesn't feel well." This puts the child in the position of knowing that the parent is ill and cannot perform. What person, not only child, would not put up with a few discomforts in the face of such a fact? Mother being in bed every morning is satisfactorily explained. The child is helping the parent when the child seeks out the only breakfast in the house, which may be vermin-ridden cereal or grain.

The parent tells the child "We're poor," or "We don't have the money"; and again the child becomes a helper to the parent by not asking or demanding items of comfort and, often, items of necessity.

Warnings by the parents to the effect that "They will take you away and put you in a home," are such a frightening reality to an already insecure child that it becomes easy for the child to lie in an attempt to deceive others regarding proper feeding in the home, the whereabouts of the parents when the child is left alone, cleanliness and other manisfestations of neglect.

These factors are brought dramatically to light in the number of neglect cases reported by other children who have already lived through the situation and are now out of the home. Police receive numerous contacts from such adult or near adult children, voicing their concern about the care of the younger siblings by the parents. Many times these older children offer homes for the younger brothers and sisters. These are drastic actions for an offspring to take against the parents, but the actions are sincere and help is requested only after long periods of soul searching. In the final analysis, the older child must take the position of the protector of the younger from the continuance of a home environment that has already taken its toll on the life of the older child.

The second and opposite effect of this childhood ignorance can be summed up in the principle of "protection through innocence." The child who knows no other life suffers less, emotionally and mentally, at an early age than a child who has a standard of comparison. It is not unusual for the ignorant child to withstand an odor offensive to others. This odor has permeated the child's life since or near birth. The child finally becomes accustomed to it, just as those persons living for years in highly industrialized neighborhoods become accustomed to the odors of industry. Where an outsider would have difficulty entering the home, the child of that home will eat, sleep and play there with an obvious unconcern for the surroundings. This is also true of the filthy bed that is shared with the other siblings — the bed that seldom, if ever, has been endowed with a sheet or other bedding. It is true of the cold, leftover beans in a grease-hardened frying pan in the middle of a table, still holding the dishes from last Sunday's attempt at feeding. The roaches on, about or in the refrigerator are of no more consequence than the lice found on the bodies of the primitives and picked off by other tribesmen and eaten. There is no one to caution the two year old about the use of the butcher knife on the floor to slice a piece of stale bologna, which is rotting because it was never placed into the refrigerator. Raw potatoes are as edible as the leftover fired potatoes still in the pan. The flies are only disturbed long enough to move the food from the drain, table or floor to the mouth. The glass on the floor is not a concern as long as it is bypassed while walking about, and the toilet has not flushed properly for a long time. A child can always find the baby's bottle full of curdled milk somewhere near the baby, unless this infant is walking. At that point the hunt may take a little longer, but once the bottle is located, almost any child older than the baby can fill it with milk and provide this need to the infant. These are the sights and smells of the neglect home; a disoriented family existance of dimly lighted rooms, spoiling food, vermin, broken glass, filthy clothes and that ever present odor that can be best described as "cabbage boiled in urine." The child who has never seen anything else — has never smelled the antiseptic smell of a clean bathroom, gazed upon a freshly made bed with sheets just brought in from an open air line and sat at a table with properly prepared food — cannot be blamed for failure to recognize the lack of a home. This, in part, answers the social worker's contention that no matter what the home conditions, these are still the parents; and the bond that exists between parent and child is to be broken only in severe circumstances. It is well known that children will play at a city dump if allowed to do so, and enjoy every minute of the adventure.

Classification of Neglect Causation

The neglect encountered by the police may be classified as to cause under four general catagories(2). There are numerous factors that may be found in each classification to account for the neglect, but each factor isolated could be placed under one of the classes presented. These classifications are: the overwhelmed parent, the incompetent parent, the unconcerned parent and severe family disorientation. Each case of neglect will fit under one or more of these cause classifications. Quite often there is an overlapping interrelationship of cause that may be distinguished by the discerning observer. The more complex the design, the more serious the neglect and the more difficult the action. In the less complex cases, less severe action will bring about desired results. One must be kept ever mindful that neglect is a family situation; and because it involves numerous people at numerous periods in life, as well as the element of privacy and intimacy of home life, very serious and extremely complex variations of improper child care can be found to exist. Entering into such a situation as an outsider requires the utmost tact and skill in dealing with the behavior of others.

The overwhelmed parent is that person no longer capable of coping with a situation in which he finds himself. This parent is suffering from neurotic reactions to the pressures of life. Very often, this has resulted in a "giving up." The person is incapable of seeing a possible solution to the dilemma and has stopped trying. Usually this has occurred long before the actual physical manifestation is evident. Overwhelmed parents are a product of our society. They are persons who have succumbed to the burdens of the age of anxiety and have lost a clear perspective on the meaning and purpose of life. They are not unconcerned. On the contrary, their concern has aided in reducing them to the present state of helplessness. They may be the victims of unrealistic goals. They may have encountered circumstantial setbacks that would overwhelm any of us. They may be the manifestations of poor emotional development or be merely adjustment failures. While they do not wish to be in their present state, they cannot visualize an escape; and so they perform the only escape they can, they withdraw. They may have begun to utilize a crutch such as alcohol or drugs. They may merely sit and ignore the world about them. They no longer face themselves or their environment. It follows that they do not have to face their children. As their own humanity dissipates, the recognition of the humanity of others, including their children, diminishes and they find themselves in a state of limbo: nowhere to go and nowhere to be. These are very pitiful people who are in desperate need of supportive assistance, not only in financial terms but in many other ways. They are isolated from the world around them and the people around them. Their existence must be one of extreme loneliness, fraught with depression. It must be realized that to be reduced to such a state indicates serious emotional instability. Dealings with such persons bring forth alibis to almost any topic mentioned. They will find reasons why the home is in the condition it is; why the children are as they are; why they are in the process of deterioration. But, they will not cease there. Any attempt to suggest another course of action will be met with numerous reasons why such a course is not practical, or alibis as to why they should not get involved. They present the impression that if anything is to be done it will have to be initiated and carried out by another. One of the reasons for failure of many workers using the casework approach with such persons has been an inability to insist on the involvement of the person in whatever plan is being attempted. This is the flaw in the overwhelmed person's life . . . no commitment to anything. It is absolutely necessary to get that person involved in an active way in any rehabilitative effort. To attempt change otherwise is merely to condone and perpetuate the existing rejection of action and responsibility. Obviously, these persons could benefit from therapy, but in most communities services of this nature are presently quite limited.

With the increase in the population, birthrate and life expectancy have become attendant problems; some of which we are not recognizing, others we have chosen to ignore. One of the results of this boom in human survival is the continued introduction of inadequate or weak individuals into our society. This means that our humanity tends to work against us in terms of the perpetuation of the race. The author is not advocating birth control, selective breeding or any other genetic manipulation; but we must recognize that increased population alone will statistically account for more incompetents in our midst. The increase of longevity due to a reduction of infant mortality will also account, in some way, for an increase in the presence of incompetents. The incidence of early marriage, with accompanying multiple pregnancies presenting parenthood problems to immature youth in multiplying numbers, swells the ranks of the incompetent parent. The failure of the society to support the efforts of educators to introduce meaningful family life curriculum into our schools has reduced the opportunities for these youthful marriage partners to receive adequate premarital training. The inability of the home to provide such training and skill in this fast-paced existence has created a void that society has been unwilling to fill. All of these factors have led to an increased number of incompetent parents; some mentally incompetent, others emotionally incompetent and still others physically incompetent.

Our society has been successful in perpetuating a romanticist attitude toward marriage and family. Youth have been conditioned from the fairy tale to the television story, that courtship is the important period when the trials and tribulations of life are successfully faced and endured. That is the adjustment period that has been presented to our youth. They have been taught that once married, it is happiness ever after. The realities of marriage, adulthood or parenthood and its attendant responsibilities have been conveniently hidden from youth by the various media employed to present this material. There is a "happiness will reign" attitude that accompanies every young bride and groom to the altar. How shocking the realizations of impending parenthood should be; but our youth are so conditioned as to fail to comprehend at this period that such preparation is needed; not just the provision of physical necessities, but the mental and emotional preparation of each parent to meeting the burdens of parenthood yet to come. This is just one more disservice to our children under the guise of protecting them from the problems of life that they will face soon enough. Is it any wonder we are faced with incompetent parents?

This subject cannot be discussed without mentioning the rising number of youthful illegitimate births. This has become a national problem, as acute as that of the rise of veneral disease among our teenagers. The author has had professional contact with numerous twelve-year-old girls who have given birth to children. What can be expected of such a mother? Possibly playing house with her infant child, little more. Who, then, raises such a child? The parent of the mother in most cases. There is a question of competency on the part of the grandparent who could not foresee a situation leading to the pregnancy of an eleven or twelve-year-old daughter, or a fourteen or fifteen-year-old daughter for that matter. It certainly presents an interesting question as to the validity of parental capability, no matter whether the grandparent raises the child or the mother raises the child. The development of the illegitimate child cannot be overlooked as a possible neglect situation.

The incompetent parent is an obvious problem when the parent is either mentally retarded or dull normal, but incompetency cannot be limited to that group, nor should it be. The student must keep in mind that many parents of normal intelligence are incompetents. It becomes a problem only in relationship to the degree of incompetency and the parental efforts to overcome any handicaps. A person of low mentality who has sought and received supportive assistance may become a much better parent than a person of higher mental capacity with a poor parental concept, but who is secure in the belief that his actions are correct. Our society requires a school counselor to have completed up to sixty hours of graduate work in order to be prepared to counsel a particular child for from one half to four hours during a nine-month period of school, while at the same time not one course in child care is required for the parent who will control the development of the child during his most formative years.(6).

Much of the neglect witnessed by professionals in the field results from the unconcerned parent. This is a parent in whom the responsibilities of parenthood have never caused a significant, meaningful commitment — the parent who does not respond to the needs or demands of the child. These are persons in arrested states of emotional development. They cannot be brought beyond a self-awareness, and their own needs and pleasures come first. These are the parents who can make children eat at a separate time and place in order not to be interrupted. These are the parents who can leave their children unattended for long periods, including overnight trips, without the worry of conscience. These are the parents whose children are being hurt, are missing school, are neighborhood nuisances and who are well on their way to being neglected into delinquency. Many of the children of these environments are prone to delinquency, as they tend to be devoid of the necessary interpersonal relationships required for normal development and personality adjustment(6,7). This gives credence to the findings of some investigators that such neglect and rejection situations lead to a continuation of the maladjustment through its transmission to the neglected or rejected child(6).

Family disorientation results in child neglect. The disorientation may take on many forms, and it may stem from many causes. Very often, it is the result of a crisis from which the family cannot recover as an adequate unit of productive emotional and personality adjustment and growth. Loss of one or both parents through death, incarceration, desertion, separation or divorce, placing the burden of continuing the equilibrium of the unit on one or more persons who are unprepared and not willing to accept the burdens involved, are all situations that are readily seen in neglect caused by this upheaval. Everyone has seen a family go down after the death of a parent, or even one of the children. It is the failure to recover from the crisis in which the opportunity for neglect is found. The longer the recovery is postponed, the greater the chance of neglect to begin. As previously mentioned, neglect is a family situation and, as such, is a progressive activity. Neglect does not occur overnight. It is the result of a pattern of living that has existed for a period of time. The longer that pattern remains, the more entrenched it becomes and the more severe the manisfestations. The answer in the cases of neglect caused by family disorientation is in the shoring up or supporting of the family to strengthen the unit as rapidly as possible. This is often done by friends and relatives, but in the cases coming to the attention of the police, there has been a failure to return the family to a productive state. This means that such a return must be accomplished through the services of the community. Society must intervene, and this intervention must be without a lag of time. The case will come to the attention of the representatives of society after it has been handled by the friends and relatives to no avail. This means that the disorientation has existed for some time and the neglect is becoming entrenched. Delay in intervention can cause permanent damage. These cases afford the greatest opportunities for constructive casework and hold the best prognosis for adequate recovery.

Manifestations of Neglect

Neglect is seen in many varying forms. It can take on several forms in one family. It may be restricted to only one of several children, or it may appear as a complete avoidance of the necessary care of all the children. It will appear in varying degrees of severity, ranging from the parent who leaves small children unattended for long periods but only occasionally, to the parent who leaves small children alone each day while working, only to return home at night and leave again for a trip to the bar or other night spot.

It can be found in migrant-labor areas, where farm laborers take the children to the field and leave them in hot cars for six to twelve hours at a time, unattended except for occasional returns to check, and sometimes not even that. It is seen in front of bars at late hours at night, when small children are found by officers asleep in a cold vehicle while the parents are inside the bar. A check with the bartender will reveal several hours of drinking have occurred, while the children are exposed to the aloneness of the vehicle and the derelicts appearing around such places.

Firemen witness the results when called to fires that have been set by unattended children playing with matches, on occasion with tragic results. It is known to hospital attendants and members of the coroner's staff, when injured or burned children are brought in for medical attention; and when the conclusion is D. O. A. (dead on arrival), while the parent is at the store, or at the neighbors', or next door.

It is seen by the police and other services in homes that are filth-ridden, too cold, with no facilities for human habitation. These homes lack food, and what food is present is in the process of spoilage due to improper handling. They are characterized by the stench of soiled and mildewed clothes as they rot on closet floors, the floors of rooms, garages, service porches and in the front room itself. It is important enough to mention that the room containing the television set will remain the better room in the home. Also, the parent's bed will be the only one with sheets and pillows with pillow cases, although not necessarily clean. Items such as poison, knives, medicines, etc., will appear in the reach of the smallest of children. Often the bathtub will stand full of dirty water that has been there long enough to form a heavy scum. This presents not only a health problem, but also a hazard of drowning in consideration of very small children. The kitchen will present evidence of dirty dishes throughout, and the general filth will be accompanied by the presence of an invasion of roaches and flies. Blinds, if there are any, are usually kept down, adding to the gloom from the dim forty-watt bulbs. The yard will reflect the house, both front and back. Some of the sights on porches can never be forgotten. There was the front porch with a broken bag of steer manure sitting just by the front door. It had been there long enough for the manure to deteriorate. By this time, the contents had been generously spread about the porch in the area of the door. There was obvious evidence of foot tracks throughout the droppings, and one could see where this had been tracked into the home on more than one occasion. This degradation of the humanity of the child is difficult to imagine, just as it is difficult to describe.

One must be mindful that dirt alone does not constitute neglect. It may be moral neglect, but it does not equal neglect with which the police are concerned, unless the dirt is so bad that it constitutes a severe sanitation and health problem that would be readily observable to most individuals. Lack of food or other necessities can be the result of poverty or financial inability as easily as neglect, so that lack of food, per se, does not establish neglect. At the same time, poverty does not excuse neglect. In other words, persons on limited means can still be clean and look after their children, while providing them but a bare subsistence. The fact there is poverty does not mean that a family has to deteriorate into a neglect situation, and the majority do not.

Some Examples of Neglected Children

The small children quarrel in the filth-strewn room. Their baby brother is lying on a bare mattress, in need of a change and drying. The infant is small and listless, too energy-deprived to fuss. An older sister, still in elementary school, comes home with a bag of potato chips. This causes a scramble for the division of the food. There is no father in the home and the mother will not return until the bars close. At that time she will probably be drunk. This is their existence, their world(8).

A report was made to the police by a physician that he had just sutured a five-year-old girl's face with a total of fifty-eight stitches. He stated that the grandmother who brought the child to his office had said that the child was playing with the dog in a bedroom in her home when a lamp was knocked over, and the child fell on glass and cut her face. An ambulance had been called and a police officer was dispatched on an ambulance follow-up. The grandmother had met the officer and the ambulance near the road quite a distance from the home. She had the child with her. No one had entered the property. Subsequent police investigation, as the result of the doctor's report, revealed a bizarre set of circumstances. The mother was separated from the father and she and her two children lived in an adjacent house on the same property as the maternal grandparents. The second child was a fourteen-month-old boy who was just beginning to walk. Because of the proximity to the grandparents home the children spent much of their time there, as did the mother. In addition, the property was large, with the houses setting back from the road. There was a large fence around the homes, with a gate that was noticable only from inside the yard. On the first occasion there, the officers were unable to gain admission. Later, by making an appointment by phone, the officers were admitted. They were given the same account of the injury as the doctor, but were told that no one was in the room with the child and dog at the time of injury. On this occasion the officers did not see the room or the dog, but were told it was a German shepherd. Arrangements were made to return the following day with representatives of the humane society.

The following day the police and humane society representatives went to the grandparents' home. Both grandparents were there, as were the mother and her two children. After considerable talk the grandfather finally brought the dog into the room. It was a young male German shepherd and, quite obviously, very nervous. When the dog was brought into the room, the humane officers were seen to react by stiffening. The grandfather held the dog by a choke collar and the dog still was not calm. At the suggestion of the chief investigating officer, the grandfather took the dog into the bedroom where the incident occurred, still holding onto the chain and protesting how gentle the dog really was; but it was obvious from the actions of the humane officers that they were not convinced. The police officer immediately noted that all lamps were intact, and when this was mentioned, the grandfather, still holding on to the dog, stated he thought the broken glass had been a light bulb and that somebody had replaced it. After two or three requests, the grandfather finally let the dog loose. The dog moved quickly from person to person. He was very high strung and nervous. He appeared to dislike a person standing over him, but became calmer if the person bent down to his level. It was the opinion of the humane officers that the dog was not trustworthy because of its temperament. This opinion was concurred in by the officer.

Returning to the front room, and beginning some discussion about safety precautions with the grandparents and the mother, the grandmother became very upset with the whole affair. At this time she admitted that the dog had bitten her granddaughter after the child had pulled its ears. She said that the dog should not be punished for the actions of the children, but instead the children would have to learn to leave animals alone. It was pointed out that the youngest child was not of sufficient age to understand the situation, but the grandmother reiterated her remarks about children learning how to treat animals. Further conversation revealed that the dog had killed a sheep earlier that day on the property. At no time would the grandparents agree to any safety practices that would tend to prevent future harm to the children. All the while, the mother sat quietly, and her only comments were in agreement with the grandmother. It was very evident that the family had a matriarchal situation, and that the grandmother exerted the strongest influence. Subsequently, petitions were filed in juvenile court and a hearing was held. The children were made court wards under the supervision of the child welfare services, but were allowed to remain in the home after the grandparents, through their attorney, agreed to keeping the dog inside a run during any occasion when the children were around. Such an agreement made at the time of police contact would have negated the necessity of a court action.

Mr. and Mrs. N were the operators of one of the newest night spots in the community. Mrs. N had five children by a previous marriage. The oldest was a twelve-year-old boy. Mr. N did not like the children, so he would not have them living where he did. Mrs. N owned a large home in a rural residential district. She left the children there and they continued to attend the same school they had always attended. In the meantime, Mr. and Mrs. N moved to an apartment at the club. Every morning at about eight o'clock Mrs. N would drive to the home in the country, a distance of about five miles. She would get the children up, and always gave the oldest boy five dollars for food for the day. She would remain about a half an hour and then would leave, not to return until the following day. To cut down expenses, the phone at the home had been disconnected. The only contact the children had with the mother was at the time of her morning call. There were no other close relatives in the area, Mrs. N's parents having died and left her the home.

The children lived like this for about eight weeks. During this period they began buying candy and soda at a small store in the area. They set up a store of their own in the garage. It was a walk up to a side window facing an alley. From this store the children sold the candy and soda to children who were returning from school. The N children were missing a considerable amount of school in order to run the store. The sales, coupled with truancy, brought an anonymous complaint to the police. An investigation ensued, culminating in the children being found alone in the home late one night. They were placed in protective custody and a note was left for the mother to contact the police. Instead, officers were contacted the following morning by Mr. N, the stepfather. He said his wife was too upset to come. He was advised that this was a matter between the mother and the officers, and the officers would not discuss the matter further with Mr. N. He left, to bring his wife and attorney back. During his absence a warrant of arrest was obtained charging the mother with neglect; and upon the return of the husband, attorney and mother, the latter was arrested. The case was adjudicated at both the juvenile court and adult court levels.

Mrs. W had only been in the state about five months. She had come to this new area with her husband and five children, the oldest aged ten years. After being here a short time the father had moved back to the home state. The mother refused to return with him, and she and the children remained. In attempting to get by, the family financial situation deteriorated rapidly. Due to residence laws, the mother could not obtain welfare assistance for the children and herself, and before long the children were being sent to the neighbors to beg for food. Some of the neighbors, trying to be of help, went to the home and after being admitted by one of the children, found the mother gone. They also found an indescribably filthy home situation. Rotten food, dirty clothes, feces in the middle of the floor and flies so thick as to give the impression of a moving wall. The yard, both front and back, was filled with old cans, broken bottles and assorted other sharp objects. The garage was filled with dirty clothes that had mildewed and were literally "hairy." This garage was attached to the home. The neighbors reported the matter to the police. Before the officers arrived, the three year old was struck by a car in front of the residence after being told by neighbors to stay out of the street. The mother finally returned home and was taken to the hospital by a neighbor to see her child. Later, when the officers entered the neighborhood, they had to stop their car before the younger brother of the hospitalized child would move, on command, from the middle of the street where he was sitting. The mother was in the home at the time. All of these factors led to the determination that the situation was one of general neglect. The children were placed in protective custody and the mother arrested. She made her first phone call to an attorney from her house. Represented by counsel at both the juvenile court hearing and her own court action, she plead guilty to neglect and the children were made court wards.

In was winter. Mr. and Mrs. B and their two children lived in a one bedroom cottage in an unincorporated area of the county. Mr.

B was twenty one, but of very low intelligence. Mrs. B was from a high income family. She was eighteen years old, not bright or very pretty, but more aggressive than her husband. As a fourteen-year-old girl, she ran away with Mr. B to another state and, after lying about her age, they were married. She immediately became pregnant. Her mother had the marriage annulled and brought her back home. Mrs. B later ran away and joined her former husband. She again became pregnant. Again her mother located her and brought her home. Before giving birth to the baby, the girl turned eighteen, left home, rejoined Mr. B and they were married again. After the marriage, they moved into the small cottage described above. Mr. B. did not work. He had become involved with some of the local hoodlum element and they were exploiting him. He turned to pimping for his wife, and she engaged in acts of prostitution. In reality, the husband's buddies were taking a cut of the income from this illegal activity. This activity occurred in the cottage. In the course of such action Mrs. B became infected with venereal disease and also was suffering from an ovarian infection. Mr. B was in turn infected by Mrs. B. This meant that Mrs. B had to curtail her activity, which caused the local group to become angered, as their cut was reduced. There was an altercation at the home one night between Mr. B and his buddies. He was roughed up and several windows at the home were broken in; the windows were broken from the outside into the house.

About one week later, a neighbor called during daylight hours and stated the two-and-one-half-year-old boy and the infant were at the home alone. Officers went to the home and found it in deplorable condition. Dirt and filth and broken glass were everywhere. They were in the process of the investigation when the parents arrived on the scene. They issued the parents a warning about the possibility of neglect and took no further action. The following night about eleven o'clock another complaint was made that the children were alone. It was a very cold night. The house was extremely cold as the windows had never been fixed. There was no heat in the home. Witnesses informed the officers that the parents had left about two thirty that afternoon and had not been seen since. The house had not changed from the description provided by the other officers the day before. There was "wall to wall" broken glass, and the older boy was walking about the house barefoot. The child could not find his shoes. There were no clean clothes. In going about the house, one stepped either on broken glass or dirty clothes. If the officers had not known the baby was there, that child would have been overlooked. As it was, the baby was hard to find. The child was in a bassinet on the floor. The whole area was so covered with dirty clothing that it was impossible to see the child. Only because the baby finally moved was he located. At about midnight, the parents appeared. They were advised of their constitutional rights and placed under arrest. The children were taken into protective custody.

Part of the procedure in that jurisdiction for the removal of children requires a physical examination at the public hospital before placement. This physical uncovered the fact the baby was suffering from extreme frost bite, in his own bed, in his own home. Had the child remained there much longer, amputation might have been necessary. The children were placed in foster-home care upon the order of the juvenile court, after a hearing. At the adult trial of both parents for neglect, they were found guilty and given probation(9).

These examples have been presented in order for the student to have a better understanding of the nature of the manisfestations of neglect, along with the variations that will surely be found from situation to situation.

The Extent of the Problem

It is very difficult to attempt to show the rate of incidence of neglect. This is true for several reasons. First, there is no actual agreement upon the definition of "neglect." Each agency, each discipline, each jurisdiction tends to evaluate neglect differently. This points to a need for a universally accepted definition of the problem, based on adequate research, as a primary objective in society's response. Secondly, many authorities view "neglect" as a problem separate from "abuse." Others tend to include neglected and abused children in the same general category. The author sees these two problems as concentric circles, interrelated, both a part of parental failure; but neglect as the broader or larger circle, with abuse contained within the full scope of neglect. Because the factors are not the same, as far as has been determined on the basis of meager studies, the two problems cannot belong to each other. This is also true of the results of the problem. While children are injured through neglect, that is a by-product of parental failure and does not have to be the outcome in order for neglect to occur. As has been stated, neglect is the endangering of the child. That alone is sufficient. The parent willfully, knowing the possible outcome of the neglectful act, places the child in danger by causing or permitting the danger to exist. In opposition, abuse results in injury being inflicted upon the person of the child by the offending party. In abuse cases, injury is a necessary part of the case. Studies or statistics that unify neglect and abuse as one, cannot give reliable accounts of the true extent of the problems, as the two are just not the same, though there are similarities and they are interrelated. Third, there have not been enough studies made of the problem of neglect. Studies to date have been concentrated on the more acute problem of abuse. Research is needed in both areas. It is hoped that the findings of the studies on abused children will result in research being made into the broader aspect of neglect. This is needed in order to increase our understanding of the type of parent with whom we must deal, to devise proper procedures for the processing of such cases, to propose upgraded services to reduce the incidences and to initiate meaningful rehabilitative programs. With our present lack of knowledge, it is impossible to correctly present the rate of incidence in order to support requests for needed services. No one can be sure our present actions in such cases are effective . . . . it may be that the course taken is wrong. Planning for future measures and protective programs cannot proceed effectively without research findings to point the way.

In the face of the lack of productive studies related to neglect, it is still possible to draw some conclusions from the known number of dependent children on probation in a given jurisdiction. These will include a majority number of neglected children. They will have been, for the most part, the more serious cases, those calling for court action in order to be properly adjudicated. Cases disposed of with a warning, cases existing in a social agency case-load, and that are being handled by workers on an unofficial basis of casework technique, or are being worked out by families, relatives and friends; as well as the cases that are being overlooked and still remain hidden, are not included in the estimate that we can presently draw. Only those officially adjudicated cases are available at this time.

> For the twelve month period ending June 30, 1964, there were between 40,000 and 45,000 dependent and neglected children known to California probation departments(10).

It is within the realm of possibility, to conclude that much neglect exists undetected. It does so because of the lack of public involvement. It does so because of a lack of understanding and agreement on objectives on the part of the professionals. It does so because many workers do not recognize its existance, while others do not know what actions should be taken when they do experience such cases. Police officers, welfare workers, public health nurses, probation officers and even juvenile court judges misunderstand the problem, or see it as only isolated incidents of parental unwillingness. Few professionals have any sophisticated comprehension regarding the problem. Until such time as the research is performed that will bring to light the factors relating to this problem and guide society toward proper remedial action in cases of neglect, it will be necessary for the professionals to work together in an atmosphere of cooperation and understanding to attain one agreed-upon objective . . . . . the protection of the neglected child.

References

1. Protective Services for Children. Report of the Assembly Interim Committee on Social Welfare, Sacramento, Assembly of the State of Calif. Jan. 1967, p. 7.
2. Flammang, C. J.: Juvenile Procedures. An unpublished study prepared for the Division of Vocational Education, Berkeley, U. of Calif. July 30, 1967, pp. 85-85.
3. Kvaraceus, William C.: Delinquent behavior and church attendance. Sociol Soc Res, 28:289, 1944.
4. Dominic, Sister M.: Religion and the Juvenile delinquent, Amer Catholic Sociol Rev, SV, Oct. 1954, p. 264.

5. Glueck, Sheldon and Eleanor: Unraveling Juvenile Delinquency, Cambridge, Harvard, U, 1950, p. 167.
6. Kaplan, Louis: Foundations of Human Behavior. New York, Harper, 1965, pp. 60, 79, 166.
7. Caplan, G.: Concepts of Mental Health and Consultation: Their Application in Public Health Social Work, U.S. Department of Health, Education, and Welfare, Children's Bureau, 1959.
8. Young, Leotyne: Wednesday's Children, New York, McGraw, 1964.
9. Examples of cases of neglect taken from the professional experience of the author.
10. National Study Service (Final Report): Planning for the Protection and Care of Neglected Children in California. Sacramento, State Soc. Welfare Board and Calif. Delinq. Prevent. Comm., Aug. 1965, p. 9.

Chapter III

THE POLICE
AND THE NEGLECTED CHILD

AMONG the responsibilities of the police in their role in juvenile enforcement, is the mission of the protection of the juvenile. The police enter into an area of responsibility every time a juvenile is victimized, either by another juvenile or by an adult. Such a mission involves police action in a number of criminal situations in which juveniles are involved as victims. These include such matters as sex, assaults, theft and, in reality, every crime that can be committed. Just as juveniles commit every crime, from the most minor misdemeanor to the most serious felony, juveniles also suffer the loss to person and property from all types of crimes being perpetrated upon them. As victims, juveniles suffer the greatest loss in the area of neglect. There are, as has been previously indicated, numerous children who are victimized by neglect in this country each year. The unfortunate part of this is the failure of the police to fully recognize the seriousness and extent of such acts. Many police departments tend to view neglect as a police problem to be handled with as little trouble to the department in terms of manpower and equipment as is possible while still perfoming a semblance of the job. This is not an outright condemnation of police agencies. Keep in mind that the whole area of neglect is confused. This confusion ranges from inadequate definitions to poorly delineated areas of responsibility. There is a quasi-social work or counseling effort connected with such cases, and this can be causal in police rejection of the totality of their role. While most police agencies are performing the functions of the police in neglect cases, they are doing so without the vitality and understanding necessary for the proper realization of the objectives of the police in the area of the protection of the juvenile.

Of all the facets of juvenile enforcement, neglect is the most misunderstood by police officers in terms of both seriousness of the offense and goals the police are attempting to attain. Neglect cases are in the area of police juvenile enforcement in which the laws and procedures, as well as the responsibility of the police, vary the greatest from jurisdiction to jurisdiction. State laws differ greatly, even in the area of placing agency responsibility, an area not always clearly defined by law. Local communities place responsibility on the police in some cases, and on social agencies in others; often both situations existing simultaneously, resulting in the first agency becoming involved as the agency of responsibility, and thus giving rise to continued interagency rivalry due to this lack of demarcation. Much of this confusion is the result of the failure of society to discover the best means of dealing with such cases. Until this knowledge is attained, the fruits of confusion will continue to be reaped.

The Reporting of Neglect

The manner in which neglect cases are reported to the police is of concern, for if the police responsibility includes such cases, it is imperative for the protection of the victims that these cases come to the attention of the police as rapidly as possible. A police agency failing to receive reports of neglect is a police agency that is not performing its task in respect to neglected children. There is no area, no group, no place in which humans reside, where neglect of children is not occurring. Rest assured that this statement is true. There is no question as to the existence of neglect, but merely as to the degree of severity of the neglect that does exist. For a police agency to feel secure in the fact that there is no neglect because it is not being reported, is erroneous and reflects:

1. *Poor reporting procedures* this indicates that the public is dubious of making such reports to the police. It may be due to poor police practices. It may be the failure of the police to adequately educate the public to the need of such reports. It may be the result of the failure of the police to keep the public informed.
2. *The failure to recognize neglect,* including the failure of the police to identify such conditions when encountered. This would indicate the need for in-service training in the area of the identification of neglect cases, as well as a continuing public education service as a

part of the police public-relations efforts.

3. *Inadequate delienation of responsibility* on the part of the police and other agencies in the community, usually a result of poor interagency liaison.

4. *Confusion established by statute.* In this event it becomes necessary for the police to involve themselves in a display of leadership, not only on the local level, but on the state level as well, to insure the enactment of laws whereby such confusion is negated and the assignment of responsibility in such cases is clearly defined.

To further demonstrate the problem of reporting as being one of police responsibility, assume for a moment that the police in a given area were no longer receiving reports of armed robberies for any one of the reasons outlined. The total effort of the department would be employed by the administor to locate the cause of the failure to report such incidents, and steps would be initiated to remedy the problem. The reason this does not occur as a police-initiated action in neglect cases is the failure of the police to view such cases in the proper perspective in relationship to the seriousness of the offense and the police responsibility. Proper reporting will not be assured until police understand neglect as what it is; and until they are cognizant of the long term effects in terms of antisocial behavior, delinquency, criminality and the continuation of the pattern of child rejection in a new generation.

The segments of the community reporting neglect may be classified according to the incidence and reliability of the reports. Further classification could be made relating to the motive for the report, but this is a classification based on an interpretation of the subjective motivation of another, and will not be presented. Suffice it to say that motivation does enter into the fact that a case is reported. Such subjectiveness, however, must not be judged by the investigators. The reason for the report is of no consequence if the investigation reveals the presence of neglect. In such situations, it is to the officer's advantage to accept the "for the benefit of the child approach." This will keep the officer from being affected in his objective analysis of the facts, by the subjectivity of the reporter's motivation.

The primary reporting source in any community is the police themselves. This is true for the same reason that the police have been charged with the protection of children and the enforcement of laws. The police are the one community agency offering twenty-four-hour service, every day of every year. The police are there. They are in the community and they see the community, not as the community wishes to be seen, not as it would like to be seen, not as it sees itself; but, in a realistic sense, the police see the wounds of the community. The police are present when the community works. They are present when it plays, when it sleeps, when it is sick and when it is injured. The police hear its complaints, its hopes, its hates. They are present on its streets, in its alleys, its businesses and its homes. Because the police are present in its homes, the law enforcement agency properly attuned to the meaning of neglect and its role in such situations is in a greater position than any other to identify and report neglect. The well trained and oriented patrolman is indispensable to the protection of children. In the course of his routine patrol duties he should have become familiar with those areas on his beat in which neglect most surely occurs. He should have made enough contacts with persons having confidence in him and his department that they will furnish the officer with information regarding cases of concern to them. Information should be forthcoming from storekeepers, service stations, bartenders, school personnel, probation officers, welfare workers, postmen, delivery men, public health nurses and recreation directors who pursue occupations in the life of the community on the officer's beat. If this information is not being passed on, it indicates the officer is not performing the basic police task, that of gathering information. He is spending too much time in his car. He is not making contacts with those important persons on his beat, at least not in such a manner as to instill confidence in those persons.

The patrolman will discover a certain amount of neglect himself. His calls taking him to numerous homes to settle disturbances, to investigate crimes, to seek witnesses and to apprehend offenders, all expose him to an eyewitness view of neglect situations. In responding to a bicycle theft, the complainant may make comments as to the care and supervision of the suspect and other children in that family. This information should not be ignored or forgotten. In contacting the friend of a burglary suspect, the officer may walk into the most serious neglect case he has ever seen. Family disturbances requiring police action are strong indicators of family disorientation. Such family situations may disclose a child on the verge of neglect, or an already well-entrenched neglect case. The officer who is content with a disposition of "settled by officer" with no report and, in many cases, no recognition of the neglect, is doing a disservice to the community, the child and to himself and his department. This child will continue to suffer the neglect imposed, until it becomes so flagrant that action is initiated by another source. The case will eventually be handled; but, in the meantime, the effects of rejection will have been established, possibly never to be overcome. A citizen, knowing of the situation and also knowing of the officer's contact in the home, can only assume the neglect was not enough to warrant any action. This citizen will watch it continue to bloom on the assumption that nothing can be done. In fact, due to the officer's poor police action, nothing was done.

The information discovered or witnessed should be passed on by the patrol division to the juvenile unit. This is true even in the smallest department, where there is no specialized juvenile unit. In such agencies, one man should be assigned, at least part of his time, on juvenile follow-up. This officer, just as those in the larger departments, must have had the benefit of specialized juvenile training, not only within the department, but from outside sources also. These include formal college courses, state and local training sessions, seminars, workshops, institutes, and the continued training services offered through membership in such associations as the International Association of the Chiefs of Police, the International Juvenile Officers Association, and state associations such as the California Juvenile Officers Association, which presents a one week annual training conference in addition to numerous other training sessions on a regional basis.

The information pertinent to neglect cases should be forwarded by the patrol unit to the juvenile specialist for several reasons. First, the investigation of such cases is complex and requires special skills and knowledge the patrolman may not possess. Such cases are best handled by an officer who is not only familiar with the mechanics of the procedures, but who has attained a degree of sophistication beyond the traditional police role in the application of modern knowledge to the attainment of desired objectives. Secondly, a neglect investigation involves more than just a cursory examination of the home. It is a tedious and time-consuming case preparation, with the possibility of two actions occurring simultaneously. This means that the patrolman would be restricted to this one action too long, and in so doing the rest of his beat would be unprotected, or another unit would have to cover. The neglect, by its nature, is a case calling for follow-up investigation. The patrolman should limit his activity to that of a preliminary investigation; obtaining names and address of victims and suspects, protecting the crime scene if immediate follow-up is indicated, and otherwise performing the tasks of the patrolman in the preliminary investigation stage. It cannot be stressed too greatly that the patrol division, as well as the rest of the police agency, including the members of the criminal investigation arm, are a primary source of the reporting of neglect. Police supervisors should be aware of this, and remain on the alert for indications of poor training on the part of their staffs as indicated by the failure of such personnel to make reports of the neglect cases with which they come in contact.

In the face of evidence of public apathy toward involvement in the matters of others; in the area of neglect, neighbors are a good reporting source. The police receive many calls from persons living in close proximity to a neglected child. The reports are usually reliable, to the extent that they report neglect. Some authorities comment on false reports of neglect(1). For the most part there are few false reports. The situation is usually one in which there is a variance as to the type of neglect or the degree of neglect. The reporters may be concerned with a situation of moral or civil neglect. This does not mean a false report; it does mean a misunderstanding of the role of the police. A false report is one in which an individual knowingly and willingly falsifies information for the purpose of obtaining a police action. A mistake or misunderstanding cannot be construed to be equal to the falsification of information. As stated before, most of these neighbors are sincere people who have witnessed a situation of such proportions as to cause them to believe that the lack of care and supervision of the child is endangering or detrimentally affecting the child. They are reporting as much for advice as to what action they should take, or to be told whether they have seen a situation for which there is cause for action, as for any other reason. They have a general concern for the children, and very often such reporting is at a cost to them: the condemnation of the reporter by the parents allowing or promoting the neglect. While the possibility of a crank call exists, for the most part the information received will be reliable. The neighbor remains one of the best reporting sources in cases of neglect.

The friends and relatives are a perplexing group. Because they represent laymen, as opposed to agency representatives, they will be included with the neighbors, but with some distinct differences. First, their information may not be as reliable, depending upon their motivation. If the relative is one who is related to the offending parent, the reliability is probably better. If there are several relatives, representing both sides of the family, the reliability is at its best; as these people have demonstrated their concern by getting together, pooling information and resources, and have hence decided that the only course of action rests with the police. In so doing they have placed themselves in a position of unity, a unity that cannot easily be explained away. Many times these relatives are the grandparents. It is not unusual to find that they have a desire for the children, that they wish custody. For this reason their reports should be verified with extreme care. Much of what is reported by grandparents amounts to moral neglect, and civil neglect constitutes the majority of the reports made by fathers or former spouses. These reports should be investigated to determine their validity unless, on the face of the report, it can be determined that the situation is not one of criminal neglect. The fact that many accurate reports of neglect situations do emanate from relatives and friends precludes catagorizing such reports as other than reliable. The warnings regarding the reliability are necessary, but in the majority of such instances the neglect is real, the reporters have been concerned for some time and often have attempted to remedy the situation, only reporting it after exhaustive efforts have met with failure.

Other siblings, either still in the home but in contact with the police or another agency on an official basis, or out of the home due to age or actions, are a good source of reporting to the police. In the majority of instances these reports are accurate and are the result of a concern, not for themselves, but for their younger brothers and sisters. These reports usually involve situations that have been in existence for a long period of time, and, as such, the case is usually acute.

Many of the children in need of protection are seen by the schools. For this reason, the schools play a large role in the protection of children. The role of the school is to identify and report such matters to the proper authorities, usually the police. This role manifests two problem procedures of reporting to the police. It is necessary that the elementary school teacher be familiar with the telltale marks of neglect. The most visible is a poor physical condition, coupled with an attempt on the part of the child to gain acceptance and some of the teacher's attention. This child is one who has suffered considerable rejection, at least in respect to his physical needs. As the child enters the school system, the opportunity for the development of a meaningful relationship appears, and the child may attempt to grasp at any means of fulfilling that need. The approaches will vary, but there will usually appear a display of need for affection by the child, who will also appear dirty and unkempt. An unkempt child is not always one who is capable of gaining the affection and the attention of the teacher. Therefore, the danger of the problem being overlooked because of the teacher's natural reluctance to become deeply involved with a disheveled and possibly smelly youngster is apparent. Teachers need to be oriented toward the problem and its manifestations at the school level. This orientation should be carried out by the educators themselves, but failing this, police leadership and advice should be offered to the administrators of the school system. Not only does the classroom teacher have a responsibility, the principals and special service personnel of the school district should also be well aware of the existence of neglect and the school's role in neglect cases. These people should be prepared to concern themselves in such cases whenever the need arises, but, more importantly, they should exert the leadership necessary to bring about proper training in staff and functional procedures for the educational community to follow in these matters.

The Schools have two staff services that are important in neglect identification and reporting. The first is the office of the school nurse. Not only is this person a trained registered nurse, with additional education in the area of public health work, but is in one of the two categories of school personnel who have access to the home. The school nurse makes many calls on many homes. In so doing, the nurse is in a position to come in contact with some of the more severe cases of neglect. The nurse, because of her professional training and her concern for children's health, is quite capable of immediate recognition of neglect. Very often the nurse identifies neglect problems and makes written acknowledgment in her own files. When the nurse fails to report such cases, it is due to improper administrative procedures in the school system, or the failure of that system to instill in these employees their role in child neglect cases. It may be stated that the school nurse remains one of the best reporting sources of child neglect.

The other school function which takes personnel into the home is school attendance work. The attendance problem is one of major concern to the schools because of the compulsory attendance laws of the state, and because the schools are given financial assistance on the basis of the average daily attendance. Most districts now employ full-time attendance officers. These persons are required to seek out both students and parents because of attendance problems, resulting in numerous contacts being made at the residence of the child. By insuring the proper orientation of such personnel toward the policies and procedures of the district in neglect cases, the incidence of reporting will more closely approximate the amount of neglect encountered. The orientation of the attendance officer is a school function, but in the instance of that function not being performed, the police should exert their influence in seeking a remedy to this void within the school district.

Police liaison with the schools is of paramount importance in juvenile enforcement in general. Properly established, it will result in mutual cooperation and will reduce delinquent problems in the schools and in the community. Without such cooperation, no successful program of delinquency control can exist. The importance of a good police-school relationship cannot be overemphasized. Such a relation is an absolute essential in juvenile work(2). Once established, the schools will readily do their part in the identification and reporting of neglect cases. The police must foster the mutual relationship by insuring the proper selection of personnel to work with the schools, the development of policy and procedures in keeping with those of the schools, and the recognition of the role of the school and the limitations of the system.

Another source of good reporters existing within a community, but a source not always tapped by the police, are the public health services, including the public health nurses or visiting nurses. These people, by virtue of their professional background and agency mission, along with the numerous home contacts they make, are as vital to the reporting of neglect cases as are the school nurses. It must be the interest of police administrators to see to it that such resources become aware of their function in this regard, and the police must become involved in developing the potential of such community services. The role of the public health nurse and services is not only in the area of identification of neglect situations and the subsequent reporting of such discoveries; but this service can be utilized to great advantage in the follow-up assistance that can be given to maintain contact with those cases that are not serious enough to warrant full action, and in areas of assisting to strengthen the ability of the family to overcome neglect caused by poor health and hygiene knowledge and practices.

The poorest reporting source, and the source that sees the most neglect, is the public welfare representative. These persons are in the homes of many of the community's neglect problems, but the incidence of reporting tends to be very low. There are several reasons for this. First, there is a definite opposition to police methods as a part of the basic philosophy of the welfare agency and its personnel. In the case of public welfare, this attitude is promulgated, in many ways, from the state level, and so it permeates the total welfare system. Secondly, the professional welfare worker has been schooled in the casework approach, and is in possession of a deep belief not only in the reliability of the method, but in the worker's ability to carry it out to a successful conclusion. The social worker desires change, and feels that by means of the training and academic background he possesses, the transformation of an individual into a productive member of society will occur if he, the worker, performs the casework effectively and properly. Hence, when confronted with cases of neglect within the case load, the worker will attempt to help the client to overcome the deficiency rather than to expose the family to police action, often mistakenly viewed as purely punitive in nature. This results in less reporting by the welfare representative. In the area of welfare, there are few workers who have any difficulty in identifying neglect. The problems arise in the failure on the part of social agencies to establish actual and practical agency responsibilities. The differences of backgrounds and philosophies existing between the police and the social agencies are significant problems that require action in the future, in order to increase the ability of these two community services to work together for the productive performance of their missions.

Protection or Prosecution?

The concepts of the protection of the child and the prosecution of the offender are at opposite poles, not only through approach and philosophy, but also in respect to investigation and evidence, and the court in which each will be adjudicated. It would appear that no question of the action that must be taken would be evident. Such is not the case. One of the more disturbing problems of the underprotected child is in relation to these two concepts. In attempting to unravel some of the problems that have been wrought in respect to the stand that might be taken, it is first noteworthy to review the police-recognized role in cases of underprotected children, and how this role has evolved to date.

The police, basically, find themselves as the enforcers of whatever laws or ordinances are set forth by the society the police serve. This is the traditional police role, and it holds today in many jurisdictions. That is to say, the police have the basic responsibility to determine if a statute has been violated, and then to seek out, apprehend and initiate a request for prosecution of the offender. At one time in our society, this simplified version of the existence of the police was quite acceptable. But with the changing times and the development of a complex society, this traditional stand can no longer produce the desired results. This is more true in the area of juvenile enforcement than in any other police function. Just as there are police administrators who still devalue the use of a limited degree of counseling on the part of the police in juvenile work, so there still exist those police personnel who see the police role in neglect cases as one of determining if a crime has been committed, to identify and apprehend the offender and seek a prosecution. There are still court jurisdictions in which the juvenile court is of the belief that in order to sustain a petition on behalf of a victim of neglect, there must first be a criminal prosecution and conviciton of the offender. This concept is based on the idea that without such a conviction for neglect, no neglect can be established. What a misconception! To hold this view relegates the juvenile court to the position of parroting the views or findings of another court. To restrict the protection afforded a juvenile by the juvenile court to that court's dependency upon the findings of a separate court, of possibly inferior jurisdiction, is to declare the juvenile court to be void of judicial powers in cases involving the protection of children. For the police to continue to hold such views, to see the protection of the child and the prosecution of the adult offender as interdependent, is to deny the basic objective of the police in cases of underprotected children. The primary concern of the police must be the protection of the child. This is the paramount objective that must be attained in these cases. No other objective will be acceptable if the police have a role in the protection of persons or property. Prosecutions are secondary. They are the results of such protection. Prosecutions, per se, are not protection. The police must come to view this objective as one that follows the protection of the child. A prosecution is the aftermath of a long series of situations, including the police action necessary to protect the child. An investigation of a neglect case may or may not result in the identification of an offender. It may or may not result in a prosecution. It is important that the child be protected, and that his environment be altered if it is one of neglect; either by means of changing the environment the child is in, or by removing the child from that surrounding. This may occur without a prosecution, by means of a juvenile court action on behalf of the dependent child. Neglect is evidenced by physical manifestations already discussed. It is not an absolute necessity to establish through evidence that X neglected the child, in order to establish that the child has been neglected. What is necessary is evidence to establish the fact of neglect.

If evidence points to one person as being the perpetrator of the neglect and a prosecution ensues, this is also a part of the police mission. It cannot be accepted that persons charged with the care and custody of children may willfully neglect their duties to these children and not be called to answer for these actions. Such would defeat the purposes of criminal justice. If a prosecution is in order, the police are under an oath to enforce the law, and by reason of this oath they are obligated to seek a prosecution within the scope of the judicial process. This is a fact many of the critics of the police fail to recognize. The police officer has his oath, often reinforced by demands that the officer proceed. The decision to prosecute is made by the district attorney. The decision to seek a prosecution is made by the police in the person of the investigating officer. Since neglect cases are usually a family situation, the decision to prosecute is one in which a grave responsibility lies. It is up to the officer to have so performed his investigation that the decision made by him will amount to the proper and most effective utilization of the administration of justice.

The Investigation of Neglect

As already stated, neglect cases are complex displays of parental or family failure. As such they do not readily fall into the scope of traditional police methods, but, rather, far exceed many of the normal police problems in relation to complexity. Neglect cases involve many persons. Family, relatives, friends, neighbors, schools and other public agencies, and private enterprise are all significant parts of the total picture. A neglect case calls for police action, requiring thorough investigation of a follow-up nature. These cases cannot be disposed of by means of the regular patrol division. The patrol officer has neither the training nor experience to properly handle the situation, and evidence of that inadequacy is demonstrated in the number of such cases that continue to be recontacted by the police on a chronic basis, because of the patrolman's failure to take appropriate action to reconcile the matter.

The officer arriving at the scene of a neglect situation should make as rapid a determination as possible regarding the gravity of the offense. In the event the problem is acute, the investigators responsible for such queries should be called in to take over. In a home situation, one of the most important pieces of evidence is the photograph. The conditions of the home giving rise to neglect identification should be photographed. These pictures must record the yard, the various rooms and any particulars in a given area that tend to bear out the contention of neglect. This calls for close ups of sinks, bathroom facilities, feces or other filth lying about, and any weapons, poisons or other dangerous items that are within the reach of small children.

The investigators should ascertain from the children, the beds that are used by the various members of the family. A record should be made of the beds utilized by each, and these should be photographed in order to retain a pictorial record of the sleeping arrangements. Usually, very unsanitary conditions will be found to exist in the bedrooms of the children. The manner of intimate living to which the child is subjected is important in establishing neglect. Outbuildings and garages must also be recorded pictorially. A survey of the existing food in the home should be made and recorded. The interior of cupboards and the refrigerator should become a part of the photographic evidence.

Overall shots of each room should be made from opposing directions, in addition to the close-ups of objects of an evidential nature. A five by seven inch identification card with the name of the case, the case number, the charge, the investigator's name and the name of the photographer should be included in each photograph. Pictures should not intentionally include the children, they should never be posed; however, in the event the children are in such a normal position as to be included in the photograph, there is no reason why such a record of the condition of the child in relation to the surroundings in which he is forced to live should not be made. It must be kept in mind that these are crime-scene photographs. There is no place in such pictorial records for persons and items that are not a part of the scene. Therefore, officers must be careful not to be included in the pictures. Further, with the exception of the identifying card, none of the photographer's or investigator's equipment should be seen. This will require that such items be moved about as the photographer's position changes. As the photographer is quite busy, the investigator should assist by performing that task, and insuring the record of the scene not be contaminated by the presence of such objects. Investigating officers should not leave the scene until the photographer is finished. This is based on the nature of the case and the place in which the photographs are being made. In the first place, the photographer needs the corroboration of the investigator that nothing was added or disturbed during the course of the photography. He needs the protection of corroboration from a charge of theft or damage. If the photographer is left alone at the scene to take the photographs, an area or object of importance might be overlooked that the investigator will find he needs at the time of a court action. One cannot expect the police photographer to be responsible for the collection of the investigator's evidence. It is the job of the investigator to remain and to insure that all the evidence he desires is recorded. In addition, if the case is one in which the parents have left the children unattended, the parents may return home while these photographs are being taken. The police photographer should not be placed in the position of having to make an arrest. By remaining with him, the investigator eliminates the need to subpoena the photographer in subsequent court action.

The photography involved will be time-consuming. But such photography is an absolute necessity. No officer can adequately describe the conditions of a home from a witness stand. Although each case will not end in court action, those acute cases calling for a full police investigation will result in juvenile court action. The need for the photographs is just as great in that court. Every case must be approached, in terms of investigation, as if it were to be both a juvenile court action and an adult jury trial. To investigate from a different perspective is folly. Due to the importance of the photographs, each picture should be double shot. Duplicate photos will insure that the photographer has corrected any mechanical errors resulting in mistakes, and no evidence will be lost. If the department has color film available, colored photos should be made a part of the record.

While awating the arrival of the photographer, the investigator may utilize that time in interviewing the children and making his written notes on the various points of significance. He should also determine the clothing that is available for the children, in the event he has made a decision that protective custody is necessary. Many times, adequate clothing is difficult to locate, but with the assistance of the older children, enough can usually be located to safely remove all the children. In the event such is not found, blankets should be obtained from the department via the patrol unit.

After recording the scene, the investigation should become a routine attempt to locate witnesses. This includes contacting the neighbors, local proprietors, landlords (including former landlords), the schools and other public agencies. This should occur only after the investigator has made a record check on the family, including a check for any outstanding warrants of arrest on other charges. This is a good technique when arriving at a home where there is no father, and an unknown boyfriend is present. He may become demanding about what is going on. Officers should remember that this is a family situation between the parent and the children and, as such, an outsider has no business being involved. Advise the person of this fact immediately, obtain his identification and record the information, and run a warrant check on the subject at that time and in his presence. This will rapidly remove any confidence he may have remaining.

In contacting witnesses, attempt to determine their knowledge of any occurrences that tend to establish a pattern or routine as related to the neglect. One of the persons to contact at the school is the nurse. She may have health records indicating that the child has a health problem and the family was so advised. The failure to seek proper health corrections, when necessary, constitutes neglect. If the family is receiving public assistance, the caseworker concerned should be contacted and interviewed regarding his knowledge of the existence of poor conditions. In many welfare departments, the worker turnover is extensive. It may be necessary to interview several workers before finding one who has had numerous contacts with the family. Don't stop with the present worker, unless that person has been on the case for sometime. Checking with the public health nurse in the area often produces valuable information. The nurse may have firsthand knowledge resulting from home visitation, as well as knowledge obtained at health clinic contacts with the family. The school record, especially of absences, should be reviewed. Absences that correspond to periods in which it has been established the parents were out of town and had left the children at home, are of particular significance. Tardys are also important, as those latenesses may be the effect of the parents oversleeping and not getting the children off to school. If a pattern can be established, the effect of the neglect in another facet of the children's lives can be presented.

Neglect may be symptomatic of incompetence or family disorientation. It may be the result of poverty, illness or family crisis. In the course of the investigation, form the first contact onward, the officer should not allow himself to become oriented toward establishing neglect. He should remain open-minded and seek the truth, whatever that may be. In doing so, evidence may come to light that will indicate that the matter is of a temporary nature, and at the same time point strongly to a cause that may be remedied by means of a referral to some service within the community. Departments whose investigative services are discovering such situations may be assured of the competence of the investigators.

Removing Children for the Purpose of Protective Custody

The police cannot leave a child unattended. To do so would cause the officer and the department to be liable for the events occurring to the child or because of the child, subsequent to leaving the child alone. How does one determine if a child is left alone and in need of care? Several factors are important in sizing up the situation:

1. *The ages and sex of the children.* Obviously, infants and very small children require more care, and of a more competent nature, than the care required for older children. Girls at all ages are in a position to have been placed in jeopardy, due mainly to the conjecture of possible happenings as a result of the invasion of the home by an outsider.

2. *The age, sex and competence of a babysitter.* There is no age that can be given as an absolute. Many young girls from large families are quite capable of babysitting, while other persons of even adult age are incompetents. Generally speaking, a child of twelve or younger years should not baby-sit for periods into the early morning hours unless that child's parents are close by and available. Any baby-sitter should have been provided with a means of immediate contact with the parents. Teen-age boys should not baby-sit young girls for long periods. A baby-sitter is not the lady next door with seven children of her own who is going to look in on the children.

The aloneness of the children, coupled with the physical surroundings, will be the best indicators. There are occasions when the parents of children will leave town for a weekend or overnight, leaving the children to care for themselves, in charge of the twelve-year-old daughter. In such cases, the police will merely baby-sit for the parents until their return home. At that time the children should be returned to the parents with a reprimand. No formal action is required in such cases, but it should be made clear to the parents that continued conduct like this will result in action being taken. What may be an adequate situation in daylight hours can be drastically changed after nightfall. In making determinations for the care of the children, officers would do well to see the situation as if these were their children.

It is important to remember that if the officer can gain entrance into the home where children are alone, so can anyone else. This immediately places the children in a position where their safety is in question. As many of these calls will be reported during nighttime hours, officers must be very careful in the approach they use with the children. The officer may have to arouse a very young child from a sound sleep. Other children may be crying or otherwise upset. There is a need to understand the situation as the child is experiencing it. It may be that the child has been forewarned about being removed from the home, and told that such a removal is a permanent factor. The child may have a dread of being taken forever from his parents. The awakening by a total stranger in the middle of the night is a traumatic experience for an adult. It is the same for a child. There are several precautions that may be taken to alleviate these problems:

1. *Use tact and patience.* The officer should display understanding and kindness. The voice should not be raised in anger, and the fretfulness of the children should not be allowed to alter the officer's attitude. The experience of coming into contact with a belligerent child should not affect the officer, as many of the children will be conditioned against the police. Such a situation calls for a well-controlled firmness on the part of the officer, but it should be tempered with kindness.

2. *Enlist the aid of the older children.* No matter the age of the older children, they are quick to respond in such a situation to assisting the younger children. This can be done by pointing out to the older ones the need for them to be leaders to keep the smaller ones from being upset. They can be utilized to locate clothes. This keeps them occupied and assists the officer. On some occasions, the younger children will also become involved in the hunt, and it turns into a game.

3. *Learn first names as rapidly as possible,* and call the child by the name the child uses. If his first name is Oglethorpe and he is called "Bo", don't insist on calling him by his real name.

4. *Use childhood terminology,* and explain what is happening. Let the children know the removal is temporary. Let them know what type of a place they are going to, and that it is just until mommy and daddy come back. They have been left alone before, and they know that the parents do come back. This gives them something to cling to, a means of judging the length of the removal. They know they are not being stolen from their parents.

5. *Do not be so big as to fail to stoop.* Literally get down to the child's level. Let him see more than just legs.

6. *Be affectionate.* Children respond to affection. An officer should not hesitate to touch the child's hand or pat his head. Lifting smaller children gives them a sense of security. Carrying one around, as the officer goes from room to room, will assist the children in seeing the humanity of the officer. Again, explain what is being done so the child understands the actions taking place. After all, it is his home.

7. *Be sure you have all children.* Ask the children if this is all. Count noses, and be sure to continue to count after taking the children to a vehicle for transportation. Don't lose or overlook a child.

8. *Leave a note for the parents.* Advise the children you are leaving a note telling the parents where the children are. Ask the children where the best place is to leave it. This involves them, and tends to reduce tensions.

9. *Assign children to one another.* If there are numerous children, assign them to each other so that there is a buddy system worked out. This will involve them in an action, and at the same time assist the officer with keeping track of the various siblings(3).

No matter the condition of the place, this is someone else's home. Take the normal precautions of turning off heaters, lights and securing the place before departing. As much clothing as can be found should be taken, unless the jurisdiction provides such.

When transporting children, all doors should be locked and seat belts should be employed. The officer should be very cognizant of his cargo and should drive with caution. Nothing could be worse than to remove a child for his own protection, and end by having the child seriously injured in an accident, including hitting his face or mouth because of a quick stop. While in the car enroute to placement, don't stop talking. The officer must keep a conversation going in order to avoid a depression from occurring in the children. This conversation may revolve about a preparation for the separation to come. That is the separation that shortly occurs between the officer and the children. At this point the officer is the only person in the world the child knows. Soon this relationship will cease, and the child will again be with strangers. Using terms such as the "nice lady," will tend to give a child a picture of a fairy-godmother type. Any term that is not harsh should be used to describe what remains in the placement procedure. Use terminology that will overcome the child's fears.

Don't lie to the child. If the question is one that the officer does not feel should be answered, tell the child, "I can't answer that", or change the subject, which is usually quite easy to do with young children. But what is told to the child should be truthful. There is no reason for an officer to lie to a young child.

In the event the parents are present at the scene, an arrest will probably accompany any removal of the children. If this occurs, attempt to have the parents, or at least the mother, accompany the placement of the children. If the parents are too emotional, this will be of no avail; and they should be removed from the scene as quickly as possible, as the upset parents will cause the situation to deteriorate for the children quite rapidly. In such a situation, the children may ask if the parents have gone to jail. If possible, refer the children to the time they will see their parents, and allow the parents the explanation of where they were. In addition, some of these cases cause very hostile parental reaction. Many things may be said, and much of it in the vernacular. Later, do not "bad mouth" the parents to the children. The officer may be mad at the situation, at the parents themselves. There may have been some force necessary in affecting the arrest, but there is no cause for the officer to editorialize to the children about how bad the parents are, or about the way the parents have neglected the children. The children were there. They know, but they aren't to be put in the position of having to listen to a stranger talk about the persons who are the closest to them in their young lives.

Officers must understand the effect of the removal on the child; at best, this will be negative. It is up to the officer to use all of his discretion in keeping the effects of the removal from being adverse and detrimental to the child. The rule to be followed is: "The removal of a child should never occur unless his immediate protection is necessary(30)." Therefore, if the situation can wait until the following day, removal is not warranted. Whenever possible, a policewoman should assist in such a removal. There is a noticable positive effect in the utilization of a woman in such cases. Children relate well to women, and a well-trained policewoman can be of invaluable assistance in the course of caring for the children during the period of time they are in police custody.

Police Decision Making in Neglect Cases

Depending on the severity and emergency nature of the encounter, the range of discretion open to the officer is wide. In the more tempered and chronic cases, the decision may be to bring the family into the police agency and institute a follow-up referral to a supportive service within the community. In some cases where there is no emergency, but the case is too involved, referral to juvenile court may be in order. This will be worked out on an appointment basis without child removal. A citation to the district attorney, with a warning from that office, may be all that is needed. But, in the event the children are in a state of immediate danger, their removal becomes necessary. Unless it is a situation in which the police are acting as a babysitter as previously described, the officer should request or file a petition at the first possible moment. This ensures there will be official review of the conditions, and adjudication. It also ensures that the parents cannot come into the picture several days or a week later and demand their children from the placement agency. It gives the placement agency the right to hold the children pending the court hearing, as the court has indicated jurisdiction by accepting the petition.

Because of the variation in the severity of the neglect, and the emergency nature of the various cases, only experience and training can serve as the foundation on which the officer may base his decision. But in any case, the decision should be based on what is in the best interest of the child. There is no room for making cases. There is no room for a punitive concern directed toward the parents. The only concern is for the children, and any decision must be made from a proper evaluation of that objective.

The Right of the Police to Intervene

Society's right to intervene in the care and custody of the children of the community has been established. It now becomes a question of what agency will exercise that right for society. Most authorities are in agreement the police have a legitimate and rightful role in this intervention(5). Protection of persons is a rightful police role. The protection of children is a part of that responsibility. The enforcement of criminal statutes is a rightful police role. As most jurisdictions have such statutes regarding neglect, the investigation of these cases is a police activity. The police have prepared for the performance of this role by the specialized training of officers for juvenile enforcement. In answer to critics of police involvement in neglect cases, it may be asserted that the police would gain such involvement by default, if for no other reason. The police are the only community service so organized as to be capable of giving this investigative protection to children on an around-the-clock basis(6,7,8).

The Contraculture and Neglect

Mention must be made of the effect of the growth of various contracultures within our society on neglect. A contraculture is a group who have left the mainstream of social existence, and have formed a culture within a culture for the purpose of being in opposition to the prevailing cultural standards. Within such a group, any action that is a defiance of the norms of the established culture will be accepted as good. Such groups are characterized by an insatiable desire to shock the "squares." Examples of contracultures are the hell's angel-type motorcycle groups, the hippies, the flower children, various militant racial and ethnic organizations and ideologies, and other groups finding their origin in a failure to adjust. These groups present unique problems regarding the care of children, ranging from having the child participate in dangerous and provoking demonstrations, to witnessing and participating in sexual deviance and utilization of dangerous drugs. These problems are heightened by the manner in which many of these people live . . . and existence so filth-ridden as to defy discreption. Children so exposed are in a position to belong to nothing but the group. They tend to be pawns of the group, to be used by the group, for the benefit of the group. They are exploited in the name of freedom, rights, intellectualism and love. The effects of such neglect on the American scene remain to be evaluated, but society may pay dearly for its tolerance. With such groups, each community, each department must prepare to meet the problem of neglect, in keeping with the manifestations of the group in the community. Police agencies must remain alert to neglect, as well as to other problems attendant to such social piracy. Action should be immediate, firm, sure and swift. The police must educate the public to the realities of such group life, and assist in removing the cloak of romanticism surrounding each contraculture. Police intelligence efforts should be expanded to include the rapid detection of this neglect.

References

1. National Study Service (Final Report): Planning for the Protection and Care of Neglected Children in California. Sacramento State Soc. Welfare Board and Calif. Delinq. Prevent. Comm. Sacramento, Aug. 1965, p. 38.
2. Kvaraceus, William C., and Ulrich, William E. in collaboration with John H. McCormick Jr., and Helen J. Keily: Delinquent Behavior: Principles and Practices. Washington, Nat. Ed. Assoc. 1959, pp. 26-32, 51, 84, 124-135, 221-224, 286.
3. Flammang, C. J.: Juvenile Procedures. An unpublished study prepared for the Division of Vocational Education. Berkeley, U. of Calif. July 30, 1967, p. 85.
4. Myren, Richard A., and Swanson, Lynn D.: Police Work with Children. U.S. Department of Health, Education, and Welfare, Children's Bureau, 1962, p. 66.
5. Eldefonso, Edward: Law Enforcement and the Youthful Offender, New York, Wiley, 1967, p. 125.
6. Kenney, J. P., and Pursuit, D. G.: Police Work With Juveniles, 2nd ed., Springfield, Thomas, 1959, p. 260.
7. Municipal Police Administration, 4th ed. Chicago, Int City Managers Assoc. 1954, p. 1.
8. Neglect, social deviance, and community action. New York, Nat. Prob. Parole Assoc. Jan. 1960, p. 22.

Chapter IV

NEGLECT – CASE HISTORIES

THIS chapter will present several case histories of neglect situations. In so doing, an attempt will be made to show more than the description of various physical facts that indicate neglect. There will be a demonstration of the decision-making process leading to the actions taken, with background histories on the persons involved. By such a presentation it is hoped the reader will be able to interpret the reasoning that lead to the final disposition of each case, thereby bringing into focus the basis of the decision-making process. These cases are excellent examples of the variety of situations with which the police are involved, and show the flexibility of judgment that is necessary to arrive at a proper disposition. The outlines may show officer error, and when these errors appear there will be an effort to point them out and to present the proper police action that should have been taken. These histories are not the final word in examples of neglect cases. Other jurisdictions have handled cases that were more serious in nature, or more classical. These cases have been chosen to demonstrate variety, and the police decision in the face of such variety.

Mrs. T and her Grandchildren

The author's contacts with this case spread over a period of ten years, spanning three professional occupations. Mrs. T was first met in 1954 when the author was a welfare caseworker, and Mrs. T and her two children were a part of the caseload. The area was an unincorporated appendage to a very small rural community. This unincorporated area was populated largely by Negroes. These people were farm laborers. Within this segment of the community were many problems. Being unincorporated, there were no paved streets, sewers, fire or police departments. Consequently, the community just grew, with homes being everything from a makeshift shack to a well-built, three-bedroom home. Life was an armed truce in the daytime, with a jungle atmosphere exhibited at night. Most homes had fences about them, with numerous large dogs to warn of night invaders. The place was anarchy, with the citizens being prey to the deviant behavior of the neighbor. What police action prevailed was in response to a called-for action. There was no patrol in the area. Other than vice operations, assault was the complaint bringing the most frequently called-for police service.

Mrs. T was white. Her mother lived with her and was an aged woman of southern extraction who continually went barefoot. The old woman's feet bore the marks of mud in the winter and dust in the summer. The home was a large but makeshift combination of additions. It was frame and had two large bedrooms, a large front room and a large kitchen area. The home had never been painted, and so gave the impression of a more dingy atmosphere than it would have if painted. As with other homes in the area, the bathroom facilities consisted of an outside toilet. There was running water into the home. The property was fenced with a combination of board and wire, and there were always several dogs about the place.

Mrs. T had been married to a Negro. Her two children were that beautiful combination of medium brown color, coupled with very fine Negro features, with expressive eyes. They were a boy and a girl. The girl was the oldest, and at this time was the only one attending school. Mrs. T and her mother both stated that the father had not appeared to be colored at the time of the marriage, and it was only afterward, when they went to visit his family, that Mrs. T learned the truth. At that time she was pregnant. The T's were living in a southern state, and with the knowledge regarding the racial background of the husband, Mrs. T convinced him they should move. They found their way to a western state and settled for a short time in an urban area. Neither of the T's liked city living, and they shortly moved to the rural community mentioned. Because of the color line, they were forced to live in the unincorporated area. Shortly afterward Mr. T became jobless, as the farm work was highly seasonal. The boy was born, and with two children and a wife to support, Mr. T could see the benefits of welfare. The requirement of being deprived of the support and care of at least one parent was easily remedied. Mr. T moved out and began working as a junk dealer in the area. This led him into several situations where he was involved with stolen property, bringing him into contact with the law. At the same time, he acquired a taste for some of the more exciting facets of life in this community, such as gambling, prostitution and drinking. He worked his way into the controlling element and began to reap the harvest of vice. This placed him in the position of having money for the first time in his life. All combined to draw him rapidly further from the family he had left, until he finally became just a shadow, hovering about the family unit. His influence reduced itself to nothingness.

In the meantime, Mrs. T's mother came to live with her, and the old lady began receiving old-age assistance after establishing eligibility. Mrs. T would do some salvage work for her husband, but this was about the extent of their contact. She began running into trouble in the acceptance of her children in the two communities. The other Negro families would not readily accept the children, and the white community of the incorporated area would not. The children were having difficulty in school, being ignored, teased or mistreated by both the colored and white children. Mrs. T could not be convinced she should move into an urban area for employment purposes, and she felt she was better off in the present situation where she was accepted in part.

By this time, the toll of such living had dissipated the woman; she carried the marks of poverty, fear and deprivation. At no time was her home well-kept, but it was not a neglect situation either. Mrs. T remained close to the home and took a vital interest in her children. She attempted to be active in the P.T.A., and for a while served as a room mother, but she was never accepted. She could feel the line drawn between her, her children and the rest of the community.

The author had a contact with Mrs. T in 1956 while employed as a welfare fraud investigator. A report came to the attention of the fraud unit, that Mr. T was living in the home. It was winter and the facts fit. Often, the laborer is out of work during the winter months. He also has the benefit of longer hours of darkness. The money from the welfare department that is received by the wife, provides food and shelter with, possibly, some spending money thrown in for good measure. The temptation is further rationalized by the fact that he is the woman's husband, and the father of the children. In an attempt to verify the complaint, a call was made at the home early one winter morning. Upon admittance, the house was searched, after Mrs. T gave her consent. Mrs. T and her children, as well as grandmother, were all sleeping in one bedroom. The other bedroom may have contained Mr. T, and with some anticipation, the door to that room was opened. Flashing a light to the left of the door, the investigators were startled to see a full-grown rooster of the fighting cock breed on the dresser. At first it was thought to be stuffed, as it stood perfectly still from the effects of the light. At that time, clucking and shuffling were heard, and it was discovered that the room was full of chickens. There were all breeds, and mostly hens. Many were in box nests. The room had been made into a chicken house, without the benefit of having removed the furniture. There were chickens roosting on the headboard of the bed, and even one hen nesting snuggly in an open drawer of a chest. The droppings from the chickens were throughout, and indicated the use of the room for this purpose for a long time. Both Mrs. T and her mother easily explained this, stating that it was winter time and the chickens could not survive outside. The health problems of such a procedure were pointed out and Mrs. T was advised to make other arrangements for the birds. She was told the case worker would check on this to be sure she had complied. It was somewhat anticlimatic, but Mr. T was not found in the home.

Later, Mrs. T contacted the investigators at their office. She told of some of the problems she had encountered, mostly in regards to the children. By this time the girl was in high school and was attempting to become a baton twirler with the high school band. There seemed to be some discrimination appearing on the scene. Mrs. T had been to the school on several occasions and she had been assured that such was not the case. She related that her daughter was not being made a majorette. She was not lodging a complaint, she was merely talking with people she felt understood.

She wanted no action, and could probably think of none herself. What she was doing was unburdening herself to someone who would listen, before she went back into that world where neither she nor her children belonged.

In 1964, as a juvenile officer for a law enforcement agency, the author again had contact with the T family. A report was received that a Mrs. E was neglecting her children by leaving them unattended for long periods. The author, accompanied by a policewoman, went to the scene to investigate. As the area was a long way from headquarters, a camera was taken to eliminate the call and wait for a police photographer, in the event such was needed. Upon reaching the scene, the house was immediately recognized as the T home. The officers were greeted by Mrs. T's mother. She was in a filthy condition. The old lady was very reluctant to allow the officers to enter the home, but after being advised that since the children were there, and a crime may be in the process of being committed in the officers' presence, admittance was in order. A cursory look about the home revealed filth and dirt everywhere. It also revealed numerous dogs, all seemingly having taken over the home. There was dog residue everywhere: on the floor, even on the beds. The grandmother's feet were caked with it, as were the feet of the two-year-old son of Mrs. E. There was an infant child of Mrs. E's in a crib, being guarded by a dog also in the crib. The dog would not allow the officers near the child. Mrs. T's mother was asked into the bedroom to remove the dog. She was still carrying on a condemning, accusatory conversation about the actions of the officers, being mainly concerned with the fact the officers were photographing the home. As the policewoman was trying to convince her that the children were being removed from the conditions of this environment and that she should cooperate by removing the dog, in order that neither the animal nor the child be hurt; the old lady walked to a corner of the bedroom, hiked her skirt, and while still in an erect, standing position, urinated into a large fruit can, never stopping her tirade and completely oblivious to the presence of the officers.

There were twenty-six dogs in the home, along with several cats. These dogs had defecated throughout the house, and none of this had been cleaned up. It was to the proportions that a scoop shovel would be needed to scrape it from the floors of every room, including the kitchen. How long this had been allowed to exist was never determined, but it was obvious that it had been going on for a month or two.

Mrs. E was the daughter of Mrs. T. She had reached eighteen, had been married, and she had two children. Her husband had deserted her, and she now lived with Mrs. T, the grandmother and her brother. Mrs. E was also receiving public assistance. An interesting sidelight is that such conditions can prevail in a home where there are three separate welfare cases, with the required presence of a caseworker entering the home on regular visits.

Both children were removed from the home at this time. Mrs. T's mother was given the information as to where the children were, and was requested to have Mrs. E contact the officers upon her return. The children were placed in protective custody, and petitions were requested via juvenile court for a hearing to determine their future care and supervision. The humane society was contacted, and that agency rounded up the animals under the statutes giving them jurisdiction.

Mrs. T and her daughter contacted the officers the following date. They had called the department at two-thirty in the morning, and they had been advised they would have to contact the investigators after eight o'clock. This is an important part of any neglect action, the time element. The children had been removed from the home about an hour and a half after the arrival of the officers at the scene. The time of the removal was 3:30 P.M. the previous day. The parent was not there at that time, neither was Mrs. T. They called the department eleven hours later, and a half an hour after the bars had closed. This information is significant. It can only be obtained if the desk officers are alerted to make note of the first contact the parent makes with the police agency after the removal of the children. The parent will contact the police almost immediately after learning about the removal. This places the time of the return of the parent to the home, almost to the minute. This information will not be obtained unless the investigators notify the desk officer and procedures are set up for desk officers on subsequent shifts to be alerted.

The information regarding the time of the parental contact was in contradiction to the story related by Mrs. E and her mother when they were interviewed by the investigators. They stated they had gone to look for work. They neglected to state what type of work they were looking for until 2:30 A.M. When this was finally brought up, they both became quite hostile, as people do when they have come to the end of a false story. The only explanation offered regarding the condition of the home was that "We like animals."

A complaint was obtained from the district attorney charging Mrs. E with neglect. At the juvenile court hearing, the children were made court wards and were placed in foster homes under the supervision of the child welfare agency. Later, at her trial, Mrs. E was convicted of neglect and placed on probation for a period of two years. The decision to prosecute was based on the activities Mrs. E had been engaged in, at a cost to her children. Mrs. E had begun hanging around bars, often with her own mother, soliciting men for acts of prostitution. It was felt, in order to attempt to bring Mrs. E to the point of reconciliation with social norms, whereby she could establish for the juvenile court her willingness to provide a decent home for the children, that the woman was in need of supervision that could best be provided by the probation department.

Mike Cooperates

Mike was a large man. He was also an aggressive person when dealing with public agencies, an experience he had encountered many times. Mike had lost a leg in an accident in 1945. Since that time he had lived by means of the receipt of public assistance. The welfare services had given Mike several opportunities at rehabilitation. He had been provided training by the state on different occasions over the years, and he had been equipped by virtue of this training to support himself and his family. Mike was fitted with an artificial leg which he refused to wear, stating that it hurt him. This leg condition was also the reason Mike gave for not following-up on the training that had been provided for him in several different occupational areas. Consequently, over the years of receiving public assistance, Mike had become institutionalized. He had learned all the tricks of the professional welfare recipient. He knew when to expect sympathy, when to make excuses and when the best defense was a good offense. He had also come to understand one of the facts about social workers. Most of them are women. With his size and aggressiveness, not many women were in a position to hold their own in an argument with him.

Mike eventually became the father of a total of ten children, all subsisting on public assistance. His wife was a good woman who put up with the discomforts that had come her way and attempted to do the best she could with what she had to work with. To make matters worse, there were many difficulties involving the children. The two oldest boys were both on probation for burglaries. The third oldest boy was a severely mentally retarded youth, who did not understand anything going on about him. One of the younger girls had lost an eye when the mentally retarded youth had stuck a stick into the child's optic. There was a ten-year-old boy who was a serious health problem. This child had deformed feet. These required special shoes, and a constant use of clean, dry, heavy white socks. Besides this, the child had a colostomy, having had a serious operation redirecting his colonic functions into a bag attached to his side. This is not an unusual condition in older adults, but it is somewhat rare to find among children. It is usually the surgical result of colon malignancy. The boy had been found to be undernourished at one time and, upon the urging of a caseworker, Mike had consented to the child being placed, on a voluntary basis, into an institution that would build up the child's nutritional deficiency and at the same time offer the care necessary for the child's other problems. The difficulty arose in the divergence of the boy's part of the family budget to the institution, to pay for a part of the child's care. Afterward, Mike became more and more belligerent toward the caseworker and the institution. Finally, he insisted in removing the child and bringing him back into the family unit.

One afternoon the case worker called the law enforcement juvenile unit. Both she and her supervisor were at the home of Mike. The caseworker was exuberent. They had finally found the children alone. Keep in mind, "alone" in this case meant in the care of the seventeen-year-old boy, in broad daylight, with the majority of the children in school. Upon arriving at the scene, the worker and supervisor advised the investigators that they wished to see the children removed; for they knew that Mike had left them alone on many occasions, and besides he was not cooperative. When questioned as to why they had never reported the fact that Mike left the children before this occasion, they stated they had never before found the children alone.

The home was found to be quite clean, but the physical condition of the building itself was very poor. In the first place, the house was not big enough for the family it was housing; besides, it was in a terrible state of repair. The best that could be said for the place was its lack of fitness for human habitation, regardless of the size of the family in occupancy. The welfare representatives were asked how long the family had lived there, and they advised that the present home had been occupied by Mike and his family for five years. It was pointed out to the caseworker and supervisor that the conditions of the house indicated no one should live there. They agreed, and were asked why the family had not been encouraged to move. The answer was classic, "we can only suggest." From the attempts to keep the place clean that were in evidence, it could only be concluded the family had remained here due to Mike's aggressiveness and the lack of insistance on the part of the welfare workers. Over the years, none had stood up to Mike, except the one who had brought about the institutional care of the young boy. Even that had been disrupted, with no further attempts to face Mike after that worker had been placed on another caseload. To the investigators, the gross negligence was on the part of the welfare agency in allowing such conditions to exist for a long period; finally culminating in the desire of the agency to remove the children from the home during daylight hours with a seventeen-year-old in charge, who was stating that the parents would soon be back. The main reason for this removal was based on the fact Mike would not cooperate.

While the investigators were waiting for the children to come home from school, Mike and his wife returned. After receiving their check earlier that date, they had gone with some relatives to town for the women to shop and the men to drink. Mike was not drunk, but he was feeling high. He became belligerent toward the welfare workers and began shouting about that agency and the employees. The officers, realizing there may be difficulty, requested the workers leave the scene, after which Mike calmed down. There were several other occasions when it was thought an arrest might have to be made, as Mike tried his aggressiveness on the officers. Finally, it was decided to cite Mike to the department for the following morning. At the time of presenting Mike with the citation, neither officer was sure he would appear because of the poor attitude he was displaying. But, the following morning Mike was waiting at the department when the officers arrived for duty. Since the most immediate problem was one of housing, and since the welfare department had demonstrated their failure to deal with this situation, Mike was advised that petitions were being requested for a juvenile court hearing to be held to determine whether the children should be allowed to remain in such surroundings. He was told that the major problem was one of housing, and that he could take the time between the petition and the court hearing (about three weeks) to seek better housing. At this, he began making alibis. He didn't have enough money, he didn't have a car, he had tried before. With each alibi, he was met with a lack of sympathy, and the burden of locating adequate housing was placed directly on him. It was pointed out to Mike that if the children were removed, his welfare would cease. He was also advised that by providing better housing, he would be demonstrating to the court his desire for the children to have a proper living environment. It was left up to him.

A few days later, Mike called to state that he had made several attempts but had found nothing yet. He was encouraged to look further, and some advice regarding where he could seek a house was given to him.

Shortly thereafter, one of the investigators left the department and police service. About six months later, while making a turn in a vehicle at a corner within a block of his home, the investigator noted the little boy with the deformed feet sitting in front of a large, well-kept home in the same middle-income neighborhood the former officer resided within. Later, in talking with his own children, the former officer heard them say, "You mean the man with one leg? That's J's daddy." It was true. Mike had found his house. The children were no longer living in a hovel in a ghetto area. Mike had given them a home in a decent area, and the children were to benefit from this new-found dignity and association with a different type of child in a different type of environment. It took awhile, but assimilation has occurred. The younger children are accepted by their peers, and may attain adulthood without the scars of deprivation that the older ones wear. For over two years Mike and his family have lived in the home. Its yard is well-kept. There has been little trouble from his children. The neighborhood has learned to accept them for what they are trying to do for themselves. The only remark the former officer has been heard to say is, "I wonder what would have happened if the large house next door had been vacant;"

The Case of Mrs. G

There were five children in the family. The oldest was seven years. This was a family of lower-class standing. There was no father in the home, and subsistance was provided by public assistance. The home was in poor condition, but was adequate for the standards that prevailed in the neighborhood. Mrs. G had been married at a young age, and there had been multiple pregnancies resulting in a large family of children while she was still quite young. Although in her early twenties, Mrs. G had deteriorated from the life she had led and appeared much older than her years. In addition to the other problems in her life, Mrs. G had become a heavy drinker, bordering on alcoholism. This had occurred as a result of her frequenting cheap bars and taverns, seeking male companionship. The promiscuous attitude of the woman had led to the birth of the last two of her children, each from different fathers. As time passed, Mrs. G's drinking became progressively worse, and ultimately she was reduced to the place where drink was the most important thing in her life. She began spending more time at bars, with her reason for seeking male companionship changing from a psychological need to a financial need. She wanted drinks bought for her. All of the problems accompanying such an existence had occurred to her at one time or another. She had been involved in bar fights, had been the victim of several assaults and batteries, and on at least one occasion, had reported that she had been the victim of a rape. All of these activities reduced her capacity for parenthood, until she reached the place of being unable to care for the physical needs of the children. She was spending so much time at bars that the children were being left unattended during long periods both day and night.

At about four o'clock in the afternoon, the welfare caseworker arrived at the home and found the children alone. This worker called her supervisor, who in turn contacted the juvenile division of a police agency. A juvenile crew was dispatched, consisting of two detective sergeants, one a policewoman. They arrived at the scene about four-thirty and found the caseworker standing outside the front door, crying. The worker had been reluctant to enter the house, as the mother was not at home, and somehow she felt this would amount to an invasion of privacy. Because of the crying, the officers did not know if the worker had been hurt or injured. It developed the worker was crying because she had failed with Mrs. G, after thinking she had made progress with the woman in attempting to upgrade the child care. The children had been found alone before by the worker, and as the conditions of the home were deplorable, the worker had attempted counseling Mrs. G; and was at the point of believing the effort had done some good when this situation had been discovered. For these reasons the worker was upset, to the extent that the officers advised her to return to her office, and they would insure the handling of the children.

The officers entered the home by the back door which led into a service porch. They encountered the seven-year-old girl, who was mentally retarded, in the process of attempting to operate a wringer type washing machine (subsequent investigation revealed the same child had been treated at a local hospital previously for having her arm caught in the wringer). A hot iron was found, having been started by the children during the mother's absence. In checking the home, the general serious neglect conditions of filth and mess were discovered, coupled with a lack of adequate food. The stench was oppressive. The policewoman found Mrs. G's infant child in a crib. The condition of the child was so bad that the officer thought the child was dead. This child was suffering from severe malnutrition accompanied by dehydration. The color was gone from the emaciated body and the skin appeared as if it would split open upon touching. To add to the garish impression, the child had an unrepaired hair lip and cleft palate. The welfare department had made arrangements for the medical attention for this condition, but to date Mrs. G had not taken advantage of this.

In talking with several neighbors, the officers determined that the mother was probably at one of several bars. They left the scene and made a check of the bars in question. The effort to locate the mother was unsuccessful and the officers returned to the home. They had been gone for a period of about forty-five minutes. As they were approaching the rear door, Mrs. G, in a very drunken condition, staggered toward them from the alley. She became belligerent when it finally dawned on her what was going on, and after the officers' attempt to identify themselves had penetrated. Because of her condition and attitude, the officers placed Mrs. G under arrest for neglect and contacted a patrol unit to transport her to jail for processing. The juvenile unit remained at the scene, called for the identification bureau and obtained the necessary photographs. The children were then placed in protective custody. Due to the condition of the baby, that child was admitted to the public hospital suffering from severe malnutrition.

Petitions were requested in order for a juvenile court hearing to occur. A complaint was obtained from the district attorney alleging child neglect against the mother. Mrs. G obtained a court-appointed attorney and pled not guilty, requesting a jury trial. The attorney was successful in obtaining a continuance of the juvenile court hearing pending the outcome of the trial of the mother on the criminal charges. This success came about through the lack of aggression on the part of the probation officer who was to present the case in the juvenile court; the lack of orientation of the judge toward neglect cases, and a proper understanding of the need for the independent protective action of the juvenile court. There should never have been a continuance granted pending the conviction of acquittal of the mother, for as previously stated, for purposes of juvenile court, the guilt or innocence of the mother has no bearing on the existence or nonexistence of the facts of neglect. The court should have recognized this fact, but with its failure to do so, the probation department had the obligation to inform the judge, and strongly recommend that the hearing be held as scheduled. The failure of the probation officer to take such a stand is based on probation's belief that they are employed for the purpose of serving the court, which is true; however, this mission does not place them in a position of remaining silent in the face of error. The obligation to speak out exists, but all too often probation officers remain quiet in the face of judicial opposition. This does not imply that the probation officer need go as far as to cause himself to be held in contempt, but there are judges who do not readily identify the objectives of their role as juvenile court judge in their entirety. Since part of the mission of the probation service is to make recommendations to the court, the fact that these are made in polite, respectful, but strongly worded terms does not mean that probation is out of line with the court. Rather, such would indicate the attempt on the part of that department to carry out one of its important functions.

Due to the court calendar, the trial of Mrs. G did not come up for some six months. The day of the trial, the defendant failed to appear, and a bench warrant was issued for her arrest. The reason for the failure was the fact Mrs. G was intoxicated, and not only had forgotten, but was in no condition to face the court. After her arrest on the bench warrant, the jury trial was altered to a court trial. This was at the request of the defense. As the woman was incapable of making bail on the subsequent arrest, the defense counsel made the request of the court in order to provide the defendant with a speedy trial.

At the trial many issues were brought forth. There was the contention that the officers were in need of a search warrant prior to entering the home, but this issue failed. The defense referred several times to the gestapo tactics of the police involved in the invasion of Mrs. G's privacy. None of these attacks prevailed; however, one error on the part of the officers proved fatal. Both officers, with a number of years of juvenile experience behind them, had left the scene for a period of about an hour to search for the mother. The issue then became the following question:

If the conditions were so serious, of a nature which placed the

children in immediate danger, why did the officers leave the children
unattended to search for the mother?

This had been a tactical error on the part of the officers and, as it
turned out, it carried the day for the defense. Mrs. G was found
not guilty and released. After this finding in adult court, her
children were returned to her. Within seven months, the same
agency and officers again found the children unattended, this time
late at night. Action on this matter went smoothly, the children
were protected by the juvenile court and Mrs. G was convicted of
the neglect that had become a part of her life.

Mrs. S Never Learned

Mrs. S was the mother of four children. Mr. S had been
well-employed and was killed in an accident. The family was left
very well-off financially upon the death of the father. The house
was located in one of the finest districts in the community, and
was now clear due to mortgage insurance. The children had the
benefit of attending some of the very new and very good schools
of that particular school district. This family should have had want
for nothing.

The reaction of the mother to the death of the father was
fearful. She began going out a lot, as it seemed she could not stand
the home any longer. This began her drinking, not so much for the
sake of alcohol, but as a means of contacting men. The woman
would become involved with first one man and then another.
Some of the men she would allow to come home when she had
been drinking heavily, but for the most part she would go off with
them. This became the pattern, with the mother leaving and not
returning for one to three days. The frequency of this increased,
until it became apparent to many who knew her that she was
seldom, if ever, at home with the children.

In the meantime, the oldest child, a girl, was in high school. She
was an attractive girl and somewhat popular. The child was very
talented in music. As the mother became increasingly absent, the
girl assumed more and more of the work around the home. Then
the mother brought a boyfriend home. The man moved in and
they began living together. This caused the daughter extreme

distress for numerous reasons, one of which was the problem of facing children at school, as the situation had become the talk of the area. As the man became more entrenched, the drinking shifted from outside and away from the home, to inside and in the presence of the children. The older daughter was still having to do the housework, look after the younger brother and sisters and also care for the adults, who were intoxicated the majority of the time. As things progressed, the girl became more detached from her surroundings and seemed outwardly to be coping with a severe problem for a young teenage girl. Then events took a turn for the worse. The man in the home began making advances toward the daughter. The girl attempted to gain assistance from the mother, but this only lead to hostile reactions on the mother's part. The mother would not believe that such was going on, and tended to feel that the girl was making up the story to have Mrs. S force the man to leave. The girl received no satisfaction from the mother. She turned to the dean of girls at her high school, and the dean of girls called in the local juvenile bureau. A policewoman responded and talked at length with the girl. By this time the girl's school work had dropped off badly and she had been having disciplinary trouble at the school. This kept the girl from being in the role of the real victim she was, and tended to decrease the empathy with which the school personnel and the policewoman greeted the situation. The girl was finally cited to appear at the police agency juvenile unit the following date, with her mother. This meant that the mother, who was now drinking heavily and who had failed to assist the daughter when requested, was now going to be asked by the daughter to go to the police over the boyfriend. This was too much. Feeling she had nowhere to turn, the daughter went home and committed suicide by shooting herself. The body was found by the mother and the boyfriend after returning home.

This child was in desperate need of help and was crying out to any one who would listen, but found no one there. At the same time, it is hard to condemn any of those involved, as they were all reacting as humans do. The mother was so wrapped up in what was going on about her that she had no time or need for the daughter. The dean of girls had been having trouble with the girl right along, but was not fully aware of the home situation, as the girl had kept this from her. On the occasion of this report, the dean felt the problem was being exaggerated, as children often do, especially those who are in borderline trouble themselves. This was the attitude that was displayed to the policewoman by the dean, and this woman also misread the problem, thinking it would keep until the following date. If either the dean or the policewoman had put themselves in the position of the child for a short time, they would have both recognized beforehand what we see so clearly now. They were asking the girl to do the impossible and, in so doing, sent the girl away with nowhere to turn.

With the demise of the girl, the mother realized the folly of bringing men home, but this did not slow down her activity. It merely shifted it outside the home. The remaining three children were very small at this time. The oldest was a girl, but she was still in the lower grades. As the mother continued her romping throughout the area, the children were consistently left alone to fend for themselves. They did not do a very good job. The house became more of a mess and the children did also. Their absentee rate at school increased, and conditions became progressively worse. Finally the police were notified and the children were picked up and placed in protective custody. The mother was charged and petitions were filed with the juvenile court. The children became court wards and were placed into foster home care. But, this did not last long. As soon as the mother was out of jail, after serving ninety days less good time, the children were returned to her.

Within a two-year period, these children were found alone on four separate occasions, and in each case were removed from the home and made court wards. In each case, the mother was charged with child neglect and received short jail sentences, but everytime she was released, her children were returned to her. On the fifth occasion, officers were summoned to the home in broad daylight. The children were home alone and they had not been attending school for several days. The house was quiet as the officers approached. They finally heard some noise inside and, after identifying themselves and requesting that the door be opened, the officers entered the house through the front window. The home was in its normally bad condition. this was to be expected. The children were another matter. They were located in the bathroom in the master bedroom, but they had locked themselves in, and no amount of persuasion could get them to open the door. The officers were able to pick the lock and bring the children out. The children were very belligerent. They had been through the mill many times, and furthermore had been coached by Mrs. S not to allow officers into the home. The fact that the officers had made their way in and located the children made them all furious.

The children were in the process of being removed when Mrs. S appeared. She was placed under arrest and advised of her rights. Mrs. S was charged with neglect again and the children were placed in protective custody. In this final instance, Mrs. S must have had enough. She got out on bail and went out of state for a period of time. When she returned, she was married to the present boyfriend, who was not a bad character. He succeeded in straightening her up where the system couldn't. The district attorney dismissed charges and the juvenile court allowed the children to return home as court wards. This action did not solve all the family problems, but apparently it kept Mrs. S at home. The neglect calls did not occur and the children went on to a little better life.

Chapter V

THE ABUSED CHILD

A POLICE investigator was called to a large metropolitan hospital. There he saw a three-month-old baby girl who was being treated for fractures of both femurs, the large bone located in the thigh. The child was in traction, but seemingly comfortable. The resident pediatrician, a female doctor, informed the officer that interviews of the child's parents had failed to reveal any information regarding the nature of the injuries. All the parents would state was that the child had been fussing and crying for about two days and, after swelling had appeared in one leg, they had brought the child to the hospital for examination. At the time of the examination it was discovered the child had sustained fractures of both legs. The admitting physician had attempted to determine from the parents the cause of the injury, but had received no concrete information. The resident was questioned by the officer regarding the manner in which such injuries could occur in a child so young. Her answer gave a detailed account of the strength and elasticity of a young child's bone structure, ending with the statement, "Someone broke her legs." This caused a discussion of the doctor's willingness to testify, and with the mention of testimony the statement just uttered disappeared into a cloud of inconsequential hypotheses, ending with the suggestion the baby may have caught her legs in the crib, thereby breaking her own bones. Even the doctor had trouble with that statement. There was no evidence that the child could sit up, or even move about to the extent that she would be capable of having both legs caught in a crib, in order for the fractures to ensue. The concept of an infant fracturing her own legs, with the pain that would accompany the attempt, was somehow farfetched. The resident stated that possibly the child's bones were brittle, and when she was questioned as to such a determination, she referred the investigator to the radiologist who had read the x-rays.

Contacting the radiologist at his office, the presence of osteogenesis imperfecta, a congenital bone disorder causing brittleness of the bone to exist, was dismissed. An attempt to question the specialist further brought his insistence he could make no statements inferring that such fractures were unusual for a child of this age to have suffered in the confines of her own home.

This case, more than any other, demonstrated clearly to the officer involved the need for medical testimony in cases of abused children. He had been in charge of such investigations before, but never had he seen a child of three months with both of the largest bones in the body fractured, and no explaination forthcoming from the parents about how such an injury could have occurred. The case in question was prior to any national interest in the "battered child syndrome(1). In frustration, the officer completed a report to be entered in the files of the department, and proceeded on to other matters. The sight of that child, and the artificial defensiveness of the doctors, were to later serve as a stimulus to action.

Law enforcement has lived with the abused child for a long time. The police have many occasions to come into contact with children abused in a variety of ways. Methods of inflicting pain and trauma have matched the number of individuals involved, and the police officer has encountered the results. With the increase in specialization in juvenile enforcement, the problem came to the attention of farsighted police personnel, who had an early recognition that numerous children were being injured and killed by the very persons who were to give them care and protection. These officers also recognized the lack of response on the part of others, including coroners and physicians. How many instances where these officers saw such cases disposed of officially as accidental cannot be enumerated, but the sum would be astounding. It is factual information that law enforcement is not a johnny-come-lately to the field of abused child protection; but, rather, it represents the one agency that has long recognized this problem(2).

The Problem

In order to deal with the abused child effectively, it is necessary to recognize the existence of two situations that must both be attacked. First there is the abuse itself. Who abuses children, what type of child is abused, what are the nature of the most debilitating injuries, what causes abusive action on the part of the parents and other caretakers, what is the rate of incidence? These and many other questions must be answered before the knowledge necessary to effectively cope with this social ill will be attained. Some of these are partially answered at this time, others are in need of research. There are exacting attendant problems dealing with effective legislation, jurisdiction, proper procedures and the extent of treatment of both victims and offenders. There are many schools of thought regarding the best course of action for those agencies and institutions which have been traditionally involved. While many of these questions and much of the confusion surrounding the abused child problem remain to be answered or clarified, the fact remains that the children are being abused.

> It is a tragic commentary on the mental and moral health of our nation that the most common cause of children deaths today is physical abuse of children by their own parents(3).

This is a dramatic and often surprising statement by a leading authority in the field. How many people are aware of this fact, and how many of those who do know the fact believe it? Therein is the second part of the problem. A lack of recognition, belief or concern over the leading cause of infant mortality. How has this disbelief developed and why does it continue to persist? As far back as 1946 a radiologist, Doctor J. Caffey, read a paper before the American Medical Association describing the clinical diagnosis of this condition by use of full-body skeletal surveys through x-rays(4). Such radiological examination of an abused child would tend to reveal multiple fractures in various stages of healing. The fractures would be telltale injuries to the joints, the ends of the long bones, or spiral fractures of the long bones. Such trauma would be the result of a wrenching or twisting; the result of an applied force. The fact that the injuries were seen during various stages of healing would indicate to the specialist the existence of a pattern of injurious action occurring over a long period of time, with little or no medical care being sought or applied to alleviate pain, suffering or deformity. The ability to seek out this information and utilize the findings in making a determination that the child is in need of protection, has been finalized by other experts in the medical field, such as Dr. Kempe of the University of Colorado Medical School, Dr. Silverman, University of Cincinnatti, and Dr. Petersen, University of California. The latter, during a presentation December 5, 1964 before the Northern California Pediatrics Association, stated that any radiologist could, if he wanted to, make such a radiological identification. At this writing, there are a majority of radiologists throughout the United States who make no such attempt at discovery. There exist a majority of pediatricians whose involvement in the care of children never reaches the proportions of requiring such diagnostic methodology. There are parents who continually accept the word of the other spouse in general, and flimsy explanations of the occurrences leading to childhood injuries. There are social workers who have never heard of the "battered child." There are coroners and pathologists equally ignorant. These same conditions extend from the neighbor to the juvenile court judge, from law enforcement to the legislature.

The reason is simple, and yet complex. In its simplified form the reason is a basic revulsion at such acts; a revulsion that causes a denial. No one wishes to believe that such events could happen, that parents charged with the care and supervision of their own children could perform in such a manner. People are the servants of their experience. For most, these experiences are the common sharing of good, effective and dedicated parents, whose self-sacrificing efforts in behalf of their offspring are legend. The general conceptualization of parenthood is one of Mother's Day and a painting of an old lady in a rocker, now hanging in the Louve of Paris. Thoughts go back to tender scenes, apple pies and affectionate admonishments. All of these concepts result from experiential impressions. Such impressions not only spring from experience, they are also subjected to the screening of conscious memory-deleting events of a painful nature, throwing out that which would disrupt an otherwise tranquil and meaningful recollection of persons, places and things. These same concepts are held by most parents about their own parental effectiveness. As most people have experienced good and decent child care, for them to attribute a lesser degree of care to relatives and friends surpasses their range of experience and, thereby, is easily rejected. It is within the context of this rejection, this denial of the possibility of such events, that the simple form of the disservice to the underprotected child exists.

In its more complex form, the reason for the blindness exhibited by society falls into three catagories. These are: the lack of knowledge of the type of person performing such acts, the present drift toward a nation of uncommitted people, and the existence of an extremely complex pace of living. An attempt will be made to analyze and clarify the meaning of each of these factors as each relates to the reason for the prevailing unawareness of the abused child problem.

First, the lack of knowledge of the type of parent involved. For humans, much time is spent searching for reasons, and this is very true of the culture of twentieth century America. As a nation, as well as individuals, the people of this country must have answers to various problems with which they become involved. This is true in personal matters as well as in domestic and international encounters. The question is invariably heard . . . "Why?" For a thinking, educated people to be denied answers causes a crisis to occur within the individuals, bringing on frustration and anxiety. As these feelings are negative, and as they in turn cause more questions, with the attendant void in relation to answers, the person attempts to counter the turmoil. To do so, there often occurs a repression of the fear of the unknown, an attempt to cover the anxiety of the undefined. Thus, if the reasons cannot be found, if there is no explanation forthcoming, there is a tendency to ignore or dismiss the unfathomable as if it did not exist. For most, the type of person who inflicts injury upon children of tender years is beyond understanding. The most that can be stated by way of explanation is that the person "must be sick." But as an answer of any depth, this is not satisfactory for thinking individuals. Therefore, persons coming into contact with such situations are left without any understanding as to why they occurred. What is required is more research to provide the answers to the questions that are asked. To date, studies of such persons who have been identified as offenders, have been very limited. Until there is an understanding of the nature of these persons, there will continue to be a denial of the existence of the offenses. This allows it to be easier to make statements to the effect that the problem is not acute, it is a limited situation, it does not occur often; and from these premises it is not difficult to postulate that the effort needed to control these acts is one of limited concern, somehow belonging to the other fellow.

Secondly, the American society has become one of uncommitted people. Not only are people not committed on the broader scale of national concerns, they lack commitment to their fields of endeavor, their families and themselves. This noncommitted attitude is continually being displayed throughout community life. It is seen not only in relation to law enforcement, but in the many facets of social action and family relations. It extends from the neighborhood to the national scene. This country suffers from a disregard for the other person, a public apathy of such a level as to worry social scientists and defy their efforts to identify the root causes of such attitudes. Basically, too few wish to become involved, and those who do often pay for their involvement mentally, emotionally, financially or physically. It is both easier and safer to remain aloof, to be unaware of environment happenings. This detachment from the concerns of others has been a major factor in the failure of the society to come to the rescue of the abused child.

The third factor affecting the failure to come to grips with this problem stems from the pace of living in twentieth century America. In the torrent of work involved in any of the fields that are necessary to the proper protection of children, abused child cases are seen as but a trickle in the deluge. They are identified as but a small amount of the caseload such agencies must handle. Every case of an underprotected child requires extensive effort in order to accomplish the desired results. For most of these agencies, it is either impossible or impractical to expend the necessary effort in terms of time, budgets and manpower needed to cope with the dilemma. Not only are many communities lacking the services that need be offered, but the agencies that do exist are suffering from increased caseloads and added responsibilities, with a lack of a corresponding increase in budgets, equipment and trained personnel. With the increase in agency services has come an increase in agency record keeping. These records emanate from the field worker. These persons are overwhelmed with reports, forms and sterotyped contacts requested by law or agency* policy. This is as true in the area of law enforcement as it is in any other. Consequently, the time needed to conduct an extensive investigation is drastically shortened by the time consumed meeting deadlines and compiling reports. These agency employees are not without their own sufferings, as the result of our progress in living. They have the same problems as the rest of the population. These problems affect them in the same manner as such situations affect others. There is a reduction in the effectiveness and capability of the employee during his time of stress. In addition, each professional is limited in the ability to function in every area of the broadened caseload presented. It is much easier to view the area of underprotected children as a small portion of concern than it is to become deeply involved in the tangle of events that seems to accompany such cases.

All of these factors are interwoven. They all effect the individual, the agency and the community. Each plays its part well and each becomes disguised within the individual's own rationalizations, causing the identification of any or all of the factors to be more difficult. Thus, the reason why the problem of abuse continues to gain but little attention may lie within the confines of the individual's failure to concern himself with an analysis of his own rationalizations. But in one way or another the factors are there, forming a thicket of protection, insulating the individual from the basic problem, with the resultant failure to recognize the existence of an abused child.

The Manifestations of Abuse

Abuse to children takes on various forms, from minor assaults on the person of the child, to the most flagrant and long range physical tortures imaginable. Children are beaten with hands, belts, sticks, clubs; they are burned with cigarettes, matches, hot irons and scalding water. They are locked out of the home and locked inside the home. They are deprived of food, beds and, in some instances, toilet facilities. Their hair is pulled out in handfuls, their arms are yanked and twisted, wrenching the bones and ligaments at the joints. They are beat about the head, causing brain damage and, in some cases, death. They are poisoned, forced to drink filthy water or other fluids that cause their stomachs to wretch; and then, they are denied medical aid for many of the injuries suffered.

For the majority of adults, a fracture of a bone is something that happens to someone else. Most have never had a broken bone, but many have participated in sports or have been employed in occupations that tend to give rise to such injuries. There are children who, before the age of four years, have suffered from three to seven or eight fractures, all as a result of their environment. It is important that this fact be kept in mind: the abused child suffers more injuries in a shorter period of time while living in the home, than most professional football players suffer in a ten-year period of being engaged in that activity. In addition, the injuries suffered by the child are, for the most part, left untreated, with the child undergoing the added pain and debility pursuant to such injuries being healed through natural process. The tragedy of abuse is in the fact that these things occur to the child while in a position of almost total dependance upon the attacker.

According to a 1963 survey by the American Humane Society, many of the injuries to these children are the results of beatings with a hair brush, fly swatter, baseball bat, sculling oar, pool cue, rubber hose, straps, belts and sticks. But other injuries are a negative testimony to the ingenuity and inventiveness of man(5). These have included burning the extremities of the child over an open flame, while other children have been dipped in scalding water or other hot liquids, or such heated liquids were thrown upon the child. In a few extreme cases, the boiling substance was administered by means of an enema tube. Parents have strangled, bitten, suffocated and drowned their child. Children have been placed in freezers, kicked, thrown into walls or onto floors, and have even had pepper stuffed down their throats. From the variety of methods of inflicting trauma, the injuries also vary from minor contusions and welts, to severely burned areas and broken bones. In the survey, one five month old child was found to have received thirty broken bones(5).

This survey was conducted in 1963, and was under the direction of Vincent DeFrancis. It was a newspaper survey on a nationwide scale. The study disclosed 662 cases, that included 178 deaths from the inflicted injuries. The majority of the cases involved children under the age of eighteen months. Very significantly, the survey discovered that children who had been removed from the home after being identified as abused had a mortality rate of 20 percent when returned to the same environment within one year. Furthermore, of the surviving 80 percent, 50 percent of those children will suffer serious trauma withing the same year(5). This information points to the extreme danger existing whenever a child is replaced into a home from which he had been taken due to sustained inflicted trauma. These findings were somewhat substantiated by a follow-up study of fifty former abuse patients at Children's Hospital, Pittsburg, Pennsylvania in the same year. From this study it was found that 14 percent of those children released back to the home were deceased. Sixty percent of this mortality rate occurred among children under ten months of age, with the majority being in the three-month age group(6).

From these figures it is apparent the major portion of the problem exists in children of tender years, many who will be under two years of age. This information has been subsequently verified by studies performed by other authorities, as well as surveys in local jurisdictions. It may be stated that the child in need of protection, the individual of greatest concern, is the child of infant or preschool years. This is a very serious matter for a number of reasons. The child of this age is under the total care and supervision of his parent. He is isolated in his environment. There is no escape, there is nowhere to go. He must remain there and suffer at the hands of the offender. Because the child is in the home twenty-four hours a day, the ability to detect or identify the situation is reduced, as the child's movements are restricted. No one with a severely bruised or beaten child allows that child to come into contact with persons who may become alarmed at the condition. To others, the caretaker may successfully explain away the injuries or marks by indicating a plausible accident the child may have suffered. In any case, the child is not subjected to the scrutiny of the general public or the suspicions of a teacher or a school nurse. The victim remains in the same place and with the same person causing the injuries. There is no way to determine the number of children who are existing in such a dilemma at this time. Many of these children will never be identified as "battered children," but will continue to suffer trauma until they are old enough to protect themselves, or until their lives are snuffed out in one moment of anger or uncontrolled emotion.

In considering the infant child, one must be cognizant of the fact that the child cannot walk. This child is confined to not only the general home environment, but more specifically to the very place he is put, be that a bed, a freezer or a bathtub full of water.

An additional problem for these children, and one causing them to be more vulnerable to continued abuse, is their lack of ability to verbalize on the injuries or talk about the conditions under which they live. Due to the tender years involved in so many abuse cases, the child is unable to communicate. He cannot tell who did what. He cannot even describe his pain or the area of the body in which the serious pain is felt. This allows abuse cases to be "mute cases," situations in which the victim is unable to communicate the circumstances surrounding his present condition. All that is provided for the child in way of expression is the ability to cry or whimper. The surprising fact is the lack of such emotional reaction after undergoing months or years of abuse. These children tend to become resigned to the severity of their existence, and their crying is often restricted to those moments of extreme pain or to the period of the infliction of the injury. As many are injured in reaction to their crying, the association between crying and further harm is readily made. Once this occurs, the parent is freed from the problem of neighbors becoming aroused at the continued screaming of a young child, and again silence works in favor of the suspect.

Many people, when hearing about the "battered child

syndrome" for the first time, react by thinking in terms of the parental right to discipline the child. These persons are visualizing a fourteen-year-old boy or girl who is no longer willingly submitting to the control of the parent, with the parent taking action by use of corporal punishment. This is a rightful parental action and one that does not require intervention, unless it goes beyond that which can be deemed reasonable. But this is not the situation found in abused child cases. For the most part, the victims are preschool age. This must be stressed, to overcome the foregoing notion of parental disciplinary rights. These victims are at such an age that discipline is not yet needed in a severe form. The situations these children find themselves in requiring discipline, are normal situations of childhood curiosity and exploration. To choke a child of two years with an electric cord to stop the child from pulling over the lamps is unnecessary; as a gentle pat on the hand, accompanied by a meaningful "no" would accomplish the same purpose, but do so with the security of love and affection. Occasionally a child of grade school years will be abused to the extent of severity, and these cases also fall into the abused child catagory; however, these children are graced with the attributes of added years. They can walk and run. They can talk and verbalize what has occurred to them. They have the benefit of the school system's protection. They will be seen by others. If questioned, they can tell what happened and can describe the act, the weapon, the circumstances and the suspect. These older children are not left as readily unprotected as the younger ones. Their ability to survive is greater, as their ability to have the matter identified, and thereby gain the protection of society, is in proportion to their increased age. This means that the main concern of society must be directed toward the protection of the infants and young preschool children. The ability to identify these cases, and the development of proper procedures for effective disposition, must be a concern of all agencies representing society's protective ability. According to Doctor William Ziering, former Chief of Pediatrics at the Fresno General Hospital, Fresno, California, and the founder and first chairman of the Fresno County Battered Child Committee:

The Battered Child Syndrome can be likened to a malignancy. In one years time, about 20 percent of the injured children will be dead. Few tumors are that devastating. For this blight on human resources the subject is qualitatively different from child neglect and consequently demands our fullest attention. Happily the subject has surfaced somewhat the past six years and is being discussed and examined critically in some areas.

At best, even with the fullest resources from the notable psychosocial services, there are no cures, only improvements. Rehabilitation or, better, habilitation must be the ultimate goal, but the issues are complex and professional personnel extremely limited.

There is no socioeconomic group nor geographical area to which the abuse is limited. It traverses the total of society, spanning the continent, and prevailing in the best as well as the worst neighborhoods. There is no community, no area without incidents of abuse. Those areas feeling secure because of the failure to have knowledge of the condition, are not as free of abuse as they are failing in the identification and recognition of the existing cases. There is a large differentation between the existence of the abuse and the discovery of the same. In areas of higher economic standards, the abused child is taken to a private physician for treatment. The explanation usually given by the parent is accepted with little or no reservation. The doctor is usually the family physician, and very often knows the family socially as well. For him to suspect this parent to be abusing the child is against his better judgment. The case goes undetected. In the areas of lower social and economic factors, the people are not as well oriented towards one physician, and in a large number of instances such families are utilizing the services of a public medical institution. These public institutions, as well as the staffs of such hospitals, are better oriented toward the identification and reporting of such incidents. The public institution accepts the majority of accident and assault cases on an emergency basis. The personnel are quite cognizant of the law, requiring the reporting of these various traumatic injuries. They are used to having the police and other investigators about and have established procedures for the dissemination of information. Because the lower class has more medical contact with such institutions, the rate of incidence among these persons appears statistically higher. This probably does not reveal the true picture, as the higher on the social and economic ladder a family may be, the less chance of identification of abuse. This will effect the rate of identification and reporting for the higher social group. There is a willingness on the part of the middle-class American to readily report the ineffectual conduct of the lower-class citizen. It is an "I told you so" attitude. This is also a part of the reason for the high proportion of lower-class families in which this problem is identified. But those persons working in the field have the best insight into the distribution of the rate of incidence. In other words, there may be a leak in information regarding a higher-class abuse case. Someone may have questioned the events surrounding the injury and reported the same to an agency, with a subsequent investigation ensuing. That investigation may not be too effective because of the nature of who is being investigated. In the end, the investigation does not reveal enough to do more than dispose of the matter as unfounded. This disposition would be in the record, but such a case would not become a part of a statistical study. At the same time, the investigator would be well aware of why this case failed to materialize. The cause could be the result of pressures brought to bear on the department or the investigator. It may be the failure to gain the cooperation of witnesses, or the result of the legal protections afforded all citizens, but more readily attainable by the upper class. In such a case it is often impossible for the investigator to have any contact with the parent. Most field workers, recognizing the existence of abused situations, also recognize there is no one group or area to which such cases are confined. Abuse can be found anywhere and in any family. The potential for child abuse is increased with the existence of certain correlative factors, but it is a social ill that can be found throughout the community.

Reporting the reception of 103 cases of abuse during the year 1962, it was concluded the rate of incidence known to one agency in a county of 400,000 was in line with known figures in other areas(7). A Denver study in 1962 revealed a total of 750 abuse cases identified, seventy-eight of which resulted in death, with another 114 sustaining permanent brain damage(1). In a study performed in Kansas involving eighty-five identified cases of abuse, the majority of the children were under three years of age, with one third being under six months. Fourteen of the cases resulted in fatalities, and all of these children were under four years(8). In the first nine months following the enactment of a state reporting law in Illinois, 363 cases were identified. Two hundred and forty-seven of these children were under five. Of these, ninety-nine were under one year. Under a U. S. Children's Bureau grant (Number H-83), Brandeis University is conducting a Nationwide Epidemiological Study of Child Abuse. The study is surveying the central reporting services of all fifty states, Washington, D. C., Puerto Rico and the Virgin Islands. In a tentative report issued in 1968, covering information from January, 1967 through December of the same year, the following facts were derived: 14 percent of the children reported to be victims were under one year old; about one third were under three and another third were between three and eight years. It should be noted that the very young child was not as markedly represented as in other studies of identified hospital populations. At the same time, the type of injury tended to be minor in a majority of cases; 76 percent were listed as abrasions, lacerations, bruises and welts, with severe injuries to the head accounting for only 7 percent of the trauma(9). The study, utilizing state reporting systems, showed a wide variation in the ability to report, with reports ranging from 1,313 in one state, to nine states reporting less than ten cases and one jurisdiction reporting none. This variation may be accounted for, in part, by difference in population; but variations in reporting laws, definition of abused children and local procedures and recognition also affect the findings. Furthermore, the two largest groups of children reported, when combined, comprise the age group from three years to twelve years. This was approximately two thirds of the reported cases. As this large group is beyond the home and into the school, the extent of the injuries would tend to be less severe and, for the most part, would result from over-discipline. This could account for the low rate of infant mortality found to exist, as well as the low rate of serious injury. The hard-to-reach cases of the younger children are not being identified. The easily identified cases of the school-age child, resulting from overt disciplinary activity, are the cases coming to the attention of the majority of the authorities throughout the nation, leaving the child of tender age still underprotected.

Definitions

In an effort to clarify some of the terminology being utilized in this chapter and in other portions of this text, the following definitions are presented to assist the reader:

1. *The Maltreatment Syndrome* as defined by Dr. Fontana is a pediatric disease presenting no signs of being battered, but having multiple minor physical evidences of emotional and at times nutritional deprivation, neglect and abuse(3).
2. *A Syndrome* is a group of signs and symptoms that occur together and characterize a disease(10).
3. *A trauma* is bodily injury produced by violence or any thermal, chemical or extrinsic agent(11).
4. *The Battered Child Syndrome* as set forth by Dr. Kempe, is a clinical condition in young children who have received serious physical abuse from a parent, often described as unrecognized trauma leading to disability or death(1).
5. *An Inflicted Trauma* is an injury received as the result of an action by another individual being performed against the person of the victim.

Factors Relating to Abuse (type of offender)

There are many factors that relate to abused child cases, and these will vary from case to case; however, at this time there are certain correlative factors that tend to point in certain directions and that can be utilized to assist in understanding the nature of the phenomenon. The majority of the information has been gathered within the past five to six years, and this area of study is still far from complete. The limited information at hand is somewhat reliable, in light of the experience of those who are working directly with such cases.

The American Humane Association survey indicated that the parents, either together or singly, inflicted 78 percent of the injuries to the offspring. The parents accounted for 75 percent of the deaths discovered in the study. This is significant to counteract the thinking that most of the injuries to children are inflicted by a parent substitute, a stepparent or a boyfriend. This study also showed the most serious injuries to be inflicted by the mother. In the majority of the situations studied, both parents were found to be living in the home. Only about one third of the mothers in these homes were working outside the home with any regularity, and subsequent studies have failed to indicate any correlation between working mothers and child abuse. The majority of the parents were in the twenty to thirty-year age group. This overcomes the commonly held impression that such parents are suffering from the results of their own young age and chronological immaturity. At the same time, the one most frequent cause of traumatic parental behavior was identified as emotional immaturity or instability(5). What is clear from such a study is the high rate of incidence in abuse cases wherein the injury is inflicted by the natural parent, sometimes with the knowledge and even the participation of the other parent. These parents are not the young teens who lack the maturity of age, but are generally older and supposedly more mature individuals. There may be found to exist a significant correlation between the early teen-age marriage and the effects of such a marriage on the parties involved at a period a few years hence, under the strain of several children and social and economic burdens. Additional study of the offending parties is desperately needed, but one of the largest handicaps to such studies is the identification of the individuals. In the majority of abuse cases, the adult offending parent is not identified as being the perpetrator.

The Brandeis study showed a trend for the perpetrators identified to have been involved previously with the abuse of the same child in 35 percent of the cases, and for them to have been involved in the abuse of this victim's brothers and sisters almost 20 percent of the time. This indicates a harsh fact: abusers tend to remain abusers. This is an incidence of repetition that cannot be ignored. Dr. Ziering, in a lecture at Fresno State College in 1963, stated;

> What is most repulsive about the whole field is that to date, there is not known, not authenticated to be one solitary case wherein a family has been successfully rehabilitated. Naturally, the ultimate resolution of this problem is to rehabilitate the family, but we must not be naive.

According to Helen Boardman, Director of Social Services, Children's Hospital, Los Angeles:

> The 1959 hospital project began with a review of the records of twelve patients believed to have inflicted trauma. Six of the patients were under twelve months of age and all were under three and one half years of age. All but one had a history of repeated injuries. All had remained with their parents after they had sustained suspected inflicted injuries. Three were dead and two had died of injuries occurring after the parents had been placed on probation following conviction for inflicted injuries. The parents of a four month old baby were, at the time the baby was admitted to Children's Hospital, awaiting preliminary Criminal Court hearing on charges of inflicting injuries on the child. The baby had remained with them while awaiting trial, only to sustain another, almost fatal, injury(12).

Margaret Stumpf, Childrens Services Supervisor, Fresno County Welfare Department, in a speech to the California State Juvenile Officers Association in Bakersfield, California in March, 1965, brought forth the concept that "rehabilitation" presupposes some previous level of effectual activity from which one has descended, and she substituted the term "habilitated" as the goal to be attained, contending that these parents were never at a state of functioning parenthood. In any event, there are numerous authorities who agree on the recidivist nature of the offending parent, and the omnipresence of danger whenever the child is placed under their care and supervision.

The only psychiatric team to have worked extensively with persons known to have inflicted trauma upon children, have done so in conjunction with the studies on the "Battered Child Syndrome" at the University of Colorado Medical School. The findings and conclusions of the psychiatrists involved are of significant interest to those endeavoring to be of some assistance in the protection of children. It should be pointed out that the area of psychiatric or psychological investigation of the personalities and disorders of the offending parties is one of great importance, but an area little touched by any adequate studies. The efforts of this team are important not only in relation to the findings, but also in the fact that the studies have occurred at all.

In a presentation to the Northern California Pediatrics Association in San Francisco December 5, 1964, Dr. Carl Pollack, one of the members of the Colorado psychiatric team, presented various facts regarding the personality conflicts of the offending parents and the manner by which treatment was being carried out at that time. The team had been working with such parents for a period of three years. It consisted of two psychiatrists, Doctors Carl Pollack and Brandt Steele, two psychologists and one medical-social worker(13).

Although the team encountered some evidence of psychosis existing in a few of the persons studied, the majority were not suffering from this malady. For the most part, it was felt, the psychotic individual was not the problem. The parent most often involved in the battering of a child was described as a person who had never experienced a well-adjusted, meaningful and successful personal relationship, including that with the individual's own parents and spouse. Because of this lack, treatment involves the tedious development of a successful personal encounter with another human, often a member of the staff. These parents were found to be narrow individuals, quick to make denials and capable of bearing punishment. This ability to endure punishment results from their experiences and long suffering at the hands of condeming relatives and friends, who have cautioned and cajoled for a long period of time in order to rebuke the parent to recognize that he is not a good parent. While such attempts at fostering insight are carried out, the person feels strongly that his parenthood is good and that he is undergoing undue criticism. This process tends to condition the parent to accept punishment from a martyred concept, fully knowing the condemner to be wrong.

There are signposts that indicate problems, and these are of importance, as the field worker will quite often be in a position to become exposed to such signs, and early identification of these cases is necessary. Dr. Pollack indicated the parent who is extremely anxious about the child's eating habits, especially at or near age one year. This problem was cited as a priority for several reasons. First, it is normal for a child to go through periods of poor eating during the infant stage. This is not unusual, nor do such actions present any serious health hazard unless continued for long and unreasonable periods. Consequently, eating-habit fluctuations are going to be experienced by every parent. The person who becomes overwrought at such activity on the part of the child is dangerously close to being in a position where battery of the child may not be too farfetched. As the child acts poorly as an eater, the parent views this as a conflict of wills between the parent and child. There is an inability to keep the situation in the proper perspective of childhood normalcy. The problem develops in how the parent will resolve this conflict. The manner by which the parent imposes his will on the child becomes crucial. In the moments of such a conflict, injury to the child may occur.

A similar serious conflict situation in the parent-child relationship occurs when the parent is overly sensitive to the child's crying. When the crying of the child becomes a conflict, both tension and anxiety occur within the parent. The parent is in need of establishing his own equilibrium. In the conflict of wills, the need for the parent to impose his will on the young child stems from the lack of the ability of the parent to relate himself to another through a mutually rewarding personal relationship.

These persons are exhibiting emotional fixations or arrested emotional development; probably in the narcistic stage, the stage of an emotional growth and development usually experienced by the three to five-year-old child. This is a period in life when the "I" figure dominates. It is characterized by selfishness, inability to share or become deeply attached to another person, and is a time when the needs of the individual are paramount. During this phase of development the individual finds difficulty in accepting or sharing blame, and alibis and denials are forthcoming in any conflict situation. As the person grows older he fails to develop emotionally beyond this stage, leaving the person maladjusted at the adult level. His reactions to conflict situations will tend to follow the pattern of the narcistic emotional level. The individual will be self-oriented, will be incapable of forming strong attachments to others and will experience little fulfillment from such relationships. Criminal psychology has discovered that such persons account for the major group of recidivist criminality. These arc the psychopaths and sociopaths who comprise a majority of our criminal population. They represent the largest group of personality disorders within society and they are the hardest to detect. For the most part they are capable of presenting a well adjusted veneer, but for only short periods of time, which is usually all that is necessary. It is over the long haul, while undergoing stress requiring adjustment or adaptation, that such persons fail to perform in acceptable behavior patterns. This is what occurs in certain child battering situations, as described by Dr. Pollack. The situation required mature, well balanced adjustment, of which the individual is incapable.

The actions of the spouse, who may be aware of the failures or tendencies of the offender, usually result in the ignoring of the danger signs, while at the same time attempting to force better parenthood upon the partner by means of argument and other pressures. This is often the approach taken, similar to that of the spouse married to an alcoholic; the hope that the situation will improve, and the attempt to cause this improvement by pointing out and demonstrating the other's shortcomings and the effects of these shortcomings. The failure to succeed in such an undertaking is the result of the inability of the offending parent to adjust to this action due to the lack of a personal commitment to the spouse. These facts indicate the offending parent to be an individual, lacking in adequate personality orientation; and any meaningful treatment would have to be accomplished by means of the utilization of trained and skilled professionals. Dr. Steele, at a seminar on the Battered Child Syndrome in 1967, agreed that at the present time psychiatry is too expensive and limited to be utilized as the basic treatment device. He suggested the use of skilled master social workers, supported by caseworkers, and a psychological resource as an alternative(14).

In further consideration of the typology of the personality of the individual, some interesting factors known from studies of delinquency may be seen as applicable in abuse cases. Delinquency, by definition, is antisocial behavior, and character deficiencies are antisocial behavior. Delinquency is but one form of behavioral deviance, abuse is another form. It must be concluded that there is some relationship between character deficiencies and delinquency. There should exist some relationship between character deficiencies and abuse. What this relationship amounts to is not known fully at this time; but in cases of abuse, it may be the early childhood personality development of the offending parent and the effect of that early childhood, when the individual was exposed to rejecting or neglecting parents. the McCords found a very high percentage of neglecting mothers and delinquent sons, in comparison to a very low percentage of affectionate and responding mothers having the same(15). They found the rejection of the mother to be more influential than the rejection of the father; and, significantly, maternal neglect was found to be more damaging than maternal abuse or cruelty on the personality of the sibling. It has also been discovered that the roots of hostility and aggression are found within the developing family(16). In clarification, it appears the primary social unit involved in the development of the individual affects the personality of that individual. Those persons designated as character disorders or character deficients are the persons with arrested emotional development, very often in the narcissistic stage. The only psychiatric group in which more delinquents than nondelinquents are found are in this category(17). Many authorities studying delinquency have found neurotics and psychotics to make up but a small portion of their caseloads(18). These and other authorities have also discovered psychoanalysis to be of little success in the treatment of criminality and delinquency(19). It is important to recognize that few persons engaged in deviant behavior, including the offending parents in abuse cases, are either neurotic or psychotic, and the greatest majority of these offenders will be character disorders. It should be additionally understood that psychotherapy has not been a significant success in the treatment of offenders. Therefore, the offending parent is the result of a complex family situation, and a family is a social institution affecting behavior in numerous ways. The character disorder personality is not only difficult to identify, but is extremely difficult to treat through therapy and casework. This is true because of the difficulty the individual has in forming any meaningful relationship with another, and this will include the therapist or the worker. In such individualized efforts at treatment, rapport is of major importance, and when treatment is employed in cases of persons incapable of establishing such rapport, the effectiveness of the treatment is substantially limited.

It would appear that the best move toward which those in the treatment field should direct themselves, would be in the area of strengthening the family unit, thus reducing anxiety-causing situations in which the offending parent tends to react in violence. More importantly, the community effort to reduce rejection and neglect, now recognized as only a minor social ill, is needed for the reduction of the number of character-disordered personalities fed into the mainstream of parental vocations.

Many of the parents abusing children are the products of rigid parents themselves. This has influenced their lives in the development of values, and these values in turn have become a ruling element of their behavior. These are unbending persons who have little tolerance for human weakness. They are persons who become disturbed over mistakes and inabilities. In their parenthood they expect too much of a child, at too early an age. They have no tolerance for, or understanding of, the normal growth and development of a child. They are quick to react to what they consider to be folly or defiance. The interpretation of what amounts to foolishness, or of what is a threat to parental respect, is based on their own recognition of a highly developed and narrow value system. The small things, laughed at or overlooked by others, become out of proportion in the eyes of such parents. The consistent childhood curiosity, movement and noise all magnify the parent's concern over the direction of authoritarian response on the part of the child. The ease of moving into a violent encounter with the sibling is ever present, with all the accompanying dangers of inflicting trauma.

This type of parent accounts for many of the cases of attacks on infants and very young children that are later explained away by the offender through the rationale of discipline. In their own rigidness, these parents are incapable of an intellectual differentation between childhood normalcy and a disciplinary situation. They are quick to attribute reason and understanding to a child of an early or prereasoning age; and are convinced of the effectiveness and rightfulness of their approach to child rearing, feeling confident that by nipping the act in the bud, they are well on their way to preventing delinquency and other antisocial acts on the part of their child. These parents are not character deficients, and they can and do establish fulfilling interpersonal relationships. They are concerned for the welfare of their children and, in their strictness, demonstrate their love and affection through the only outlet their rigidity has left them. But, this same rigidity has placed the burden of strong values upon them, and their ability to respond to a change of such a value system is very limited. They have exerted self-discipline over their lives for such a length of time as to be quite incapable of reducing the sterness by which they exercise their every act. The intolerance for lessened standards and values in others will stand as a wall between the individual and the person attempting a change. They are so certain of their standards that the worker will be met with hostility in such encounters. The prognosis in these cases is very dim.

Mrs. Edith Lee, supervising probation officer of the San Francisco Juvenile Court, has stated the need to recognize the type of child being abused; and she has indicated that the concern aimed toward the typological determination of the offending parent has tended to reduce proper identification of the relationship between the type of child and the incidence of abuse. Her comments are noteworthy, as they present the other side of the coin, and in the present state of indecision in such matters, the thoughts of Mrs. Lee should be given consideration(20). Illegitimate children are often subjected to injury, and, surprisingly, often the hostility emanates from the mother. The children of multiple pregnancies, with limited spacing between are such an overwhelming problem for many parents as to lead to a high susceptibility to abuse. The child who is born later, after the other children have entered school, and upsets the newly found equilibrium of the family, may bear the brunt of parental wrath. This is displayed by the mother toward the child because she is unable to sustain or display her feelings toward the father. Very often, the children become the scapegoat for difficulties existing between the parents, but which the parents never unleash toward each other or otherwise find a reasonable outlet for. Other children, failing to meet parental expectations, are vulnerable to abuse. Children suffering from neurological handicaps, hard to identify and who appear not to be trying, in their attempts to compensate develop annoying mannerisms and are quite subject to violent parental response. There are situations where the child resembles the other parent or some other person the offending parent has a deep hostility toward. The child receives the vengence intended for another. These and other situations, such as the placement of the child within the family structure, or parental difficulties not associated directly with the children, have been experienced by most field workers in abuse cases, pointing to the need for research into the typology of the child as well as that of the parent.

The problem of the child being made a scapegoat for adult troubles is a real one. It accounts for the fact that in many abuse cases one child is singled out for the receipt of such treatment, while the other children thrive normally. In cases of this nature, the immediate removal of the abused child from the environment is necessary for the child's protection. However, this does not lessen the need for a scapegoat. Actually, the removal of the one child may become the cause of a transfer of hostility toward another child. This may be the result of an upsetting of the family equilibrium, maintained through the parental hostility toward the original scapegoat now removed. The parent is placed in the position of seeking a new outlet for these hostilities and negative reactions. According to Dr. Pollack, it is important to keep a surveillance on the family after the removal of a child, for the purpose of determining if a transfer occurs and another child is endangered.

Predictable Actions of the Offender

With the increase in interest in the "battered child syndrome" over the past few years, some fundamental knowledge of the behavior of the offending parents has formed recognized patterns. One of the earliest of these discoveries, a fact now universally recognized, but which as late as ten years ago was a point of controversy, is that abuse will occur to only one of several children within a family. It is not necessarily a uniformly administered social ill within a family unit. As workers became more concerned with the problem of abuse, the newfound recognition brought about more serious observations of the phenomenon. From these observations, certain predictable behavior patterns of the offenders in abuse cases have been identified. These patterns are significant indicators of a battered child when found in conjunction with inflicted traumas. In and of themselves such actions prove nothing, but in the totality of the situation they give rise to the surety of being on the right track in pursuing the investigation. The patterns also form part of the circumstantial information necessary for presentation in juvenile court, to establish the inadequacy of the child's environment and aid in arriving at a proper decision in the protection of the child.

The parents tend to be medical butterflies in seeking treatment for the injuries they inflict. While the family may be known to one physician and one hospital in conjunction with normal medical attention, when the abuse results in trauma requiring emergency care, the child is usually taken to physicians or hospitals where the family is not known. Furthermore, the child, if reinjured, will be taken to another location for treatment. By this means the parents are able to cover the pattern of their activity, with few, if any, of the physicians or institutions discovering the preceeding injury. This is a highly characteristic behavior on the part of the offender. It has been such a significant factor as to give rise to the development of state and local clearing houses for the gathering and dissemination of the medical and agency contacts of known abuse cases, in an attempt to counter the failure to identify the case because of limited background information.

Whenever an injury is brought to a physician, the medical history of what caused the injury is pursued. In abuse cases, physicians have found the first contact with the parent to result in very poor accounts of the history of the trauma, with the parent often becoming belligerent if pressed for clarification or better definition of the cause of the injury. In many instances, the parent will leave the office or the hospital indignant and hostile, only to return later with the other spouse, a relative or friend, and at that time give a coherent and rational account of the circumstances in a friendly and cooperative manner. This occurs often enough to be included as a method of operation. Whenever such actions are encountered by members of the medical team, suspicions should increase. An injured child of parents acting in such a manner should be exposed to full-body x-ray survey.

At the point of presenting a cooperative medical history, and in subsequent conversations with investigators and workers, the parent will relate any of the following facts:

1. The child cried excessively, explaining that this child's crying is different than other children's. This child will be said to cry almost constantly, and the parent will relate that nothing seems to help. The professional should be aware of any physical reactions that would tend to indicate serious anxiety on the part of the parent during the period of describing the excessive crying.
2. The child is often reported to be a poor eater, and the parent will give lengthy descriptions of the attempts that have been made to increase the child's eating habits. This report of failure to eat is significant in child abuse cases, as very often the abuse has occurred as a result of the parent's concern with this real or imagined problem.
3. Because abused children tend to be undernourished, retarded walkers or talkers, pale and listless, the parent will contend that the child has not developed normally. By this, the parent is attempting to explain the cause of the failure of the child to have met the standards of size or development for a child of its age.
4. Due to the number of bruises appearing on the body of an abused child, the parent will make vague statements about the fact the child bruises easily. This information will be based on the parent's observation, or what someone has told the parent. That someone may have been the spouse, a relative, a friend or a member of the medical profession. In the latter instance, very few parents will be able to give the name of the physician, and usually the location will be in another community or another state.
5. Because of the listlessness of the child, it will often be said the child does not respond to "tender loving care." This may be stated to counteract the child's obvious fear of the parent, or failure to respond to the presence of the parent(21).

These actions and statements are classical predictors of the abused child case. Whenever encountered, the level of suspicion should be increased, as the child being examined, treated or investigated is usually suffering from inflicted trauma. To overlook the meaning of these indicators is to place the child in danger of further injury that could easily lead to permanent damage or death. Only through the recognition of the universality of the predictors, can many cases of abuse be identified. For persons working in the field these should become significant guidelines, readily recognized as indicating contact with a possible battered child.

The Key to the Protection of Children

The abused child is a medical-social problem with legal overtones. Unlike neglect, abuse involves injury to children. This fact isolates the importance of the medical aspect of the problem. No one other than a physician can adequately describe the injuries involved and the meaning of such trauma. No police officer, no caseworker, no probation officer can present this information, other than to describe the superficial location by personal observations. The meaning of such trauma requires medical recognition. The key to the protection of the battered child is the medical profession. Without the testimony of the physician, no physically abused child can be protected from the environment giving rise to the trauma. It is of importance to recognize the general failure of the medical profession to meet this need. An area of controversy that continues to exist is the mandatory reporting of abuse cases by physicians. At the present time all states have enacted such legislation, requiring physicians and others to report cases of abuse and protecting the reporter from civil liability as the result of such a report. This legislation, the majority of which has been passed into law in the last six years, has failed to substantially increase the physicians's activity in this respect. The Brandeis study indicated the private medical doctor to have reported less that 9 percent of the six thousand cases, while hospitals and the police combined to report an approximate 50 percent.

Why this lack of commitment on the part of the physician? There appear to be several reasons. Some are presented by the doctors themselves, and others are arrived at through the experience of attempting to increase the physician's participation. The medical profession has contended for sometime that the fear of legal liability when reporting caused a reluctance to become involved. This contention was made in the face of several facts. There have been but few cases of such litigation, and all have been resolved in favor of the physician. In reporting the abuse of a child, the physician is treating the child, not the parent. The question of patient-doctor communication does not extend to a third party, to wit the parent. Anything the doctor recognizes in the totality of the nature of the injury is of his concern and, as such, is also his responsibility. The physician has the moral as well as the legal responsibility to report his findings and his suspicions, to the proper agencies as a part of his treatment of the patient. It will take such a report to insure the future safety of the patient. With society's recognition of the physician's fear of liability, laws were enacted to offer the doctor the necessary protection. The existence of such laws has not increased his willingness to report.

In California, the physician-patient privileged communication does not extend to criminal actions. That jurisdiction still passed a protection-from-liability law, granting immunity from civil suits to the physician. This was incorporated, as in other states, with a mandatory reporting law. These concessions to the physician have not increased that profession's involvement to any measureable degree.

One of the points made by doctors is that as individuals they do not encounter cases of abuse. This is in contradiction to the estimated number of ten thousand cases now believed to occur in this country yearly. There is increasing evidence of the willful misdiagnosing of abuse cases by physicians in order to reduce their involvement. This information has become a concern of some of the physicians interested in this problem.

Physicians do not like to become involved in court actions. A court appearance causes the doctor to lose time with his practice, and takes him away from patients who do need his services. At the same time, there is a financial loss due to the time spent in court. This cannot be disputed, nor may it be overlooked. When in court, the doctor is unable to take care of his practice; and his time, which is valuable, goes unpaid and, in many cases, unrewarded in what he is attempting to accomplish in the case in court. The developing of a reputation of reporting may result in the reduction of the volume of a practice, as many persons, through lack of understanding of what the physician is doing, are fearful to take their child to the doctor because of a mistaken belief he is indulging in the indiscriminate reporting of parental failure. Additionally, many court cases have involved the subpoenaing of physicians when they were not needed, resulting in unnecessary loss of time. Prosecutors and probation officers, as well as judges, have not gone to the lengths they should in an attempt to alleviate mix-ups and long periods of sitting in court waiting to be called as a witness. In one case in which the defense counsel became annoyed at the physician during the defense efforts to cross-examine the doctor, the physician was refused dismissal from the court room by the defense and was made to wait throughout an afternoon session in which his testimony was not needed and not called for. There was no effort on the part of the prosecutor or the judge to correct this flagrant disrespect for a member of another profession. Very often, the doctor will show up at court and no one there is prepared to greet him or insure his proper orientation to the proceedings and the court surroundings. These little courtesies would be to the advantage of all concerned, for many physicians complain about the treatment they receive during these court appearances.

The abuse of children tends to be repulsive to most persons, and most people who hear about cases of battered children, or who otherwise are exposed to the existence of the problem, are impressed by the injuries the children suffer. This is not true of a group who have dedicated their lives to the treatment of human ills and injuries. There are no horrible injuries that can be described that will tend to melt the heart of the doctor who has spent his day in surgery or the emergency room, working to save the life of a person more seriously injured. It is not because these people are professionally cold to the sufferings of their fellow man, but rather, it represents the ability to view the traumas in a clinical manner, not an emotional manner. The one group that is the most difficult to impress with the seriousness of this syndrome is the medical profession. They are concerned with numerous syndromes, many of which are more serious and far-reaching than the abused child. They cannot devote their full time and energies toward the effective reduction of a social ill, and they may be right in the observation that such is not their role.

All of these reasons stated, it must still be recognized that the involvement of the physician is of absolute necessity to the protection of these children. To do so does not require the doctor to name a suspect or describe the manner by which the trauma was inflicted, other than to state that such an injury coupled with the other medical findings do not support the medical history as provided by the parents. It is the doctor's role to testify to the inconsistency of the injury in relation to the manner in which the parents described its cause. In addition, he should be able to state his opinion, based on his medical findings, that the present environment of the child is not conducive to the child's health and safety, and that continued exposure to such an environment would be detrimental to the best interests of the child. It is not necessary that the doctor allege who the responsible party may have been. He needs no proof beyond his medical findings and professional opinion regarding the condition of the child. With this alone he is armed to report, and has the moral and legal obligation to report the suspicion of a battered child case. It must be through the continued and increased efforts of the members of the medical profession that a realistic commitment to the combating of this problem will occur.

The Need for Immediate Protection

The difficulties involved in the removal of children from their homes has already been presented and the facts therein cannot be disputed. There exists in such action the potential for extreme emotional trauma to occur to the child. As previously stated, the manner by which the removal is performed can do much to alleviate the hazards of removal and lessen the shock that the child will experience. The actual removal of a child requires tact, patience, understanding and skill. Although the potential for emotional upset is present in this manuver, much damage can be avoided by utilizing proper procedures. There are those who are against the removal of a child from his home *in toto,* and these people feel that the taking of a child from this primary environment should only occur in extreme emergencies. In matters involving battered children, the extreme emergency exists in any situation in which traumatic injury of a severe nature has been inflicted upon a young child. This calls for a decision on the part of the agency responding to the initial call. For the most part, this agency will be representative of law enforcement. Therefore, the decision to remove a child for his protection is, for the most part, a police decision. As such, the police must have some guidelines for the enactment of a removal. It is difficult to present more than a general set of rules for the officer to follow because of the variations in abuse cases; but in an attempt to clarify the decision making process, the following aspects of the problem should be utilized to form the basis of the police decision that protection is necessary:

1. The age of the victim is a primary consideration, for this fact will serve to establish the ability of the victim to seek protection or avoid an attack. No infant or child under three years should be allowed to remain in the home if that child has sustained an injury deemed to be unreasonable. This includes excessive bruising, evidence the child has been burned, struck about the head or has experienced the administration of an uncontrolled spanking or strapping.

   Older children, with limited marks and no serious injuries, may be left in the home pending other immediate action, including a referral to another agency. This action should include the warning of the parent that the child has been advised to seek aid, in the event of a subsequent attack pending the outcome of the action.

2. The extent of the injuries are of concern and are good indicators of the hazards involved in leaving the child in the present situation. Inflicted burns should result in removal and juvenile court action. This statement is based on the severity of the pain accompanying such an injury, and the opportunity for damaging infection as a complication often encountered. As everyone has experienced the discomfort of a minor burn, the willful infliction of a burn on the person of a child indicates the ability to administer severe injury on the child. No child should be left in such a hazardous environment. Removal for the protection of the individual should occur pending the official action to be taken.

   In a small child, any injury inflicted to the head or abdominal region, by the fist or other weapon, would be of such a dangerous nature in relation to the willful administration of that injury as to require immediate protection. With older children, the injury would have to be viewed in light of its severity and the circumstances under which it was administered.

3. Unreasonable disciplinary action, resulting in extreme bruising or indiscriminate striking of various parts of the child's body, would indicate a danger to the child of remaining in that home during the period of pending action. Such overt discipline points to very extreme family disorientation, with an accompanying lack of

self-control on the part of the persons administering the discipline. This is a hostile environment and represents a real hazard to the health and safety of the child.

4. Any use of bizarre or unusual punishment indicates extreme personal problems, emotional disturbance or psychotic manifestations. A situation of this type requires immediate protection of the child. There should be no hesitancy on the part of those charged with making this decision. The removal is necessary to prevent any further pain or injury from being inflicted upon the person of the victim.

Those agencies charged with the initial investigation of abuse cases must be aware of the negligence involved in their failure to take appropriate preventative action of an immediate nature. As agents of that agency, the responsibility of carrying out the functions of the agency is theirs. To arbitrarily leave a child in a situation where the victim may be reinjured or death may result, is a negligent act caused by the ommission of the performance of a duty. Such an agent, as well as the agency and governmental unit involved, have contributed to the degree of the victim's safety, either by taking action or failing to take action. This may or may not amount to a legal negligent act, depending upon the jurisdiction, but in all cases it is an act of moral failure. It is past the time for agencies to stop considering the protection of a child as something less than the protection of other citizens, and to realize that the children involved in this problem are, in many cases, in a position of absolute reliance on the adults around them, including the agency involved. These cases need the development of procedures and methods to insure protection, and this is the responsibility of the agencies charged with the initial response to the complaint. It is noteworthy to quote from the Statement of Principles Concerning Mandatory Reporting as developed by the Trauma Committee, Children's Hospital of Los Angeles;

Infliction of injuries (physical assault) on a child should be considered at least equally as serious as assault on an adult, or the infliction of a gunshot wound.

In further consideration of the need for the immediate protection of the child, the following statement by Helen Boardman should be given credence:

Is the purpose to rehabilitate the families? With the exception of the adults involved in the assault, everyone agrees that they need help. These adults characteristically deny problems for which they need help. This denial bears no relationship to any possible legal action. Experience at this hospital with over 200 such families has demonstrated that the only sure way to get them to see a psychiatrist is by court order. Even the University of Colorado Medical Center psychiatric team, which has engaged in hot pursuit of these adults in order to involve them in a psychiatrically-oriented relationship, admits that court orders are necessary; for how many is not stated. Assumptions that the problems of adults who assault children are now well understood and that rehabilitative services are available can result in betrayal of responsibilities to the child, to the family, and to the community. That welfare agencies throughout the 50 states at this time or in the forseeable future have effective rehabilitation resources for all these adults is an undocumented, possibly dangerous, hypothesis. These do not exist in Los Angeles County.

In a democracy should we perpetuate a distrust of, even hostility towards, the legally constituted authority for enforcing laws? Social workers generally resist the use of authority, and may even refuse to communicate with an authoritarian agency. The solution is not for social workers to absorb a law enforcement responsibility but to learn to work with law enforcement and to share responsibilities(22).

According to Dr. Katherine Bain:

> . . . At present, the only solution in many cases is to remove the child from the home by court order. Many of the parents are themselves so psychologically damaged that they are beyond the reach of our present therapeutic measures. We need studies of the kinds of parents who abuse their children and of criteria that will identify those parents that can be helped. Some beginnings along those lines are recorded by the Children's Bureau Clearinghouse for Research in Child Life(23).

In an article entitled Psychiatric Implications of Physical Abuse of Children, Dr. Irving Kaufman, Director of the Center for Child and Family Study, indicated the relationship in the parent-child interaction to be so severe as to present a real hazard to the life and health of the child. Dr. Kaufman presented the need for action to remove the child from the environment in such recognized situations.

The importance of the protection of the child is evidenced in statements by Dr. James S. Apthorp, Pediatrics Trauma Coordinator, Childrens Hospital of Los Angeles:

... But when nonaccidental inflicted trauma is identified, our main objective is to get the child's environment changed.

My purpose in testifying is to protect the child — not to see the parents prosecuted. The important consideration is that the battered-child syndrome is not self-limiting. The hazards of repetition are great unless the patient is separated from the source of the trauma.

The only preventive measure we have is to intervene and change the child's environment.

The report to law enforcement authorities and appearance in court are part of the medical treatment and part of the principle of prophylactic care. Cases should be reported in order to prevent recurrence(24).

In further support of the need for immediate protection of the abused child, it is well to reiterate the limitations on the ability to predict the behavior of adult offenders. Although some success in treating the adult has been reported, those present at the Children's Bureau Meeting on Abused Children in 1962 were cautious in their optimism. At that time, Dr. Leontyne Young stated she could not cite a single instance of successful treatment, while Dr. Leon Eisenberg, Professor of Child Psychiatry, Johns Hopkins Hospital indicated:

It must be squarely faced that some types of psychological illnesses are malignant and untreatable(25).

It is imperative that those persons working with these cases be aware of the danger the child is facing, and recognize that misguided hesitancy in the intervention of society in the parent-child relationship may result in increasing the degree of the danger through the misinterpretation by the offending parent of the agency's failure to act.

References

1. Kempe, C. Henry: The battered child syndrome, JAMA, 181:1, 1962.
2. Flammang, C. J.: From a speech given to the Northern Calif. Pediat. Assoc., San Francisco, Dec. 5, 1964.
3. Fontana, Vincent J.: The Maltreated Child, Springfield, Thomas, 1964, pp. viii, 10.
4. Caffey, J.: Multiple fractures in the long bones of infants suffering from chronic subdural hematome. Amer. J. Roentgen., 56 (No. 2):163-175, 1946.

5. DeFrancis, Vincent: Child Abuse — Preview of a Nationwide Survey. Denver, Am. Humane Assoc. Child. Div., May 1963, pp. 4-9.
6. Elmer, Elizabeth: Identification of abused children. Children Reproduced by U. S. Department of Health, Education, and Welfare, Sept.-Oct. 1963, p. 183.
7. Flammang, C. J.: From a speech at the Fresno County Abused Child Seminar. Fresno, Calif. April 5, 1963.
8. Rubin, Jean: The need for intervention. Public Welfare, July 1966, p. 231.
9. Tenative Summary of Child Abuse Reports Received From States Between January 1, 1967 and December 31, 1967. The Florence Heller Graduate School for Advanced Studies in Social Welfare, Nationwide Epidemiologic Study of Child Abuse (Children's Bureau Grant No. H-83), Waltham, Brandeis U., 1968.
10. Barnhart, Clarence L. (Ed.): The American College Dictionary. New York, Random, 1952, p. 1289.
11. Nielson, Willaim A. (Ed.): Webster's New International Dictionary of the English Language, 2nd ed. Springfield, Merriam, 1961, p. 2559.
12. Boardman, Helen E. (Director, Social Services, Children's Hospital of Los Angeles): A project to rescue children from inflicted injuries. Social Work, 7 (No. 1):43-44, 1962.
13. Pollack, Carl: From a speech before the Northern Calif. Pediat. Assoc. San Francisco, December 5, 1964.
14. Steele, Brandt: From a speech at a seminar on the Battered Child Syndrome. Las Vegas, Nevada Southern U. Aug. 1967.
15. McCord, Willaim, and Joan: Origins of Crime. New York, Columbia, 1959, pp. 98ff.
16. Toby, Jackson: The differential impact of family organization. Amer Sociol Rev. 22 (No. 5):502-512, 1957.
17. Jeffery, C. Ray and Ina A.: Prevention through the family. In Amos, W. E. and Wellford, C. F. (Eds.): Delinquency Prevention — Theory and Practice. Englewood Cliffs, Prentice-Hall, 1967, p. 77.
18. Cavan, Ruth: Juvenile Delinquency. Philadelphia, Lippincott, 1962, pp. 62-63.
19. Witmer, Helen, and Tufts, Edith: The effectiveness of delinquency prevention programs. Publication No. 350, Children's Bureau, U. S. Department of Health, Education, and Welfare, 1954, p. 37.
20. Earl, Howard G.: 10,000 children battered and starved. Hundred die. Today's Health, Sept. 1965, pp. 24-31.
21. Flammang, C. J.: Juvenile Procedures. An unpublished study prepared for the Division of Vocational Education, Berkeley, U. of Calif. July 30, 1967, p. 84.
22. Boardman, Helen: From an unpublished paper prepared by Mrs. Boardman, Director of Social Service, Children's Hospital of Los Angeles, December 12, 1966.

23. Bain, Katherine: (Deputy Chief, Childrens Bureau, Department of Health, Education, and Welfare): Commentary: The physically abused child. Pediatrics, 31 (No. 6):896, 1962.
24. Battered children and abusive parents. Roche Med Image, 10 (No. 4):29-31, 1968. By Permission of Dr. James S. Apthorp.
25. U. S. Department of Health, Education, and Welfare, Children's Bureau: Report of meeting on Physical Abuse of Infants and Young Children. Washington, Jan. 15, 1962, p. 4.

Chapter VI

THE BRANDEIS STUDY

THE Florence Heller Graduate School at Brandeis University undertook a nationwide study of the epidemiology of child abuse for the United States Children's Bureau, a study designed to analyze officially reported incidents of child abuse in 1967(1). This was to be the first full-scale, in-depth study of the extent of child abuse on a nationwide level. The need for the study was apparent. There had been numerous limited studies of the problem, but the knowledge of the magnitude of abuse was based on incomplete findings or assumptions drawn from the early research, which tended to be quite limited in scope. With the increasing emphasis on the problem of abuse, the need for research to ascertain the extent of the problem was evident.

The degree of difficulty in such an undertaking should be recognized by the reader. First, the study was to be nationwide. This meant that all states and some other jurisdictions must not only cooperate, but there would have to also be skillful organization, liasion and follow-up. Secondly, jurisdictions would not have the same definitions, conceptions or reporting procedures. This caused the establishment of controls to screen the reported incidents in order to eliminate those not coming within the scope of the study. Third, the compiling of the information was done utilizing the epidemiological approach, a method that has been used to only a limited extent. Fourth, the data collected had to undergo analysis, after which competent conclusions were to be drawn based on skillful interpretation. The planning, organization, computation and interpretation involved in such a study are extensive and can only be performed by skilled researchers. The accomplishments of the Brandeis study are yet to be fully appreciated, but the impact of this effort will certainly be an influence upon the future avenues society will follow in dealing with the problem of the abused child.

As the first step in the planned study, David G. Gil, D. S. W., principal investigator, launched a press survey in July, 1965. This survey, extending for a period of six months, was a collection of newspaper accounts of child abuse. It should be noted that the survey was similar to the one conducted by another group in 1962(2).

There are some weaknesses to such a survey. Obviously, not all such cases receive newspaper coverage, for those that are to be printed must be considered newsworthy. Furthermore, there is a margin of error in the obtaining of the clippings, thus some cases are overlooked. The reliability factor increases with the seriousness of the incident, with fatalities being the most accurately reported by news media.

During the period of this survey, 412 cases were reported. These involved a total of 502 children. Nonfatal injuries were reported to have occurred to 338 children, while 164 were fatalities(3).

Survey of Public Knowledge, Attitudes and Opinions

It was discovered that there was no existing information relating to the knowledge, attitudes or opinions held by the general public regarding child abuse. This was a void the researchers felt should be filled before proceeding. A survey was designed by Brandeis University and was administered by the National Opinion Research Center of the University of Chicago(4). The survey was conducted in October, 1965. In order to narrow the focus on abuse, the survey was based on a definition of child abuse as being:

> . . . an occurrance in which a caretaker, usually an adult, injures a child not by accident but in anger or deliberately(4).

The interviewers in the survey defined child abuse as follows:

> I want to make clear exactly what I mean. Child abuse is when an adult physically injures a child, not by accident, but in anger or deliberately . . . it would always be someone who is at least temporarily taking care of the child(4).

The survey was first directed toward how much knowledge the public possessed about child abuse. The respondents numbered 1,520. Of this sampling, 82.6 percent had some knowledge of the problem to which they had been exposed in the past year. The source of this general knowledge was surveyed, and it was discovered that the greater majority had obtained this knowledge from newspapers, radio and television.

The knowledge of the individual regarding specific cases of abuse coming to his attention within the past year revealed almost eighty percent of those interviewed to be aware of such a case. Again, the source of this specific knowledge was found to be the news media.

The public's knowledge of community resources, and the use of those resources, came under scrutiny. This information was obtained through questions about the respondent's exposure to educational programs or presentations on the problem. The identity of the sponsoring organizations as well as the individual's attendance or participation, all became desirable information. Their knowledge of agencies that would assist in the protection of children was also obtained.

The findings indicated that the public's awareness of community resources was divided about equally between those who had some information about resources and those who had none. The public appeared to have limited knowledge about educational programs dealing with child abuse, and such items as attendance or participation were equally low. This information, coupled with the fact that most persons seem to gain their knowledge of the problem from news media, would point out the failure of various agencies, groups and organizations in reaching the general public by means of educational programming. This should indicate the need to devise new methods of successful dissemination of information on the part of such groups.

The individuals were asked certain questions that would tend to indicate the extent of the existence of leanings toward abuse within the general population. Included in the questions were some asking for the personal propensity toward abuse on the part of the respondent. Over half of the responses indicated a belief that anyone could, under the proper circumstances, abuse a child. Less than 40 percent thought the opposite. The personal question directed to the individual about his ability to be so disposed resulted in a converse finding. Where over half felt anyone could abuse a child, less than 25 percent admitted they might have the capacity. This was found to be influenced by the age and sex of the person, with males being more inclined to admit the capability than women; while both sexes over fifty-five years of age tended to be less willing to admit an ability to abuse a child. Additionally, questions regarding how close an individual had come to harming a child in his care or custody resulted in fewer admissions, about 16 percent. Of the 242 persons admitting they had been close to abuse on at least one occasion of child care, six admitted they had actually abused a child. This number was 4 percent of the total questioned.

The reaction of the individual to cases of child abuse that might occur in the neighborhood was found to indicate few persons who thought they would make direct contact with the child's family. At the same time, 47 percent felt they would notify welfare authorities, while almost 24 percent indicated they would contact law enforcement. In contrast, almost 77 percent thought they would try to stop abuse and protect the child from being hurt, if the abuse were to occur in their presence.

It should be noted that these were hypothetical questions, asking for reactions to events that had not occurred. The normal human reaction to overindicate what one "would do," as opposed to what "was done," reduces the reliability of the actions as responded to in these fictional situations. This is evidenced by the responses made by individuals who had stated their knowledge of abuse cases prior to the questioning. In these situations, where the respondents admitted having been confronted with an abuse case, 62 percent took no action at all. In contrast to the 47 percent who stated they would report a hypothetical case to the welfare agency, those persons facing real incidents made reports to that agency 37 percent of the time. A law enforcement agency received the report 47 percent of the time in which actual instances were experienced. Again, the human reaction to seek assistance from an emergency service in a situation calling for such service, is shown when the individual is faced with an actual event.

Within their knowledge, 14 percent of the respondents indicated the case was the first incident of abuse that had occurred in the victim's family, but 60 percent of the cases were situations wherein abuse had occurred before. This tends to support the contention that offenders are prone to be recidivists. Over 40 percent of the children were abused by their fathers, and 31 percent were abused by the mother. Stepfathers accounted for 16 percent of the abuse in the cases related. One quarter of the offenders were between twenty and twenty-four years of age. The age group from twenty-five to twenty-nine accounted for 12 percent of the offenders, while another quarter fell in the thirty to thirty-five age bracket.

In the cases reported to law enforcement, an arrest ensued 43 percent of the time, but court appearances occurred only 34 percent of the time. This supports the thought that many cases culminate in arrests prior to complete and thorough investigations. It also indicates the inability of the prosecution method to protect children.

It appeared that a case of rumored abuse would not bring the same reaction as a case of known abuse. The respondents were more prone to become involved in situations where they had some knowledge of the incident occurring, and less in situations of hearsay reports. The protection of the child brought forth the opinion that only as a last resort should a child be removed from the home, in a little over 50 percent of the group questioned. The opposite opinion was related by 36 percent of the respondents. This division became greater in response to the action that should be taken against the perpetrator. Almost 70 percent felt that the offender should undergo supervision and treatment; while about 30 percent demonstrated punitive leanings. It was found that those favoring supervision and treatment were set apart from the others by education.

The primary responsibility for official handling of abuse cases was reported to be the welfare agency by about 55 percent of the respondents, while less than 23 percent would place the responsibility with law enforcement. Just what is meant by the term "primary," is not clear. If it is synonymous with "initial," this placement of responsibility with welfare may not be warranted. On the other hand, if the term applies to the long-range casework assistance given to a family and the supervision of the child, such a placement of responsibility would undoubtedly have value.

This survey was a part of a much broader study of child abuse. It was designed to encounter a representative sample of the noninstitutional population of this country who were over twenty-one. In so doing, the researchers were able to discover facts relating to the knowledge of the problem, as well as information about opinions and attitudes prevailing within the general society towards child abuse. Of all the findings, the researchers appeared to have made the most significant determinations regarding the awareness of the general public to the existence and function of child protective services. The study indicated that such an awareness was quite low, pointing to the fact that those agencies were in need of increasing their ability to gain recognition.

In respect to the extent of the problem, the researchers cautioned against overstatement of the theoretical statistical findings, The following quotation reveals the thinking of the Brandeis team:

> Central to this discussion, however, should be the recognition that child abuse is not a monolithic phenomenon. And as such, it should not evoke a monolithic response. Physical child abuse may range in severity from a slap mark or bruise to fatality. It seems important, therefore, to retain proper perspective on the phenomenon in face of the glut of recent publicity which child abuse has received — some of it pretty lurid. Publicity meant to gain support for legislation and protective services should guard against intemperance and overstatement, lest it foster unrealistic guilt feelings and punitiveness. Certainly, nobody concerned can profit from a witchhunt. Until more comprehensive data are available on incidence and distribution of child abuse in subsegments of the U. S. population, it would seem wise to hold to the opinion voiced by the majority of respondents in the present survey: almost anybody at some time could injure a child in his care. Physicians, especially pediatricians, psychiatrists, social workers, marital counselors and clergymen might well routinely counsel married persons and those contemplating marriage about stresses and strains associated with the child-caring role and the likelihood that they will be tempted some day to strike out against a child because of frustration and anger(4).

The California Pilot Study

In September, 1965, the State of California amended its mandatory reporting law and established a central registry in the bureau of criminal investigation and identification. Within five months the registry had received over 1,600 incidents of reported abuse. Brandeis selected at random 421 incidents. These were screened against the definition of abuse. By that means 247 incidents were eliminated, leaving 123 incidents classified as abuse by the researchers.

The 123 reported abuse cases were followed to the locales where they had occurred. From the information thus collected, it was learned that 140 children were involved in the incidents. Of these, less than 12 percent were under one year, while almost 17 percent were between one and three. Almost one-third of the victims involved in the incidents were between three years and nine years of age. The largest single group was between nine and twelve years of age, and amounted to almost 16 percent(5). It is interesting to note that half of the children in the incidents reported were between three years and twelve years, while almost 30 percent were between birth and three years. With the better expectations for discovery existing within the older age groups, it is noteworthy that the pilot study resulted in about 30 percent of the cases being identified within the most difficult age group for discovery. Other findings of interest included: about 73 percent of the male household heads were involved in the incident reported, and 32 percent had been involved in previous incidents as the perpetrator; less than 44 percent of the female household heads had been involved in the present incident, while less than 15 percent of the females had been previous perpetrators. The majority of families had never received public assistance and were urban dwellers. Three-fourths of the perpetrators were between twenty and forty years of age, and in 66 percent of the incidents, they were the biological parents. Over one-third of the perpetrators had a previous involvement as abusers. The resource of first contact for assistance after the incident was the police in over 80 percent of the reported cases, but there was no social agency follow-up after the incident in the greater majority of the cases. It should be noted that the California system at the time of the pilot study would be a strong factor in determining the emphasis on police at the time of the initial incident, as would the same system preclude social agency involvement in many instances where such follow-up may have been advisable. Neither of these findings could be utilized to establish support for the involvement of one agency over another. These results would appear to conform to the California system at that time.

The Nationwide Epidemiologic Study of Child Abuse

Brandeis University then launched the nationwide study of child abuse incidents reported through legal sources throughout the country. At first it was to be a one year study, but was later extended to include the second year. The study began in January, 1967, and, with the extention, continued until the end of 1968. In addition to surveying each state, the District of Columbia and several territories, the study also included a comprehensive section that involved all cases reported legally in thirty-eight representative cities and counties(6).

With the exception of Texas, every state operated a central registry of child-abuse incidents. Of these the majority were established especially for the Brandeis study, while in several states the registries existed under state law. Texas participated by the use of the standard state child-welfare form. In addition to the registry reports, there was developed a method to screen out cases that did not fall within the definition of abuse as used in the study. All but three states utilized this method from the outset.

In addition to the general survey and the comprehensive study, there was a press survey on fatal cases that was in effect from July, 1967 to December of the same year.

The information has not been completely tabulated at the time of this writing. Therefore, in all areas of the survey and study, the final figures are not available. Enough of the study has been completed to begin to draw some conclusions. The findings available will be reviewed for the reader's benefit.

In the year 1967, 23 percent of the incidents were reported by California, a state containing only 10 percent of the national population. This amount is probably based on the fact that such reports in that state are within the police system, and law enforcement undoubtedly performs this role with more compliance than other agencies. The figures probably do not reflect a true higher-incident rate.

In that year there were about 6,000 abused children identified in the general nationwide study. Of these, 52 percent were boys. There was a slight gain in that percentage in the comprehensive areas, but in consideration of age distribution, that was found to be similar. About 34 percent of the victims were under three years of age in the nationwide study, with 49 percent being between three and twelve years. These victims were reported in the nationwide survey to have past involvement with abuse in almost 35 percent of the group, while in the comprehensive communities there was positive recognition of previous abuse for a little over 50 percent of the children. This indicates the recidivist nature of the problem.

There were about 1,500 cases reported from the comprehensive areas, and these amounted to about 25 percent of the national reports. From this group, incidents involving the abuse of 773 children resulted in the identification or suspicion of 768 persons being involved as perpetrators. Of this sample, positive identity of the offender occurred by means of court action in about 22 percent of the cases, and by other means in a little over 45 percent. It remained suspected in almost 32 percent of the incidents. The biological parents accounted for about 72 percent of the perpetrators, of which the majority were mothers. This higher percent of female offenders must be viewed in light of the fact that almost 30 percent of the sample families were fatherless.

Stepparents were implicated as 14 percent of those identified or suspected, with the largest majority by far being the stepfather. When the perpetrators are compared to the total number of families in the comprehensive areas, including those in which the offender remained unknown, the figures take on a converse aspect. Of the 542 fathers or stepfathers living in the homes of the total comprehensive sample, 331, or about 62 percent were perpetrators or suspect; while only 341 of the 764 mother figures were so identified. This would be about 45 percent in respect to the females. Furthermore, of the 331 males, 96 — or about 30 percent — were stepfathers.

Since over 89 percent of the perpetrators were parents or parent substitutes, the characteristics of the parents present a fairly accurate picture of the offender. It was found that they had little education and, for the most part, were of low economic means. Minority group members were representative of 62 percent of the offenders, and only about 13 percent of the perpetrators had criminal records. Significantly, 60 percent had encountered some social or behavioral problems during the year preceeding the study. This figure would tend to support the contention of the correlation between abuse and personal or family disorientation.

Over 90 percent of the incidents occurred in the victim's home. Forty percent of the cases were reported to have happened between three in the afternoon and nine in the evening, with 11 percent occurring between nine and midnight.

Regarding the injuries suffered in the cases involved in the comprehensive areas, about 50 percent were minor, 41 percent were serious, 5 percent caused permanent damage, while 3 percent were fatal. Of these figures, medical diagnosis verified the injuries in about 85 percent of the cases. It should be noted that in over 90 percent of the cases there was no permanent damage to the victim, while in about half of the cases the injuries were not considered serious.

> In view of these findings, one must certainly question the view of many concerned professional and lay persons, according to which, physical abuse of children constitutes a major cause of death and maiming of children throughout the nation(6).

It is the view of the researchers, that the incidence of child abuse is not as great as once suspected. This view must be recognized to be within the definition of abuse as set forth for this study, as well as being subject to any reliability factors yet to be encountered.

The research encountered a failure to report fatalities, and in order to obtain some findings regarding this aspect of abuse, a press survey was conducted. This survey extended over a period of six months and consisted of daily search of newspapers throughout the study area. The results were 164 cases of abuse that were fatal. About 90 percent of the cases were not reported through the regular registry channels and were known to the newspapers only. This fact casts some doubt on the reliability of the total amount of abuse, nationwide, as indicated by the respective state registries. The three major means of inflicting trauma in the cases resulting in deaths were: beatings by use of weapons or instruments, 43.2 percent; beatings utilizing the hands, 37.9 percent, and burns and scalds, 10.3 percent.

The researchers discovered most abuse to have occurred within the victim's home, but rarely were the victim and the offender alone. In almost two-thirds of the cases, other siblings were in the home; however, data relative to the ages and ability of the other children to testify has not been made available. Depending upon these facts, the victims may have been in the same position as being alone with the perpetrator, for a child who would not qualify as a witness would afford no assistance. The ages and witness ability of the other siblings would have a definite bearing on whether to classify the incident as witnessed. In about 30 percent of the cases the other parent or parent substitute was present; and in 6.2 percent of the cases another adult member of the household witnessed the act, and adults not residing in the home were present in 7.8 percent of the incidents. In the great majority of cases, only one perpetrator was involved, and only one child was abused in more than 80 percent of the incidents.

Who obtained assistance for the child was determined and found to include the offender himself securing the help in almost 25 percent of the incidents. With the addition of other members of the household, it was found that in more than 60 percent of the cases a member of the victim's own family sought assistance for the child. Delay in such instances may be crucial to the safety of the child. In over 30 percent of the situations help was sought within three hours or less, while in another 30 percent of the cases it was from three hours to one day before assistance was procured. Anywhere from one to day to one week was required in about 22 percent of the incidents, with the percentage dropping off rapidly after that.

The choice for the initial assistance was the medical services in the majority of incidents. In over 50 percent of the cases a hospital or clinic was chosen, and in 6 percent of the situations a private physician was utilized. The medical group was followed by the police in almost 25 percent of the cases, again pointing out the emergency service as being frequent choice. Social agencies were contacted in about 15 percent of the incidents explored. It is interesting to note the following figures that deal with the source of an official report of the incident, after the case was taken to one of the initial resources for assistance. Hospitals reported 53 percent of the abuse, while private medical doctors reported less than 3 percent. This meant that the doctor, although seeing 6 percent of the cases, reported less than half of the cases brought to his attention. In contrast, the hospitals reported more effectively. The police reported over 21 percent of the cases, while the social agency made official reports in less than 9 percent of the incidents, or a little more than half of the 15 percent originally brought to their attention.

The research found social agencies to be the third choice for initial assistance in the abuse cases, but in the follow-up stage those agencies were involved with either the child or the family over 90 percent of the time in the comprehensive communities. In this same sample, 37.5 percent of the children were removed from the family after the incident, and counseling services were indicated in over 80 percent of the cases. In consideration of prosecutions, it should be noted that indictments were secured in only 17.9 percent of the cases. There was a considerable drop between the charge and conviction, with less than 13 percent being found guilty. Of these, 7.2 percent received jail sentences. Data on the extent of the injuries, age of the victim and sex of the perpetrator in these cases have not been made available. It should be noted that such information would have a bearing on the fact that an offender was incarcerated as a result of a conviction.

From this study it would appear that abuse may be uniform in symptoms, but diverse in causation. Further study of the 773 cases in the comprehensive areas revealed some conclusions regarding the typology of abuse. The first type, and one of the major types, is the result of a disciplinary action getting out of hand, but linked to either a real or imagined undesirable behavior act on the part of the child. This reason appeared in some form between 60 and 70 percent of the time. It is interesting that in such instances the behavior of the child was deemed by impartial observers to have been in conflict with normal community standards only 23 percent of the time. This indicates such perpetrators are rigid persons with severe value systems. It is important to recognize that the majority of the cases in this sample were from a low socioeconomic level as well as a lower educational attainment.

> Studies of child-rearing patterns have found a strong association between the use of physical means in disciplining children and low socioeconomic status(6).

Situations wherein the offender tended to reject the child were listed as the second type. This was a constant rejection of the child himself, not the result of any specific act or circumstance. A third type was considered to have been instigated by the child, and was listed as relating to some behavioral pattern that was persistent and annoying. A fourth type was a situation wherein the child was abused as the result of trouble or argument between the adult caretakers. This type occurred in less than 10 percent of the cases, but should remain as a consideration.

The fifth and sixth types related to injury to a child victim of a sexual attack and a sadistic gratification, respectively. Neither type occurred extensively.

The person who describes himself as a severe or strict disciplinarian appeared in situations where the attack was linked to a value system and was the seventh type. It was discovered to exist in over 30 percent of the incidents.

Type number eight was related to a significant mental or emotional deviation on the part of the offender and occurred in over 48 percent of the cases. Another large percentage was typed as number nine and was a situation wherein the abuse occurred along with neglect. This type was found in 35.2 percent of the incidents.

Type number ten was the defined "battered child syndrome," but was discovered in only 15 percent of the cases. This may be a significant finding if one recognizes that the incidents in the Brandeis study were officially reported through public legal channels. The fact that the syndrome requires medical diagnosis and that physicians in private practice were so poorly represented as reporters within the study could account for the small number in this group.

Type number eleven occurred as a result of the offender being drunk, but was not a great amount. In contrast, type number twelve, wherein the perpetrator succumbed to stress, appeared in over 62 percent of the incidents. These are life-stress situations, wherein the individual appears to be overwhelmed when faced with certain undesirable circumstances.

The last two types, thirteen and fourteen, relate to the mother figure being gone from the home for a short period, during which time the child has been left in the care of a male friend or a female friend and an injury is inflicted.

The researchers indicate the typology to be limited, but it will be subjected to further analysis. It seems important to attempt to pursue this area of the problem, as many of the facts of causation may be identified through this technique. In any event, each type is an area of consideration to assist in the formulation of any prevention programs.

The enormity of the project must be recognized; a research effort spanning a continent over a period of three years. Obviously, the results are just being examined. The true worth of the study remains to be uncovered. This effort has been a tremendous attempt to unravel a perplexing social phenomenon. The final conclusions of the Brandeis team will undoubtedly be of assistance in the efforts of society to successfully provide for the protection of children. Those persons taking part in the project should be due the recognition of a grateful nation.

References

1. The Forence Heller Graduate School for Advanced Studies in Social Welfare, Brandeis University, Waltham, Mass. (U. S. Children's Bureau Grant No. H-83). Permission to utilize material granted September 3, 1968 by Dr. Gil in a telephone conversation.
2. DeFrancis, Vincent: Child Abuse — Preview of a Nationwide Survey. Denver, Am. Humane Assoc., Chil. Div., May 1963.
3. Gil, David G.: First steps in a nationwide study of child abuse. Reprint Series No. 20, Reprinted from The Social Work Practice, 1966, Waltham, Brandeis U. 1966, pp. 1, 74-75.
4. Gil, David G., and John H. Noble: Public Knowledge, Attitudes and Opinions About Physical Child Abuse in the United States, No. 14 Papers in Social Welfare, Waltham, Brandeis U. Sept. 1967, pp. 2-4, 10-13, 15-16, 18-19, 23, 26, 31-32, 35, 37-38.
5. Gil, David G.: California Pilot Study, Waltham, Brandeis U., 1966.
6. Gil, David G.: Nationwide Survey of Legally Reported Physical Abuse of Children, No. 15 Papers in Social Welfare. Waltham, Brandeis U., May 1968, pp. 4-6, 8-9, 11, 16-26.

Chapter VII

THE POLICE AND THE ABUSED CHILD

THE basic reason giving the police a rightful role in the protection of children from abuse is the traditional police function of the protection of persons and property. This is a function no other agency is prepared to perform. Within the performance of this function the police have the training and experience; and they are the one agency most capable of giving immediate protection to the children, necessary in cases of abuse. Additionally, the police are the only institution of a protective nature offering twenty-four-hour emergency service. This constant availability places the police in a unique position in relation to the underprotected child. Unless there is developed an agency with the manpower and the period of service availability presently possessed by the police, no restriction of the initial role of the police in abuse cases should occur. The police role is one of primary reaction to an emergency situation. It has as a part of that function the ability to initiate an investigation into the circumstances surrounding a complaint, thereby verifying the need for societal intervention. The police possess the ability for quick response to complaints, and the potential for immediate action is a part of the service law enforcement is prepared to render.

The police mission covers the total area of abuse; first, under the police responsibility in juvenile matters, in relation to the protection of the juvenile; and secondly, under the penal statutes of most jurisdictions, making the abuse of children a criminal act, the enforcement of which is a traditional police concern. Those critics of police involvement in abused-child cases are opposing such intervention from a misunderstood conception of the police role and punitive prevention(1,2). They offer no alternatives other than the removal of the responsibility from the police after police contact and police determination to make a referral. In other words, the critics have failed to remove the police from the field even in those jurisdictions where the police responsibility in abuse cases has been restricted to the preliminary investigation stage. The reason for the failure to completely remove the police from any activity in abuse cases is the inability of the social agencies to meet the needs of children after closing hours, the limitations of such agencies in responding to called-for service, and the lack of the manpower and procedures to adequately protect children during the initial phase of the situation. There can be no reasonable explanation for the removal of the police from performing their rightful duties in the area of underprotected children. The initial called-for service should be performed by the police, the only agency capable of offering the needed service of emergency action and evidentary investigation(3).

The juvenile court stands as the ultimate protector of the child in most jurisdictions. Such proceedings are based on evidence, although the degree of evidence differs from a criminal proceeding and more closely approximates the requirements of a civil action. This means that the information needed to sustain a juvenile court petition must qualify as evidence under rules of the admissibility of such facts. Consequently, a major part of the initial or precourt investigation of an abuse case must be handled by persons trained in the rules of evidence in order for the information collected to be admitted into a juvenile court hearing at a later date. It is only necessary for those skeptics of this contention to refer to the Gault decision of the U. S. Supreme Court to observe the intention of that body to insure the rights of the persons coming before a juvenile court, in order to forsee the stringent application of evidentary rules in the future(4).

With the advent of juvenile enforcement specialization, police agencies have developed a core of well-trained and properly oriented personnel, capable of handling such cases and performing in a professional manner. As these specialized units have existed for over twenty years, former juvenile officers are now in command positions throughout departments everywhere. This increases the ability for the formulation of administrative practices and procedures, insuring the effective utilization of methods in keeping with the objectives of society in the protection afforded children. The fact that other disciplines disagree with the concept of police involvement in the protection of children is usually based on a subjective interpretation of the police decision during the second stage of the action in such cases. If these philosophies would, instead, concentrate their analysis on the first or initial stage of an abuse case — that stage where the first contact is made in a situation of an emergency nature — or when the case is still in the investigative stage, their criticism of police intervention would be reduced. Instead, their concern is narrowed to the controversy involved in whether to prosecute or protect.

Protection vs Prosecution

There is no question of the validity of the assertion that the protection of the child is of paramount concern in cases of abuse. It remains the primary responsibility of society, and the validity of society's right of intervention is based on this presumption. No agency or representative of society charged with carrying out the obligation of the community to protect children can logically conceptualize any other reason for action in abused-child cases. It is, therefore, the primary function of the police in such cases to protect the child. There is no reason for any other goal to preempt this objective, and to allow such a preemption would be in conflict with the basic obligations placed upon the police by society in situations involving the battered child. For many jurisdictions, this concept of primary protection is an established fact; but in too many other instances, ignorance of the problem and the objectives of society have deterred police recognition of this concern. It is up to the police to insure that such misdirection is altered, and that proper and effective orientation to the "battered child syndrome" occurs. Every other question involved in an abuse case must give way to the precedence of the protection of the child. From the moment of original police contact to the final police disposition, all law enforcement activity should be geared to the protection of the victim. It is evident that such an objective involves relegating the traditional police function of the identification and apprehension of the offender to a secondary responsibility. In the course of the police investigation, as well as in police decision-making, the primacy of protection must exist.

To many this will be a concept of a revoluntionary nature, to others it may be totally unacceptable, but this is the way in abuse cases. Just as other areas of juvenile enforcement have caused a departure from the traditional police approach, so in cases of abuse, new directions for the performance of the police function must be assimilated into the efforts of society to cope with a perplexing problem. It is the responsibility of police administrators to familiarize themselves with the "battered child syndrome" and its various ramifications, and, from this foundation, to develop the necessary policies and procedures that will bring about effectual police participation in this community activity. It is not enough for a handful of juvenile specialists to attempt to provide the full scope of police action. The police administrator is the one who must provide the leadership and foresight into police participation in this area of enforcement. This leadership will not be forthcoming until the administrator has developed the knowledge and understanding of child abuse, in order to be adequately prepared for the role the administrative hierarchy should perform. That role is leadership. Leadership not only within the field of enforcement, but on the community level as well, seeking the integration of police activity into the total effort of society. To perform this task requires a reorientation of police objectives that can only be executed by those in command. Police participation in abuse cases will be as effectual as the understanding of the problem by police administrators.

There is a controversy regarding the prosecution of adult offenders in cases of child battery. From disciplines such as the social and behavioral sciences, the arrest and prosecution of an offender is not seen to be of value in the restoration of the family to a productive child environment; but, instead, is thought to be a damaging experience in any attempt to rehabilitate the family unit. Prosecutors and police officials often are of the opinion that swift and sure punishment is the best deterrent to criminality. It is within this area that the conflict arises between law enforcement and other disciplines. The concept of deterring others by getting offenders off the streets and behind bars caused the California Peace Officers Association, supported by the California Juvenile Officers Association, to obtain a change in the penal statute relating to child neglect in 1963. Through their efforts Penal Code 273a was changed from a misdemeanor to a felony, with law enforcement being assured of a decisive victory in the protection of children when the revision was enacted. Soon afterward, the truth of the revision became known in its practical application. It turned out, up and down the state, that prosecutors were reluctant to file such a serious charge against neglecting parents, as the sentences received from the Superior Courts were not in keeping with the amount of time, money and effort needed to bring a felony case to a successful conclusion. Most of the suspects were requesting jury trials. Juries were found to be reluctant to convict a mother of five to eight children, knowing that the law called for a prison sentence in such matters and being unaware of lessened sentences and probation. Even after obtaining a conviction, the prosecutor recognized the sentence given by the higher court would be far less, in most cases, than the misdemeanor sentences formerly passed down by the justice and municipal court systems. Thus, law enforcement in California learned a hard lesson, but it is one that has been forgotten only too soon. That lesson is the futility of increasing penalties beyond the objectives of society. The community has its own concepts of how such cases should be corrected, and the underlying recognition of the family nature of abuse cases found its application in the judicial process relating to the administration of Section 273a. Thus law enforcement experienced a period of a sharp decline in the number of neglect issues brought to trial, and this remained so until the situation was remedied in 1965 by an amendment to Section 273a giving an option to the prosecutor of either charging a felony or a misdemeanor, as the circumstances warranted.

It is within the family nature of the offense of child abuse that unique differences are found. At the time of intervention, the family is not a productive unit of society, but instead is a destructive unit, capable of rendering harm to one or more individuals who are members of that family. The ultimate end of societal action is the formation of a productive unit. Severence of the individual from the unit is a temporary means to insure the safety of the victim, but it is not intended to be a permanent characteristic of community response. How the eventual reunion of the family will occur, or what services will be offered by society to effect such a unification is not a direct police concern. It is, rather, only important that the police recognize the ultimate end of a community action in abuse cases.

> Every community should have a well-defined and well-known program to afford protection to children abainst abuse and neglect. The focus of this program should be on the welfare of the child and not on the prosecution of the parents(5).

It is important for the police to be involved in this community planning and for the leadership of the police to be apparent(8).

The decision to prosecute parents inflicting trauma upon their children is a law enforcement decision. It must be arrived at through the combined efforts of the police and the prosecutor, with the final decision resting with the district attorney. This involves the secondary purpose of police activity in abuse cases: the police responsibility to enforce the law. Society has placed abuse under criminal statutes, and, as such, the violators of those statutes are subject to criminal action. These are police functions. They are functions that are not shared with other disciplines involved in the protection of children. The identification, apprehension and prosecution of the adult is a mission of law enforcement. As this mission belongs to no other group, no other group has the right to attempt to make the decisions involved. It is within the authority of law enforcement, which has the responsibility of the criminal action against the adult offender, to make the decisions necessary. Such a responsibility may be attacked by other groups, it may be disagreed with, but its factual application is to be carried out as a part of the police function. It is, then, a police consideration, and the decision in the matter of an adult offender in an abuse case is originally a police decision. This decision cannot be abdicated by law enforcement, nor should it be abridged by other disciplines(6). But, such a decision must be based on certain criteria, some of which are similar to normal investigative procedures, with others being peculiar to the nature of abuse cases. The criteria for deciding in favor of a prosecution of the adult offender in a battered child situation are as follows:

1. The availability of medical testimony supporting the allegation of inflicted trauma is essential to the successful prosecution of such

cases. This entails a medical diagnosis of the existence of inflicted trauma.

2. The evidence of the inflicted trauma should be supported by accompanying evidence of other maltreatment falling into the area of repeated inflicted injury or general neglect. This evidence should point to a pattern of behavior by which it may be demonstrated that the child has been subjected to an environment tending to place him in a hazardous situation. Such a pattern is beneficial in overcoming the defense position of a disciplinary approach being the motivation for the specific act of battery or assault.

3. The existence of physical evidence such as the weapon employed, and illustrative evidence of a photographic nature clearly indicating the condition of the child as a result of the attack.

4. The location and availability of witnesses whose testimony will support either the specific violent act or the existence of previous conditions indicating a pattern of hazardous experiences the child was caused to endure through the willful acts of the adult offender.

5. There should be a need for a control over the parent that can only be obtained through the criminal court prosecution. These control situations are often cases where parents are in need of court referral to family service agencies, psychological counseling, psychiatric evaluations; or in situations where the child has been removed from the home and there is concern regarding a transfer of hostility demonstrating a need for family contact on a continuing basis by a supervising agency service(5).

6. The effect of a criminal action against the parent, in relation to the parent and the child, must be a consideration. Further alienation of the parent-child relationship may be a negative outcome of the prosecution of the adult offender. This is especially true in the event that the victim or any of the siblings are utilized as witnesses against the parents(5).

7. Consideration must be given to the effect of a prosecution on the ability for a service agency to continue a rehabilitative or therapeutic program for the reorientation of the family unit. Since the eventual reunion of the family is the ultimate goal of society in abuse cases, no preliminary action of society should abrogate the chances of the success of this attempt(5).

No decisions to prosecute should be made prior to a complete and exhaustive investigation establishing that a crime has been committed, identifying the suspect and fixing the degree or seriousness of the offense. It should be recognized that there is no evidence that the prosecution of the adult in any way deters the repeated infliction of injury upon children; it cannot be equated, in light of present knowledge, to the protection of children. It may well be a positive utilization of punitive prevention, but there is no empirical data to base this conclusion upon. Therefore, the prosecution of the adult must be seen as a secondary function of law enforcement in abuse cases. It is originally a police decision, based on criteria for the successful utilization of the judicial process to perform additional positive tasks in the overall objectives of society. No features of child protection should be attributed to a criminal prosecution.

Reporting of Cases of Abuse

No child can be protected from inflicted injuries unless the situation is brought to the attention of society's appointed representatives. Since the evidence to date points to the high incidence of repeated traumatic infliction upon the person of the victim if left unaided in the damaging environment, one of the most crucial aspect of the "battered child syndrome" is the need for swift and accurate reporting after identification.

The first problem encountered in reporting is the identification of the case. This is a problem fraught with facets of denial and indecision. It has been pointed out by some authorities that the denial of the existence of the abused child problem exists at every level of society, from the abusing parent and nonabusing spouse, to relatives, physicians, social workers, police and others who have roles to play(7).

While others are in positions to identify cases of abuse, the profession with the most authoritative background for an identification is medicine. Dr. Samuel Wishik, Professor of Maternal and Child Health, Graduate School of Public Health, University of Pittsburg, has presented certain criteria upon which mandatory reporting of abuse would occur:

1. Extreme cases of multiple lesions definitely diagnosed.
2. The existence of a characteristic age, usually under two years.
3. The general health of the child indicative of neglect.
4. Disproportionate amount of soft-tissue injury.
5. Characteristic distribution of fractures.
6. Evidence that injuries occurred at different times and are in various stages of healing.

7. A questionable cause of the recent trauma.
8. Suspicious family medical or social history.
9. History of previous episodes.
10. No new lesions or bruises occurring during a period when the child is either hospitalized or otherwise removed from the damaging environment(8).
11. No other medical explanation will adequately indicate a satisfactory answer(8).
12. The recognition of a single injury that appears to have been inflicted by means of a severe beating or an extrinsic element, such as a caustic agent or fire(8).

By utilizing these criteria, the identification of cases needing referral to protective agencies will increase to a significant number of those being brought to physicians for treatment.

The criteria not calling for technical medical diagnosis may be utilized by others coming in contact with battered children. This will be true of the nonoffending spouse, relatives, friends and neighbors, school officials, nurses and para medical personnel, caseworkers, probation-parole officers, police and fire personnel and numerous others to whom the syndrome is exposed. The fact of denial must be overcome. It can only be overcome by an increase in the level of suspicion when encountering the existence of several or more of these criteria. Persons involved in such recognition must then overcome their own indecision. This indecision stems from a hesitancy to become involved, a concern for falsely accusing someone and a failure to understand the method of reporting employed in that particular community.

First, in consideration of the existence of apathy, the individual must realize the danger to the child should the failure to report occur. If the person is unaware of this danger, or is unaware of the "battered child syndrome," the apathy may persist. There is no way of overcoming this problem on the individual layman level other than through the use of the public media, whereby a number of individuals may be educated. But, in cases of public or semipublic servants, there is no reason for the continuation of the ignorance concerning the abused child problem. It is an indictment of the administrations of the various services and agencies for the uninformed and noninvolved employee to continue to exist. Steps should be taken to correct the lack of training, whenever and wherever it is encountered in medical, social and other public service.

No one is required to accuse anyone when reporting the existence of an abused child case. The only report that is necessary is the one that identifies the criteria pointing to possible or suspected inflicted trauma. The identity of the perpetrator does not identify the injury. The existence of inadequately explained trauma is the "battered child syndrome," and this information is all that need be reported.

Every community should establish and publicize the manner in which cases of abuse should be reported, and to whom such reports should be directed. In the absence of such community standards, cases will go unreported, as the persons coming into contact with the case will fail to understand what action should be taken and who should initiate the action. When it is recognized that such a void exists within the community, the police have the responsibility to point this out and attempt to work through community channels to develop such a reporting procedure. If no response is received from the community, the police should add their own reporting system in abuse cases to their public relations program in order to educate the population to report these incidents to law enforcement.

The Tentative Summary of Child Abuse Reports, by Brandeis University, indicated the sources of reporting incidents of cases to statewide clearinghouses, on a national level, during the period from January, 1967 to December, 1967, as follows: hospitals or clinics reported 1,421 incidents, amounting to about 24 percent of the total reported. This number was followed closely by the police, who made reports in 1,294 of the cases studied, or approximately 22 percent of the total. The schools reported 250 cases, 12 percent of the number Brandeis studied. (The reader is cautioned that the cases reported by the schools do not represent those in extreme need of protection.) The combined reporting of these three agencies or institutions amounts to an excess of 50 percent of the total reported cases during a one-year period, on a nationwide basis.

The study also recorded the private medical physician as reporting 406 cases, or about 7 percent of the national report;

while the public social agency reported 561 cases, or 9 percent. The two groups seeing possibly the largest number of abuse cases are combined, reporting few more than the schools. The cases not seen by the schools are seen in great numbers by the medical or social professions, and are either not being recognized or are not being reported under our present reporting systems. There are probably some of both reasons for the failure of these two groups to report. The existence of the denial of the problem would account for the failure to identify some of the encounters; but it should be emphasized that the reluctance of these two groups to report to the police cases of abuse, undoubtedly accounts for large numbers of the younger children, not of school age, being denied the protective actions of society. This reluctance to report through the present channels, set by society for that purpose, is demonstrated by both of the professions with limited reporting. It represents a desire on the part of these disciplines to circumvent police or law enforcement activity in the field of child protection. This negativism must be overcome, as an attempt to remove the police from the performance of this function will not occur for the reasons already presented. To alter these attitudes will require effort, not only on the part of law enforcement, but also on the part of members of the medical and social work professions, who themselves are capable of visualizing police involvement, and utilizing such involvement on a positive basis.

The Investigation of Abuse

The investigation of abuse cases is too often assigned by police supervisors to a detective assault or homicide detail. This tendency should be immediately ceased and, in its place, the assignment of such cases should be to officers trained in juvenile procedures, with specialized training and experience in cases of abuse and neglect. There are valid reasons for this contention, many of which have been covered at various places in this text, but the foremost reasons are two: lack of interest in these investigations by officers oriented toward the apprehension of adult offenders, and the lack of sophistication on the part of these officers to depart from traditional police methodology. These two factors combine to form the catalytic action that will cause an inadequate investigation or the failure to protect the child in keeping with the objectives of society.

It is important for police administrators to become aware of the need for specialized police procedures to deal with this problem. While certain aspects of the investigation are similar to other police investigative techniques, there are facts pertinent to abuse cases causing the investigation to be of a singular nature. To begin with, the identity of the perpetrator is most difficult to obtain, especially in cases involving the very young child. The syndrome may exist, and medical testimony may be in strong support of the contention that the injury was inflicted by an external and nonaccidental force. The object causing the injury may be unknown. There usually will be no witnesses beyond the victim, who, due to age or condition, is unable to testify. The crime may have been committed in the confines of the home and, within the protection of this environment, be unknown to others. An investigation of a traditional police nature, intent on identifying the person responsible, will quickly run into difficulties. At the same time, the protection of the child will become relegated to secondary importance, and this will be detrimental to the reason for involvement in the case.

Seven objectives in the investigation of a child-abuse complaint have been isolated. These are:

1. To determine all facts concerning the incident under investigation.
2. To establish the identity of the person or persons responsible.
3. The collection and preservation of evidence.
4. The immediate protection of the child.
5. The apprehension of the violator.
6. The juvenile court action.
7. The adult prosecution.

In many of the cases in which the police will become involved, the investigative process will fail to uncover either the full facts of how the crime took place or the identity of the responsible party. These failures will lead to the failure to prosecute. This means that the majority of police actions in these cases will be directed toward the juvenile court action, not the adult court. The evidence to be sought will be similar in either action, so that in the process of preparing a case for juvenile court presentation, the officer is also gathering evidence that can be used in adult criminal action if that should arise.

The first determination to be made is whether the circumstances more readily fit neglect than abuse. In other words, many cases of abuse are such that it is easier to present the matter as being one in which the injuries are the result of the failure of the parent to offer proper care and supervision than it is to attempt to show the parent actually and willfully attacked the child. This is very true in situations where the child had been denied medical attention for an obviously serious injury for any considerable period of time. The best approach in such a matter may be from the aspect of the parental failure, and not from the position that the parent inflicted the injury. The ability to establish the parental failure to seek medical aid is fairly simple, where the attempt to prove inflicted trauma may be quite difficult. This determination of the direction to take in the investigation must be made early in the case, in order for the officer to keep from going in a direction leading him nowhere. The outcome of this determination is as pertinent in juvenile court as in a prosecution.

Consider for a moment the parent who has established a record of taking the children and herself to one family physician on many occasions for colds, check ups, etc.; but on the several occasions when the child has evidenced injury, the child was not taken to a physician until a few weeks after each injury, and then was never taken to the family physician, but was always taken to doctors in other communities. In such a matter, this area of the parental activity may be a situation wherein the parent failed to take proper care of the child or to seek proper care for the child; or to seek proper care for the child, while having demonstrated in the past a concern for the health of herself and the children by establishing a lengthy record of medical treatment with one physician.

Another example of making the determination of the direction the investigation should follow occurs in situations involving the death of the child. Very often, a homicide investigation is begun which sometimes even culminates in arrests for murder. However, few such investigations are successful in resulting in convictions. Quite often the police are not called into the investigation until the postmortem has been performed. By this time valuable evidence from the person of the victim and the crime scene itself has been lost. Because of this loss of evidence, such cases should follow the regular lines of an abuse or neglect investigation, with the contention being that the death of the child is not an important issue. The existence of the circumstances leading to the death of the child is the issue. It is often easier to establish that the neglect or abuse the child suffered at the hands of the caretaker brought on a condition resulting in the final demise of the child. By doing so, the contention is that the act of neglect or abuse preceding the death of the child is the crime, not the death itself. The facts of neglect or abuse would stand whether the child had lived or not. The death of the child is not the primary issue, the neglect or abuse is the concern.

When it is determined that the protection of the child, through the juvenile court action, is the primary purpose of the investigation, all police activity will be directed toward the successful completion of that act. The child and his environment become the paramount concern of the officer and the target of the investigation. This is in opposition to the attempt on the part of the investigators to trace the activity of the suspected parent through the period when the injury may have been inflicted. At the same time, the establishment of the situation the child was forced to endure will be sufficient for a juvenile court protective action, and in some cases may lead to information being uncovered that will sustain a prosecution.

The investigator should visit the crime scene. This is important and should be done at the earliest possible time after the discovery of the incident. These cases often involve the claim that the baby fell from a bed, crib, high chair, stroller or other place. If the victim is gone from the home due to protective service, hospitalization or death; the crime scene, including the item from which it is claimed the child may have fallen is often altered. No measurements or photographs can be taken, and the officer has difficulty familiarizing himself with the scene in order to properly form any questions for subsequent interviews or interrogations. It must be kept in mind, if the parent is the suspect, that such a crime scene visitation at the home or in contact with the parent will require the admonishment of the rights of the accused. But it is very often wise in abuse cases not to enter into actual interrogation of the suspect on the first contact. Rather, the suspected party should be allowed to describe the circumstances in an interview situation, without interrogative pressure on the part of the investigator. There is plenty of time for interrogation later, after more background has been gathered. This is very true in cases where the child is deceased, or has already been removed from the home. Either of these facts remove any emergency nature from the conduct of the investigation. In these investigations, speed is only of an essence until the protection of the child occurs. After that has been insured, the investigation should be slowed down, and enter into a methodically paced police action.

In the collection and preservation of evidence, police should be careful to obtain evidence of any nature, admissible or not. This is because of the ability for some pieces of inadmissible evidence, such as hearsay, to be utilized by social agencies in their subsequent efforts in a case, after court adjudication. This means that the officer should involve himself in the determination of background family and social history as well as the pertinent aspects of criminal evidential collection. Within the scope of the evidence to be obtained in abuse cases will be any evidence of neglect to the victim or any of the other siblings. Evidence of this nature may serve to be the only basis for court action at a later date. Therefore, the procedures for the use of photography as described in Chapter III are important in abuse case investigations; as well as the procedures for searching out witnesses to poor family situations involving not only the victim of the abuse, but any of the other siblings. For this reason it is important to canvass neighborhoods, not only the presently occupied area, but other areas in which the family may have resided in the past. It is imperative to contact the school if there are other children in the family who are of school age. Very substantial evidence may be uncovered from this source. The school is also the place to interview any older children or their friends who may have knowledge regarding the case.

The identification of the weapon is important, if that can be accomplished. Quite often in cases of very young children this is not possible, but in situations involving children of school age, the weapon can be identified by the victim. In any event, if the investigation leads to the identification of the weapon, this should be obtained, marked and placed in evidence.

The most significant evidence apart from medical testimony will be photographs indicating the visual effect of the injuries to the victim. These should be taken as soon as possible after the child has come to the attention of the medical services or the police. Photographs should be made of all bruises, marks, leisons, burns or areas requiring medical treatment. The pictures should be in both black and white and color. Color photos are excellent illustrative evidence in court, but the collection of photographic displays should not be limited to color for several reasons. Police photographers are just in the process of becoming familiar with the use of color photographs. Many who are competent with black and white film are found to be unreliable in obtaining properly exposed colored shots. The problems are compounded depending on the natural skin coloring of the child. If the child is dark-skinned and the photograph in color is over-exposed or dark itself, the bruises or marks tend to blend with the coloring of the child to the degree that the photographs are of little value. The same child photographed in black and white will tend to show marks much better. All black and white pictures should be double shot. Because of the expense of colored film and processing, single shots would be sufficient if augmented by the black and white film. Each investigator is in a position to size up the competence of the police photographer, but, as a general rule, the better photographers are more willing to accept the suggestion of the number of pictures to be taken and the type of film to be utilized. The investigator should remain at the scene when the photographs are being made and should assist the photographer in pointing out the marks and bruises that need to be recorded. The use of case identification cards in the photographs remains necessary.

A majority of photographs will have to be obtained while the child is at the hospital or doctor's office. Therefore, the police should be sure to use the procedures of that institution or doctor in the proper channeling of the request to obtain photographs. As a general rule, photographing a child at the doctor's office should be avoided, as most doctors will be reluctant to allow this procedure. Hospitals and other medical institutions will have regular procedures for obtaining permission for photographing the victim, and these procedures should be followed as long as they do not directly interfere with the collection of evidence. In the event such a situation would occur, contacting the district attorney will alleviate much of the problem and will result in the acceleration of obtaining the photographs, as well as placing the argumentative stage of gaining the permission in the hands of the prosecutor. If such procedures set by a hospital continually are found to be a hurdle, the police administrators should involve themselves in a change of policy at that institution by working through the hospital administrator's office. The investigator should not become involved in these administrative matters, nor should an officer attempt to circumvent the normal channels of administrative protocol in order to gain such evidence.

Just as in other investigations, photographs of the crime scene should be obtained. In the event of death or serious injury requiring hospitalization, the suspect or parents will not be too surprised to have the officers conducting an investigation. If an approach is used indicating the investigation is merely routine, many of the permission difficulties in obtaining crime-scene photographs after the victim has been removed from the scene will be overcome. It should be remembered that many of these cases will come to the attention of the police from the hospital level, and often the child will have been in the institution for one or two days prior to the report being made. It often requires the medical team that length of time to assure themselves of the existence of a "battered child syndrome." This means that crime-scene visitation will normally occur after the victim has been away from the scene for a period of from one to three days. Therefore, a tactful and subtle approach must be used in order to gain the parental cooperation necessary for permission to view and photograph the scene of the alleged injury. Very often this scene will be important as negative evidence, tending to establish the improbability of the injury occuring in the manner described by the parent and as demonstrated by the crime scene. The scene being discussed is the scene area the parents indicate caused the injury. It may or may not be, in reality, the true scene of the injury. As in any other falsifications, the scene as described by the parent might not support the injuries located by the physician, in keeping with the age and development of the victim. Just the same, this false scene may be strong negative evidence, tending to overcome the account of the injury by the parent. It should always be visited and recorded.

If the child is deceased, photographs should be obtained of the body prior to the postmortem examination and also during the performance of that medical process, at which time the various stages of the autopsy should be recorded photographically. These photographs will assist the pathologist in court when presenting testimony regarding his findings. They are also helpful in bringing out medical testimony regarding other conditions the child may have possessed, such as skin disorders, rickets or malnutrition, all of which would tend to support a general neglect situation. In cases where the victim is alive and photographs have already been made, it is a good idea to rephotograph the child several hours or a day later, as at that time it may be found the marks or bruises in question have developed a better contrast between the normal skin coloring and the mark itself.

Evidence of a laboratory nature should be obtained whenever possible. An example: in cases where the victim has been scratched, fingernail scrapings should be made of the suspect's fingernails. To obtain these, it may be necessary to place the suspect under arrest or obtain a search warrant. Few people will submit voluntarily to such procedure, in light of recent national trends relating to police actions. Any weapons should be submitted for laboratory examination in an attempt to locate hair, skin or flesh particles that would relate the weapon to the injury.

Obviously, much of the investigation of an abused child case will be involved in contacts with the medical profession. The importance of the medical role in the protection of the battered child has already been discussed in Chapter V, but it is of such a priority that the following review of that role is significant. Elizabeth Elmer summarized the time lag between the early efforts of Caffey and further recognition of the problem.

In 1946, Caffey reported his observations that subdural hematoma in infants was frequently accompanied by injuries to the long bones. Implicit in this report was the possibility of inflicted trauma as the cause of the patient's injuries. However, the implications of the observations were not picked up by another writer until 1953, when Silverman (Dr. Fredrick N. Silverman, Director of the Division of Roentgenology, Children's Hospital of Cincinnati) described multiple bone injuries as the most common bone disease of infancy. In various quarters efforts were made to pin the entity to organic disease, but these hypotheses gradually proved erroneous.

Elmer felt that the tardy recognition of the problem could be attributed to society's discomfort at facing its existence(10). Further study resulted in medical involvement in the establishment of diagnostic measurements such as the marked discrepancy between the clinical manifestations observed by the physician and the historical data supplied by the parents. Other observations by the medical team are significant and should be of interest to the investigator.

The fact that no new lesions, either of the soft tissue or of the bone, occur while the child is in the hospital or in a protected environment lends added weight to the diagnosis and tends to exclude many diseases of the skeletal or hemopoietic systems in which lesions may occur spontaneously or after minor trauma(11).

Dr. Kempe favored full-bodied radiological surveys of the skeletal structure of the victim, and found that such efforts provided objective confirmation in cases of child abuse considerations. Radiological findings are capable of documenting the healing stages of the bone lesions.

To the informed physician, the bones tell a story the child is too young or too frightened to tell(11).

Dr. Kempe made a strong summary of the importance of x-ray examination when he related:

The radiological manifestations of trauma are specific, and the metaphyseal lesions in particular occur in no disease of which we are aware. The findings permit a radiologic diagnosis even then the clinical history seems to refute the possibility of trauma(11).

It becomes imperative in the conduct of the investigation of an abuse case, that not only the examining physician be contacted, but all specialists who have had any contact with the case must also be interviewed. This means that the investigator may begin with an intern or a resident. The original examining physician may be a general practitioner or a pediatrician. But beyond these doctors may lie the radiologist, a pathologist, an orthopod or any number of consultants representing various specialized branches of the medical field. It is not enough to obtain the opinion of the general practitioner in relation to the x-ray findings of an orthopedic condition. These areas are ones requiring specialization, and the physician who reads x-rays or does other work of a consultive nature will have to be contacted in order to complete a thorough investigation.

To make such contacts productive, the officer should be familiar with the working routines of physicians and some of the professional protocol involved in such contacts. When should a doctor be contacted? What questions should be asked? What information can be expected from various specialists? It is important to recognize that the practicing physician will be available at certain hours each day. His time will be rationed, and it is necessary for the investigator to make these contacts with a well-planned list of questions and information to be obtained. A busy doctor with patients waiting will not be willing to give an officer an extended length of time to gather his thoughts. Nor will the doctor voluntarily provide information that the investigator is not aware should be requested. It is difficult to question anyone on matters that one is not himself familiar with. This is very true in the interviewing of the physician. The investigator must know beforehand what information he is seeking, and how the questions must be phrased to obtain the answers desired. This ability will come about through the investigator doing his homework. An officer working abuse cases should have an above average understanding of the common medical terminology utilized to describe the condition. He should have a basic understanding of the medical ramifications of the syndrome, and he should be well aware of the mutual interplay of the medical field as it occurs between the practicing physician and the specialist or consultant. This information may be obtained from a local pediatrician, general practitioner or specialist. It could be received from the public health officer in the area and may be further supplemented by contacts with the paramedical team members such as x-ray technicians, nurses and medical social workers. Technical knowledge about the syndrome may be discovered by referring to *The Battered Child Syndrome*(12). This work should be read by investigators involved in abuse cases and it should become a part of every department's library for purposes of reference.

Referring to the matter of when to contact doctors, the officer should keep in mind that the police do not wish to be kept waiting and the investigator's time is limited. Too many trips to the same office without finding the doctor in is poor utilization of that time. The investigator should discover when the doctor has office hours and at what time it is best to make the contact. This information can be discovered in general by talking with pharmaceutical salesmen. These men know the best times to contact general practitioners, pediatricians and other practicing physicians. They can give the investigator general tips on how to approach the doctor, how to make contact with the receptionist to gain cooperation in facilitating early doctor contact, and in some instances they can give information regarding specific physicians. Of course, a call to the doctor's office and the making of an appointment is always a beneficial approach. Officers should realize that many of the radiologists and pathologists will observe longer office hours than the physician with a large patient practice. This is due to the supportive and consultive nature of the work performed by the specialist for the benefit of other practitioners. The chances of finding these physicians in are better than with the doctor engaged in office visitation, house calls and hospital rounds.

The fact that the officer is dealing with a professional person must be kept in mind. There is certain protocol that will assist the officer in his contact. First, the physician should be addressed as doctor, not as "doc." This man has undergone years of study and work to attain that degree, and it should be utilized as a sign of respect for his membership in the profession. The utilization of the proper term will tend to place the officer's contact on a professional basis, and this will be appreciated by the physician. The officer should not attempt to impress the doctor with his knowledge of medicine, but should approach the doctor as a layman; just what he is, no more. Nor should any disagreement or argument regarding the nature of the medical findings ensue. The doctor is the authority, not the investigator. If the physician says something "off the record," it is the responsibility of the investigator to inform him whether this information can be treated as such. As a professional contact, the ethics should remain professional. In consideration of what the doctor has said, the investigator must not allow any subjectiveness to enter his reporting of the information. Words or meanings should not be added that were not intended by the physician. The reason is simple. If this occurs, the doctor will fail to back such statements when on the witness stand and they will be meaningless. Many officers in their attempts to make the case will go beyond the context of the physician's statement. The prosecutor or probation officer will base a case on this information, only to have it fall flat when presented in court. The officer must be careful in his reporting of the statements made by medical persons. If a startling statement is made, indicating an allegation of abuse, the investigator should immediately question the doctor's willingness to testify to that fact. If he persists, then utilize the information, but if he backs off from the strength of the original statement, this fact should be recorded along with the context of the original observation in the officer's case report.

The investigation should include contacts with the nursing and other staff personnel, in situations where the child is hospitalized. This should include the forewarning of the personnel to be on the look out for certain facts, and to record such facts on the chart, initialed and dated. Some of the information desired includes the child's eating habits after admission, the child's responsiveness to affection and care, the visiting routine of the parents, especially the suspected parent, and the child's reactions to such visits. The crying the child does, should also be recorded. These pieces of information, as well as anything that would tend to overcome the assertions of the parents as presented in the medical history, constitute useful evidence in developing the totality of the case. Unless the staff is oriented to maintain a record of these manifestations, the information will be lost. In the absence of administrative orientation, the investigator should assume the responsibility, and work out the procedure or orientation through the superintendent of nurses or other hospital channels.

No abuse investigation is complete, until all agencies coming into contact with such cases are checked regarding previous records. This includes welfare and psychiatric services, public health, mental hygiene, other police agencies, and any physicians or hospitals that may have been utilized by this family in the past. The records should be checked, not only under the name of the victim, but under the parents names and the names of any of the other siblings. This clearing of records, may well present evidence of important significance to the investigation. In the event the jurisdiction has a local or state clearinghouse or index for the repository of battered child information, these resources should be advised of the existance of the new case, and a request for a clearance of their records would be in order. As in any investigation, records are no more important than their utilization.

Summary

The police role in the protection of children has been set forth as a rightful function of the police(13). This role is primary in the police concern in child abuse cases. No other consideration should take precedence to the need to protect the victim from a repeated inflicted trauma, during the initial contact stage of the police involvement. At the same time, recognition must be given the fact a crime may have been committed, and the police have a function to perform in the investigation of that fact. This is within the scope of traditional law enforcement, and as such it remains a police decision not to be interfered with, or abridged by representatives of other professions or services. To aid the police in making a determination of the direction of their investigation, certain criteria were set forth upon which the decision of whether to prosecute or not can be based.

The problems of reporting indicated the two groups with the most frequent encounters with younger children being victimized through abuse, are the poorest reporters, accounting in part for the continued lack of scientific data on battered children. The need to work with these groups from outside and inside the professions, was pointed out as the best method of increasing the reporting willingness of the medical and social welfare segments of the community.

The need for the utilization of well-trained and sophisticated officers to investigate abuse cases was presented in an attempt to overcome the prevailing thoughts of many police administrators that abuse investigations are the same as other police actions, and the failure to recognize the need for departures from traditional police orientation. The investigator's need for specific training in the area of physician contact points out the requirement for the assignment of specialists to this type of investigation. This places the burden for self-reorientation on the police administrator, in order for his increase in knowledge and understanding of the "battered child syndrome" to better prepare him to perform the administrator's function of leadership and development. Unless the police take the time and make the effort necessary for better performance in the area of abuse cases, the role of the police in these cases will be reduced, limiting the police function in the protection of children.

References

1. Brandstatter, A. F., and Brennan, James J.: Prevention through the police. In Amos, W. E. and Wellford, C. F. (Eds.): Delinquency Prevention — Theory and Practice. Englewood Cliffs, Prentice-Hall, 1967, pp. 90,91.
2. Lejins, Peter P.: The field of prevention. In Amos, W. E. and Welford, C. F. (Eds.): Delinquency Prevention — Theory and Practice. Englewood Cliffs, Prentice-Hall, 1967, p. 3.
3. Standards for Specialized Courts Dealing With Children. U. S. Department of Health, Education, and Welfare, Children's Bureau Publication No. 346, 1964.
   Child Welfare Services, U. S. Department of Health, Education, and Welfare, Children's Bureau Publication No. 359, 1957.
4. No. 116, October Term, 1966, U. S. Supreme Court: In the matter of the application of Paul I. Gault and Majorie Gault, father and mother of Gerald Francis Gault, a minor, appellants — On appeal from the Supreme Court of Arizona.
5. Myren, Richard A., and Swanson, Lynn D.: Police Work With Children. U. S. Department of Health, Education, and Welfare, Children's Bureau, 1962, pp. 59, 67.

6. Flammang, C. J.: From a speech delivered at the Battered Child Seminar, Las Vegas, Nevada Southern U., Aug. 1967.
7. Pollack, Carl, M. D.: From a Speech Before The Northern California Pediatrics Association, San Francisco, December 5, 1964.
8. Report of Meeting on Physical Abuse of Infants and Young Children: Basic Provisions of Needed State Legislation. U. S. Department of Health, Education, and Welfare, Children's Bureau, May 25, 1962, pp. 6-7.
9. Tentative Summary of Child Abuse Reports Received From States Between January 1, 1967 and December 31, 1967. The Florence Heller Graduate School for Advanced Studies in Social Welfare, Nationwide Epidemiologic Study of Child Abuse (Children's Bureau Grant No. H-83), Waltham, Brandeis U., 1968.
10. Elmer, Elizabeth: Identification of abused children. Children Reproduced by U. S. Department of Health, Education, and Welfare, Sept.-Oct. 1963, p. 181.
11. Kempe, C. Henry: The battered child syndrome. JAMA, 181:18, 1962.
12. Helfer, Ray E., and Kempe, C. Henry: The Battered Child Syndrome. Chicago, U. of Chicago, 1968.
13. Municipal Police Administration. 5th ed. Chicago, Int. City Manager's Assoc. 1961, pp. 222-223.

Chapter VIII

THE ABUSED CHILD – CASE HISTORIES

T HE case histories presented in this chapter are unique in that they are not unique. They are representative of abused-child situations occurring throughout the country every year. None of the events, none of the injuries, none of the outcomes are unusual. Each case is different from the other in many of its circumstances, but all are similar in the oneness of the "battered child syndrome." In each narrative, an attempt will be made to indicate the various stages of crucial decision-making, as well as the results of indecision and lack of knowledge. The police procedures involved in the cases outlined are not intended to be the ultimate in police practice, but merely are the methods employed by one agency within its community structure. Many police and community failures will be discovered and attempts will be made to point out these errors, with some dialogue on how each could be avoided. It should be stated that all cases herein are situations occurring within one jurisdiction and acted upon by one law enforcement agency. By this means, the reader will be able to judge the severity of cases that may be discovered in a given area if the proper identification and reporting occurs.

Maribelle Goes Home

It was spring, 1962, on a Thursday night, when the juvenile officer was contacted at his home and advised to pick up his partner and proceed to the admitting department of the public hospital. A child was there who appeared to have met with foul play. The officers, on stand by, arrived at the hospital and were met by a female pediatrics resident. The doctor informed the officers that the child was comatose. The officers were led to a cart in a hall of the emergency area where the child was seen lying on her back with eyes closed. The child had bruises all over the body, including the abdomen and the genitals. The resident stated that the child's left elbow and shoulder were fractured, her right elbow evidenced older bone damage, and her unconcious condition was the effect of the damage incurred when she suffered a fracture of the frontal bone of the skull. In addition, the child had third degree scald burns on both legs extending to the knees.

The identification bureau was contacted and dispatched a photographer. Complete photographic recording of the injuries and marks was made. The mother of the child was present at the hospital and was questioned regarding the child's condition, but she was unable to give any account of the injuries other than to state that the girl had fallen off the swing in the backyard about two weeks before. Because of the serious condition of the child and the vague statements of the mother, this woman was placed under arrest and further questioning was attempted, with little being added by the effort. Since the woman was of Mexican descent, an officer from the U. S. Border Patrol, who was at the hospital, was requested to assist as an interpreter. His questioning of the woman in the Spanish language also did not reveal any new facts. The border patrolman consented to assist further with the investigation, and the officers and the woman departed from the hospital and went to the woman's home.

Arriving there, she showed the officers the swing where it was contended her daughter had been hurt earlier, and also showed the officers around the house. Her two daughters of junior high-school age were in the home, as was her husband and her seventeen-year-old son. The husband and the son had just arrived home from work. The daughters stated that they had gotten home from school about 2.45 P. M., and had found their mother with the victim in the front room. The victim was bundled in blankets and lying on the couch, apparently asleep. The mother told the girls to go to a house on the corner and get a neighbor, as she had to take Maribelle to the doctor.

The discrepancy in the time element was noted, as it related to the time the girls had returned from school and the time the victim had arrived at the hospital, but no mention was made of this while at the home. The husband, who spoke no English, was advised by the border patrolman in his native tongue of some of the facts of the case, and that the child was in the hospital and his wife was under arrest. He was visibly shaken with this information, and both he and the seventeen-year-old son were requested to go to the Border Patrol Office.

The officers took the suspect to the Border Patrol Office and began an interrogation. In the meantime, the husband and son appeared. Interrogation of the mother revealed little new information at this time, but the Border Patrol was able to discover that the husband was an alien. He began to relate an unusual set of circumstances. The couple were married in Mexico, but his wife was an American citizen by birth. He had obtained papers and the family had come to the United States when the seventeen-year-old boy was fourteen-years-old, which accounted for this boy's inability to speak English. The younger girls were placed in school, but the boy never was given the opportunity. The husband mentioned that the couple had a younger boy, age four, but this child did not live with them. He said the mother had given the boy to her parents just after the child's birth, and the boy had been raised by his grandparents. It developed that the grandparents lived across the street from the suspect's house, but the husband said that his wife seldom visited in that home and admitted he did not see his youngest son often. He gave as the reason for the mother relinquishing the child the fact that she felt they had enough children, and thought her parents would do a better job in the raising of the child.

When questioned regarding Maribelle, the husband indicated that the child was not theirs. This came as a complete surprise to the officers concerned in the investigation, as the mother had indicated for hospital records and during interrogation that the child was hers. This new and startling information was pursued with the husband, and he related the following facts: the family had gone to Mexico on a visit at Christmas time and had returned to the United States after the first of January. While at an uncle's home in Mexico, they had met a woman who had five children and was pregnant with the sixth. The woman had indicated she would like to send Maribelle to the United States. According to the husband's story, he and his wife agreed to bring the child to the United States and raise her as their own. He admitted he was aware this was an illegal act of transporting an alien into the country, but stated he did not feel anyone would find out. After bringing her to their home, the husband said he developed an affection for the child and that he had accepted her as his own daughter. It was discovered that the husband and the older son were gone from the home about twelve hours each day for employment purposes. As a result of these long hours, neither he nor his son came into much contact with Maribelle, as she would go to bed soon after their arrival at the home in the evening and she would not be awake at the time they left the house in the morning. The man denied any knowledge of the child's injuries and stated that his wife did not spank any of the children. He claimed that he did not either, as he did not believe in physical discipline. The wife had not apprised him about the child's fall off the swing or the injury to the girl's left arm. The husband could not add further pertinent information. A written statement was obtained from him by the Border Patrol. The story related by the father was verified by an interrogation of the son.

The mother was again interrogated, and when she was confronted with the information provided by the husband, she admitted the child did not belong to them. She began by indicating the child was her niece but, after some prodding, admitted the child was the daughter of a stranger the family had met while in Mexico. As the woman had displayed her ability to falsify information, the interrogative process was increased, and some of the questionable actions of the woman were pressed. This brought about an explanation of the day's events, in search for medical assistance for the unconscious child. The neighbor woman was summoned, because the husband had the family car. It was learned that the grandparents also had a car and lived considerably closer, but no attempt to contact them had been made, as the mother did not want them to know of the child's condition. When the neighbor arrived, they took the child and, at the mother's request, drove across town to a doctor's office about six miles from the family home. She admitted she had never been to that doctor, nor had any members of her family, but she knew of the whereabouts of the office, as she had a friend who had worked for the physician for a while in the past. Arriving there, the doctor refused to treat the child in her condition and advised the mother to take the child to another doctor. The mother said they drove to the second doctor's office and he came out to the car, viewed the condition of the child and told the mother to take the child to the public hospital. It is important to note that the public hospital was located only four blocks from the home, yet the mother had driven a total of thirteen miles and had made two stops before going to that emergency center. She admitted she had tried to obtain private care for the child, as she was aware the child was not hers but was an illegal entrant into the country. When it was pointed out that she had lied to the hospital about her relationship to the child and had lied to the officers also, so that this concept could be given little credence, she made no answer. It was suggested that she had attempted to circumvent the public hospital because of the condition of the child, and again the woman would make no response.

Questioning regarding the child's injuries brought little concrete information. The woman maintained that the child was anemic and that the real mother had told them the child bruised easily, before they brought the child to this country. She admitted she had never taken the child to a doctor after arriving here to determine the cause of the bruising she contended occurred regularly. The injury to the left arm she attempted to explain by the statement that the child had fallen off the swing while the mother was hanging up clothes sometime earlier. There was no attempt to explain why there were two fractures of that arm in various stages of healing, nor could the fracture of the right arm be explained. The mother denied ever spanking this child or any of her children. The scalds were explained by stating that the day before the child was taken to the hospital, the mother was washing clothes on the back porch. She had boiled a pan of hot water and had that pan sitting on the floor. The child, playing on the porch, had fallen into the pan of water. The mother had treated the child's wounds herself with compresses. None of the other family members were aware of this accident, as she had put Maribelle to bed and told the rest the child was sick. It was admitted the child had cried frequently during the night and into the next day. On the day of the hospitalization, it was contended Maribelle had gone into the front room and had attempted to lift a large pottery bank belonging to one of the older girls. This had been dropped, or the child had fallen onto it, knocking herself out. The mother claimed to have been out, hanging up clothes at the time.

This was the extent of the explanations during that interrogation. There were many discrepancies in the story as related by the mother. As an example, the swing the child fell from was very low and over a heavily grassed area. It would be impossible to sustain fractures at two joints (the elbow and the shoulder) from such a fall by a three-and-a-half-year-old child. Secondly, the scalds were only in the front portion of the legs, mostly to the right side of each. They extended from the knees downward, to just above the ankle. The larger portion of the scalds was near the knees. The child had been barefoot at the time she was supposed to have fallen into the water, yet her feet were not burned. With the large portion of the scalds at the knees, and the position of the scalds on the legs, it appeared that the child had the hot water thrown on her while in a standing position. Regarding the injury to the head on the final day, the mother's contention that she was outside hanging up clothes on the line was not true, as there were no clothes on the line or to be hung, and subsequent investigation revealed no one else had moved any clothing that had been washed and hung up.

A search of the woman's purse revealed several letters from creditors, threatening to repossess the car and some of the furniture. Furthermore, there were papers indicating a small claims suit had been filed, in the amount of $220, to collect back bills from this family. A letter from the real mother of the child, and dated just three weeks before, was asking for $150. Questioning about this money to be sent to the mother of the child brought the response that they were trying to help this woman in Mexico, but they had not been able to send the money yet. Questions were directed to the mother for an explanation of how a family that was in financial trouble could afford to offer such assistance to another person out of kindness, but these brought no response. The interrogation was terminated, and the woman was placed in jail. The husband and son were released.

The following day the Border Patrol inspector contacted the

police investigators and related he had information that the reason the child had been brought into the country was for purposes of selling Maribelle as a "black market baby." This information is very significant. With it much of the mystery of why the child was brought into the United States was clarified. It was the answer to why a family, in debt and having already given up their own child of the same age, would bring another child into their home. It explained the financial arrangement between the real mother and the foster parents. It also fit the situation in relation to motive. A lower-income family in debt as much as this one was desperate. This scheme would appear as a good means of obtaining some large sum of money quickly. What happend afterwards was the undoing of the plan, and brought the harm to the child. After bringing the child to the United States, the family held out for a large sum they could not collect from anyone. This placed the child in their home a longer period than anticipated, with a woman who wanted no more children, as evidenced by the fact that she gave up her own last born. The frustration of having the child underfoot and the inability to sell the child, caused an explosive situation to develop between the child and the mother, with the woman reacting on numerous occasions violently toward the child. This resulted in severe injuries occurring that almost claimed the life of Maribelle.

This case occurred prior to the Escobedo decision of the United States Supreme Court. Consequently, rules governing interrogations were not as restrictive as they are at the present time. The liberal approvals by the courts of low bail and, in some cases, the release of suspects on their own recognizance, had not come into vogue yet. This allowed the suspect to be held in jail from the Thursday night of her arrest until the following Tuesday morning, without having to be filed on with formal charges. The weekend period was not considered in the time element involved in the administration of justice. During this period of incarceration, the suspect received no visitors. As will be seen later, this information was of significance in the outcome of the case.

There was a police hold on the child at the public hospital. The child remained comatose, and her condition was listed as critical.

It was unknown if Maribelle would live or die. This had a bearing on the investigation, as at any moment the case may have been a homicide.

Investigators contacted the neighbor who took the child to the hospital. She stated that she was not well acquainted with the family, but the suspect's daughter had come to her home on the date in question and had requested transportation to take a sick child to the doctor. She said the child was wrapped, so that the neighbor was unable to see Maribelle at the time they had left the home. The mother had directed the witness to the physician's office, and then while the driver remained in the car, had taken the child into the doctor. Later, the mother and Maribelle had returned, and the neighbor was directed to drive to a second physician's office. There, the doctor came out to the car, and the neighbor overheard the conversation and had seen the child for the first time. The witness indicated that the doctor had become angry with the mother and had told the woman to "take that child to the hospital." The neighbor drove the child and the suspect to the hospital and left them at the emergency room. The mother later admitted during a subsequent interrogation that she had been told by the first doctor that the child was almost dead and that hospitalization was necessary. The idea of going to a second doctor was the mother's. It was only after the second doctor refused to attempt to handle the case in his office that the suspect decided to go to the hospital.

The Border Patrol arranged, with the assistance of the Mexican consul, to bring the real mother of the child to that jurisdiction in order for her to be utilized in the investigation. This woman would arrive the Monday following the arrest.

The investigators contacted neighbors on either side of the residence of the suspect, but none of those people were able to relate any information about the care and custody of the child in question. Both school-age daughters were contacted at the school and questioned in the presence of school authorities. It developed from this questioning the mother was prone to spank and hit her children. Both girls related that they had been spanked often, and both admitted they had seen their mother spank Maribelle on several occasions. The oldest girl, thirteen, told investigators she had broken her own pottery bank about one week before the date in question, in order to obtain money from it to go to a movie. She said that her mother knew this. The other girl stated that her bank was still intact, and neither girl could recall any other banks in the home, nor could either state they had seen any broken pottery the day when they had returned home from school and had found Maribelle on the couch with their mother.

By this time, the photographs of the victim were developed, and these were taken to the jail and the mother was interrogated regarding each mark found on the child. There were clear handprints on the child's back and bruises in the area of the shoulder blade. The woman was questioned about these marks and stated the child had been hurt, and the mother had placed adhesive over the wound. When the adhesive was taken off it left the bruise that appeared to be a hand print. She stated that the marks that looked as if they had been made on the child's back and chest by a strapping or beating with a stick or cord, had been on the child when she was brought from Mexico three months before. No explanation was forthcoming about a dark bruised area extending across the abdomen of the child, and the woman denied that she had ever seen such a mark, but admitted that she had dressed the child each day. A new piece of information was brought out about the fractured right arm. This allegedly happened when Maribelle fell from the high chair while eating (subsequent investigation revealed the family did not own or possess a high chair). The woman maintained her innocence of any acts affecting the child and denied knowledge of how the majority of the marks and wounds had occurred.

The real mother of the child arrived on Monday and was taken to the hospital, with the Mexican consul present at all times. The doctors explained the condition of the child to the mother and she saw the child, as well as viewed the photographs of the girl. Later, at the Border Patrol office, the mother of Maribelle was interrogated in the presence of the Mexican consul. The woman was very upset when shown the pictures, and the injuries were described. She denied that the child had ever been ill. She denied that her daughter had a blood disorder causing her to bruise easily. She stated that none of the bruises were on the body of the child when Maribelle was allowed to come to the United States. The woman denied that she had sold the child, but stated she was expecting money from them, as the family had indicated they would help with her financial needs if she would allow them to take Maribelle. She maintained that Maribelle was to be returned during the summer. Arrangements were made to meet with the mother, the Mexican consul and the Border Patrol the following date in order to have the district attorney take a statement from the woman, as that representative had indicated that no complaint would be filed unless the mother's statements were recorded.

Later that evening it was learned the suspect was being represented by an attorney who's ethics had always been in question. The following morning the defense attorney accompanied the real mother to the district attorney's office and she gave a statement in the presence of the same persons who had witnessed her statement from the day before. At this time, the woman had completely changed her story, and even identified marks on the child in the same wording as the suspect had done, including the explanation of the adhesive tape making bruises. This information could have gotten to the mother from only one source, the defense attorney, as he had been the only other person to have visited the suspect in jail, a visit he had made the night before. Obviously the woman had been coached, but there was nothing that could be done. This was a necessary witness to any prosecution; without her no prosecution would have been successful. Because of this turn of events, the suspect was released from jail with no charges filed.

As Maribelle was an illegal entrant, an immigration hold was placed on her at the hospital. The Border Patrol contacted the U. S. Attorney, and a prosecution for illegally bringing an alien into the country was instituted against the mother and her husband. They were later to plead guilty and receive one year probation. Maribelle recovered and was deported to Mexico four months later. The taxpayer picked up the hospital bill. As an additional sidelight, Maribelle was one of the cases included in the nationwide study by the Denver chapter of the American Humane Association.

There were many inadequacies involved in the dispositional

actions in this case. The majority reflected the lack of recognition of the "battered child syndrome" on the part of all concerned, from the resident physician, as well as both private physicians, to the investigators and the district attorney's representative. There was an apparent inability on the part of the investigating officers to formulate proper questioning of the resident physician. The resident was either not able or not willing to relate the implications involved in the injuries suffered by the victim and the inability of the mother to reconcile the trauma to incidents of cause. At no time did this physician indicate a diagnosis of a traumatic syndrome. The investigators never performed the discerning task of deciding whether the case should be approached from the general neglect or the child-abuse viewpoint. Consequently, their efforts were divided in an attempt to establish evidence supporting both. The interrogations of the suspect were lengthy and numerous during the period of incarceration. This was the result of a sincere effort to obtain a meaningful admission, but in the end the results were negative. None of the interrogations had been recorded by any means. The only corroboration to the many conflicting stories given by the suspect would have been by means of the officers' testimony. This may have been sufficient to have established a case of neglect — especially in light of the trip seeking medical attention — but the district attorney's representative was hesitant to take this matter into court. The latter's indecision was based on the misunderstanding of the prosecutor regarding the approach to be taken in a neglect case. This was not unusual, as the majority of these attorneys have little or no experience with such cases. There was no effective communication between the hospital medical staff and the investigators during the course of the investigation; therefore, any further contribution by that service was eliminated. The two private physicians were never contacted during the investigation, on the assumption that they would add no meaningful information. No police investigation has room for preconceived notions on the part of the investigators. There was no action through the juvenile court, as this was felt to be unnecessary because of the alien status of the child. This may have been true, but the decision should have been made by the juvenile court, not by the police.

A crucial mistake was not protecting the real mother, a material witness, between her arrival and the time she was to give a statement to the district attorney. This was a tactical error on the part of the officers. The only effective effort performed during the whole case was by the U. S. Border Patrol, not only in respect to the very efficient investigation they conducted relating to the federal statutes, but also in the splendid cooperation rendered by this service to the local enforcement officers (this cooperation was recognized on the part of local law enforcement, and due to a letter of appreciation sent to the federal agency, U. S. Border Patrol Inspector Dale Bartlett received a special commendation for his service). Many facts about this case served to instruct the investigators in the complexities of abuse cases. The problem is the failure of such officers in passing on to others the benefits of these lessons. The mistakes tend to teach the person in error, but seldom are they utilized to instruct others. For several years now, neither of the investigators involved in this case have been connected with abuse investigations. Their insight and knowledge have lain dormant since. It should be noted that there is a need for a method of retaining such knowledge within the community.

Not an Eighty Percenter

A three-year-old girl was brought to the public hospital for examination, on referral from a private physician. As the child's condition was indicative of neglect, the case was referred by the resident physician to the chief of pediatrics. Full body x-rays were taken as a part of the medical work-up that was routine in such cases. These x-rays revealed many old fractures that had been allowed to heal without medical attention. While reviewing the hospital record and the x-rays, the pediatrics chief noted multiple fractures of the left arm. Examining the child on this date in January, 1963, the doctor discovered a large swollen area in the region of the left elbow. All of the fractures in that area were in various stages of healing. It was medically determined there was nothing wrong with the child's bone structure to cause such injuries. The chart described the father as being uncooperative when bringing the child in for treatment, and indicated that he had left the hospital, returning a short time later with his wife, and that the wife gave a cooperative medical history. This history included the fact that the family had nine children, the oldest twelve, the youngest about two years. The victim, Sylvia, was the next to the last child. Both parents said the child had become ill over a gradual period, and had stopped using her left arm about a month before. Additionally, the child was alleged not to have developed properly, and it was related that she could not walk. Sylvia was described as a poor eater, and the mother said the child failed to respond to the parent's attempts to feed her. The fact that Sylvia would not respond to tender care and affection was alleged, with the mother indicating that the child would not even respond to the other children in the home. Both parents indicated that they felt the child was not mentally normal. Neither parent could offer any explanation of the cause of the injuries.

At the time of admittance to the hospital, the child weighed only nineteen pounds and evidenced the effects of severe undernourishment. While in the hospital, the child gained three pounds in less than three days, a weight gain described by the chief of pediatrics as the same as a man of 190 pounds gaining thirty pounds in the same period. This physician recommended that the child not be returned to the parents, as the child's hospital development indicated a lack of home care as an underlying cause of the girl's general condition. He referred the matter to law enforcement, and juvenile investigators began an investigation by contacting the doctor at the hospital.

One significant notation was recorded on the child's chart by the nurse who had given Sylvia the first tray of food the child received while in the hospital. The nurse recorded that when the tray was removed, the child cried for more, and additional food was supplied. It was further noted that the second tray was devoid of food upon the staffs' return to remove it. This information was in direct conflict to the medical history of not eating and poor eating habits. Additionally, the child was in a strange situation in the hospital, where eating habits should have fallen off, not improved. Besides, in the hospital, the tray was set on a bedside stand, and the child was left to feed herself through the bars of the crib. The importance of the observations of the nurse cannot be discounted. Here was a child, undernourished and ill, who's parents had stated they could not get her to eat, who was capable of feeding herself under such conditions on the occassion of her first hospital meal. The fact that the nurse had recorded the information, and then had signed the record so that she could be identified, showed the orientation efforts of the pediatrics chief in setting up procedures to be followed in battered-child cases.

With the chief pediatrician, the officer went to the room where the child was asleep in her crib. The doctor woke the child out of a sound sleep, picked her from the crib and set her on the floor. The investigator, stooping over, indicated with his hands for the child to come to him across the room. Sylvia, a child reported not to walk or respond to affection by her own parents, toddled across the room on her frail legs, hardly capable of supporting her weight, and, smiling all the while, threw her arms around the neck of this total stranger and allowed herself to be lifted and carried about. There was a definite response in this child's actions, response to any attention shown her. This child was not only starved for nourishment, but also for affection. A police hold was placed on the child, so that parental removal would not occur during the course of the investigation.

Investigators went to the family home in a lower socioeconomic area, fully expecting to find a serious neglect situation involving all of the children. Arriving at the house just before noon, the officers located the mother in the back yard, but discovered that the woman did not speak English. Shortly thereafter, the children began arriving from school for their lunch. It was noted that all of the children were clean and well-groomed. They displayed manners and courtesies indicative of good home training. In addition, the children were extremely well-behaved and displayed the qualities of which most parents would be proud. The oldest child, the twelve-year-old daughter, was a very pretty child, and a girl who made an immediate impression for her sincerity and ability. This child was to act as an interpreter on this occasion. The mother allowed the officers to view the home on request, and the place was found to be spotless. It was one of the cleanest homes either of the officers had ever been in, and, at the same time, the children displayed all of the benefits of large-family life:

joy, friendship, helpfulness and that inner beauty that is experienced as a part of some people. With the exception of the one child lying in the hospital, this situation could only be described as evidence of a solid family unit.

The mother related that the family had come to this community several years before. She stated that the father was an alien, but that she was a citizen by birth. Of the nine children, seven were girls. The father had regular employment and, although the family was on a limited income, they were receiving no public assistance. Regarding the injuries Sylvia had endured, the mother said she had noted a swelling about the left shoulder. This, she thought, had been the result of a mosquito bite, giving some idea of the length of time the condition had existed — as this was now winter, and at least six months after the last mosquito hatch. Later, a swelling appeared at the child's elbow, and it was after this that the child's general condition began to deteriorate. The reason for taking the child to a doctor was Sylvia's fussing and apparent fever during the few days prior to taking her for treatment. At that time the concern was not so much for the arm, but was caused by the child's fussing and crying.

The investigation led to the school where the children were in attendance. It was discovered that the oldest girl was a high academic achiever. She was in accelerated classes in math and language and was very well thought of by her teachers. The school had never had any trouble with the girl. She was a model student. At the elementary school the other children attended, several were reported to be of superior intelligence and all were good students. Neither school gave any adverse criticism of the children or the condition they displayed while in school.

Based on these facts, there was no evidence to support a neglect prosecution. This does not mean that Sylvia had not suffered neglect. It does mean that no court or jury would be in a position to convict parents of neglect of one child, when it was evident that their efforts with eight other siblings were so successful. Still, Sylvia did need the protection of society. The investigation had failed to uncover abuse, but the condition of the child was indicative of both neglect and abuse. Petitions were requested via juvenile court, alleging the home environment to be detrimental to the health and safety of Sylvia, but not contending that the other children were in jeopardy. The allegations were supported by medical testimony and the court made Sylvia a dependent ward. She was placed in a foster home under the supervision of the probation department. That agency was ordered to supervise the case on a weekly basis.

Sylvia was at the first foster home for about six months. During this time, she began talking in sentences, developed her toilet training and evidenced good eating habits, with the exception that the foster mother complained the child "gobbled" her food. This child improved daily, developing the desire to stand up for herself with other children in the home and claiming the items of play that were rightfully hers. Physically she gained weight, extended her height and grew into a very pretty child. She became attached to the foster parents and would get up early in the morning to eat with them before the foster father would leave for work. During this period the parents of the child were granted visiting privileges in the foster home. They would visit Sylvia almost every week. At such times, the child was noted by the foster parents to respond to the father, but she had to be told by him to go to the mother. There seemed to be a sincere desire on the part of the parents to have the child back in the home and, after several weeks, the mother began contacting the probation department about having Sylvia returned. These contacts involved phone calls and several visits by the mother to the probation office.

In August, the foster parents were transferred to another community, and Sylvia was moved to a second foster home. Here the child's development continued to improve, and she soon was a chubby little girl of three and a half years. She was reported to be talkative, a helper around the house, who liked to remain in the company of the foster mother, and father when the latter was at home.

On the anniversary date of her removal from the home there was a juvenile court rehearing. At that time the judge took under consideration the return of Sylvia to her natural parents. The mother was now pregnant with the tenth child. The probation officer recommended an adjustment period, during which Sylvia would go home for short weekend visits with her family. This was to continue until after the birth of the expected child. The recommendation was based on a question of the mother's reaction to the return of the child, when the mother would have to cope with a readjustment to Sylvia during the last stages of her pregnancy. As the juvenile court accepted this recommendation, it can only be assumed that there was some anxiety and reluctance on the part of the supervising probation officer and the court regarding the ability of the mother to accept this child; although the mother was continually asking for her return. The probation officer also requested a psychological examination of the mother. Arrangements for this work up were made with the county psychologist, but in the final analysis it was found the language barrier was too extensive for productive findings. A significant failure was the lack of an attempt to seek other psychological efforts by a practitioner who could overcome the language difficulty. It was in the province of the juvenile court to have ordered the county to pay for such an examination, and with the willingness of the mother to undergo the diagnostic evaluation, it was to be an error on the part of the court and the probation office for not pursuing this effort.

During the next few months, when the home visits began, the foster parents related that some problems occurred. On one occasion, the mother refused to follow feeding instructions for the child as given by the foster parent. It caused a regression in the child's behavior for a period of five days following her return to the foster home. After these visitations Sylvia would attempt to obtain reassurances from the foster parents that she would not have to go back home to live. During the visits, friends, relatives and even the other siblings could not believe that this was the same child, because of her condition and behavior.

In June the court ordered the child returned to the home, still a court ward, and to undergo weekly supervision in the home by the probation officer. The new baby had been born by this time. Because of the month of the year, all of the children were to begin staying at home all day, as school was out. There was the new baby, and Sylvia had returned. This meant a disruption of the normal routine of the mother, and with the new baby there would be added duties and obligations. The father was a good, hard-working individual, but he was from a background in which the care of children and other household duties were to be left to the mother. The probation supervision of the case was to extend until the following September, when it was to be relinquished to the child welfare authorities. At this point the system began to break down.

The original probation officer received a high position with the state parole agency and left the probation department. Before leaving, this officer briefed her replacement on the situation involving Sylvia. The second officer was a good conscientious worker, but several other officers had left the department for other positions or other reasons. This left the department shorthanded, and the remaining officers had to assume extra caseloads. For some reason the agency encountered difficulty in replacing the personnel. By this time the summer vacation schedule was well under way, and this created more work on less personnel. All of these factors contributed to a failure of the agency to supervise the case weekly. In the meantime, new personnel coming onto the job had to be oriented and trained. This became the task of the older officers in terms of service. Finally, in August, a probation officer made a visit at Sylvia's home. This officer had never seen Sylvia. There was no criteria for the officer to base a determination of condition upon. The language barrier again presented itself, and the best that can be stated of that visit was its cursory nature. Nothing was determined or discovered. The officer took the statements of the mother and recorded them. She also noted that the child was very quiet and shy, an opposite transition from the outgoing, verbal and happy child who had left the foster home. Because of the lack of familiarity with the child, this quiet attitude was of no exceptional concern to the probation officer and was merely mentioned as an afterthought in the narrative of the probation record.

In September, the probation department advised the welfare service that transfer of the case would occur. The child welfare agency responded that it would assume jurisdiction, and requested a case summary and a court order giving that agency jurisdiction. The case summary was sent within the following nine days, but no court order accompanied the summary. The welfare service assumed that it was in the process of being initiated, and withheld contact with the case. At the same time, probation did not feel a court order was necessary, and did not ask for one. That agency assumed that the case was being supervised by the welfare service. Neither agency checked with the other and, as a consequence, the case went unsupervised for a period of two or more weeks.

On October 26, 1964, Sylvia was dead on arrival at a private physician's office, approximately five months after she had been returned to her parent's home. The investigation by the coroner's office disclosed that the victim's mother attributed the death to a fall from a lower bed of a bunk-bed set in one of the bedrooms of the family home. Apparently, Sylvia had died immediately. The mother could give no other account of the cause of death. Because of the history of the case and the circumstances surrounding the death, an autopsy was ordered. Photographs of the body were taken by the law enforcement identification bureau.

The postmortem examination revealed no apparent injuries, and no organic or clinical cause of the demise of the child. The examiner listed the cause of death as "cerebral edema due to shock, due to trauma." The pathologist had full skeletal surveys of the body performed, and even removed the spinal column searching for clues that would give a reason for the death of the child. The day following the child's death, which was the day of the autopsy, bruises were more pronounced on the body of the victim, and these were recorded by the police photographer.

An investigation was conducted by the officers working on the original case. The mother was contacted at the home, and the older daughter acted as an interpreter. The mother stated that she had been in the process of preparing the baby's bottle, and both she and the infant were in the kitchen. The victim and two younger sisters were in the girls' bedroom playing. The mother said she heard the eighteen-month-old child crying, and entered the bedroom and discovered that the child had fallen from one of the beds. The mother scolded the children and returned to the kitchen. She said a short time later the three-year-old came into the kitchen and told the mother that Sylvia was dead. The mother said that she went into the room and found the victim face down on the floor between the beds. When attempts at revival failed (attempts the mother performed by rubbing alcohol on the child's body), and as she noted the child was turning blue, the mother called a friend who took her and the child to the private doctor's office.

An interview of the oldest child revealed that some of the bruises on the victim had occurred when the eighteen-month-old child had bitten Sylvia on various occasions. Other bruises were said to have occurred when the victim would have tantrums, throw herself on the floor or hit herself, including striking her head against the wall or on the floor. The oldest girl also said that the child pulled her own hair out, and gave this as an explanation of the scalp wound found on the victim's head at the time of the medical examination. She related that her sister had developed a bad temper after coming home, and had gotten to the point where she cried constantly.

A subsequent interrogation of the mother was conducted in the family home. Actually the interrogation took place in the bedroom where the death had occurred. In order to assist the interrogative process, a Border Patrolman accompanied the investigators for the purpose of acting as an interpreter. The mother described the position she had found the child in, and other incidents of the date in question. For the first time in the course of two investigations and other official contacts over a period of eighteen months, the mother admitted that she did not respond to the victim as she did the other children. She said that when Sylvia was about one year old, the child who was now three had been born. Sylvia became jealous of the new baby, and tended to regress. It was at this time the child began to fuss and cry, have tantrums, and became a bad eater. The mother said her reactions to Sylvia were hostile, and that she had never told anyone about this before. She had so much trouble with Sylvia during that period of time that she became rough in her treatment of the child, yanking her about and spanking her often, usually much harder than she spanked the other children. As the hostility of the mother developed, she noted that Sylvia ceased to respond well toward her, and therein developed an entanglement that was never altered. Each person responded in a negative manner to the other, and each reaction would heighten the hostility and tension that grew between the mother and this child.

The mother admitted that the child had regressed badly after returning to the home. It was stated that Sylvia became fussy and started her crying almost immediately after returning, and that by the middle of July, the child was again having temper tantrums, was withdrawn and had become such a poor eater that the mother had to spoon-feed her. Sylvia was no longer toilet trained and would not converse in sentences. Because of these actions on the part of the child, the mother's hostilities admittedly redeveloped in reaction. This meant that the vicious circle of personal interplay between these two had begun again. According to the mother, by the time the probation officer made her call at the home in August, Sylvia was a problem and was losing weight because she would not eat. The mother recognized and volunteered the fact of her failure to report the regression of the child to the probation authorities. This failure, according to the mother, had contributed to the death of the child, for had she made the report of the child's true condition, the mother felt that Sylvia would have been removed from the home. The mother readily admitted she had lied to the probation officer on the date of the August visit. She also admitted that she was aware the child was a court ward, and that as such, she, the mother, had a responsibility to report to the court any situations that would be of concern. She said she had been to the probation office on occasions, and that she knew how to make contact with that agency by phone, in addition to personal contact. The reason she willingly withheld the information about Sylvia's condition was her fear that the child would be removed from her custody. In summing up this failure to report, the mother felt that it had contributed to the death of her daughter. At a later date the mother gave a full statement of these facts to the district attorney.

In recounting the events of the day Sylvia died, the mother said she was awakened about five o'clock in the morning. Sylvia was crying, and the mother got the child up to go to the bathroom. The mother felt this action should have stopped the child's crying, but as Sylvia continued to cry on the way, her mother admittedly became angry and sat the child hard onto the toilet, shaking her by her shoulders. Later, Sylvia, still whimpering, was taken back to her bed and placed back into it in a manner described by the mother as "rough." The parent went into the kitchen and began fixing her husband's lunch he carried on the job. Later she got the children up and ready for school. There were no more incidents until after the children left for class. At that time the mother was with the baby in the kitchen and the other children were in the girls' bedroom. After the one child had been shaken from a fall off the bed, the mother went into the bedroom and scolded all of the children about jumping on the beds. She admitted that she directed most of her remarks to Sylvia, and that she told Sylvia that she would spank her if there was anymore trouble. After leaving the room, she again heard the children jumping on the beds, and returned to the room, making them all sit down quietly on a bed. In doing so, the mother took Sylvia by the upper arms and sat her down harshly on the bed. The children were told to sit, and the mother admitted that she again threatened to spank them. Entering the hallway and returning to the kitchen, the mother was followed by her three-year-old daughter who told her, "Sylvia's dead." With this, the mother returned to the room and found the child lying on the floor, face down. The information elicited in this interrogation was later given to the district attorney by the mother, in an officially recorded statement.

On the basis of the possibility of a transference of aggression to one of the other children, a complaint was issued by the district attorney charging child neglect; in that the mother, by her failure to report the child's condition to the juvenile court or the probation department, had placed the child in danger. The woman was charged only after intensive background research by the district attorney staff member, of both the law and the "battered child syndrome." This attorney did his homework well, and after twelve hours of consultation on various occasions with the investigators, arrived at the place where he no longer was concentrating on the death of the child, but on the date of the probation visitation. He understood the reason for the prosecution, being that of obtaining a conviction for the purpose of placing the mother on a period of adult probation, and thereby allowing a supervising agency into the home to watch for a disruption of the equilibrium of the family. There were no punitive aspects to this prosecution whatsoever. The mother was not arrested, but was taken directly to court, and arrangements were made with the judge to release the woman on her word to appear. At this point the system began to break down again. The staff member from the district attorney's office was placed on another case. All of his research and understanding of the matter was lost. The attorney assigned to the case had no such sophistication, and to the day in court, could not understand why the death of the child was not the main concern. In court, the day was lost, through the presentation in which the death of the child was made the paramount issue by the district attorney's representative. Since there was no evidence to support such a contention, the case was dismissed for lack of evidence.

In a speech several months after the death of this child, the juvenile court judge, who had returned Sylvia to the home, told an audience that not only do the parents have a right to their child, but the child has a right to his parents. The judge proceeded to quote the findings of the DeFrancis' study, indicating that 20 percent of the children returned to the home after a battering will be dead within one year. The judge then said:

> This means that eighty percent of them will live, and I'm interested in that eighty per cent.

It is too bad Sylvia was not an "eighty percenter."

During the course of the investigation, all of the children older than Sylvia were interviewed, as was the neighbor woman who took the mother and the child to the private physician. The doctors were contacted, both the pathologist and the private physician. The investigation covered a span of four weeks and many man hours. Yet, it should be noted that at no time were the causes of any injuries or evidence of any injuries to this child discovered. The most noteworthy finding was the lack of serious injury. It appeared as if Sylvia had died of fright. The circumstances of the morning of her death, coupled with the child's negative experiences, brought on a shock condition resulting in cardiac arrest. The pathologist was of the opinion that immediate and effective resuscitation may have saved the child. The mother was totally unaware of such a procedure, and attempted revival by a means tragically archaic in its application.

It remains that an investigation of the case revealed nothing concrete indicating direct abuse of the child, and evidence of wilful neglect by the mother was found lacking in a court contest. This case is an example of the difficulty encountered in such situations, and supports the contention of the primacy of protection of the child as law enforcement's initial function in abuse cases.

To Protect the Child

Elizabeth was a small and frail child, first contacted at the elementary school she attended, in response to an anonymous complaint that the child was being mistreated at home. In the presence of the principal, Elizabeth was questioned in a general way in an attempt to illicit information supporting the allegation. The child was shy but friendly. She did not appear neglected, but her clothes were not the best. However, the area serviced by the school was a lower-class area, and poor clothing was seen on many of the children. Elizabeth denied that anything was wrong at her home, and as there was no evidence of mistreatment that could be identified, no further action was taken.

Almost one year later, another call was made regarding this child, and other investigators contacted the school and interviewed the alleged victim. The results were the same, with one exception. The fact that no action was taken brought out the identity of the informer. The information was coming from an aunt of the child, one of the mother's sisters. The woman called again and, giving her name, advised law enforcement that the conditions under which Elizabeth was forced to live were cruel and inhuman. It was related that the child was one of three children, having a brother older than her nine years and a sister two years younger. The treatment of these children differed dramatically. Where the other siblings were dressed well, Elizabeth wore old clothes. She was often not allowed to eat at the table with the rest of the children, but instead was made to wait until the family had finished their meal, and then was fed cold food on the service porch, without the benefit of a table. Literally, the child was eating off the floor. Many times she was not allowed to be in the room where the other children were watching television, but was made to stay on the rear porch, sometimes in the dark. The aunt stated that on numerous occasions when her family visited in the home they would not see Elizabeth at all, but the other children were present and the center of attention. It was understood by members of the family that the child was beaten at times, but none had ever seen this. They had seen marks on the child indicating such actions.

Investigators went to the school on a date that was by chance only. There was no reason for this call on this date, the officers just happening to be in the area of the school and deciding to interview the child. The little girl was brought into the principal's office. She was in a worn, drab wash dress that hung too loosely on her small frame. The shoes she wore were boys shoes and were scuffed and shabby. The child's shy manner gave way to a friendly grin in her reactions to initial conversation indicating that the officers remembered her. On this occasion a very simple, "yes, this morning" came as the response to the question of whether she had been spanked recently. The policewoman took the child into a bathroom off the principal's office and discovered that the child had suffered a serious beating very recently. There were numerous bruises and hematomas about the child's back, from high near the shoulder blades to just above her knees. In addition, there were some heavy marks across the area of the child's kidneys, as well as some miscellaneous bruises and marks on the front portion of her body. This child had been beaten, and the beating had been administered in an indiscriminate manner. Further questioning revealed that the spanking had occurred before school on this date. Elizabeth said she had been on the porch and her mother had gotten angry with her for putting a rag in the hot water tank. The child's explanation of this act was not clear, and the matter was not pressed further at that time. She recounted the spanking as being administered with a stick, which was one of the legs to a chalk board. She said it stood against the door frame just inside the service porch, when one entered from the inside of the house. The child cried and screamed during the beating, and related that this action seemed to infuriate the mother. Elizabeth's older brother had left for school before the beating, as he was playing baseball and liked to practice on the playground before school began. Elizabeth stated that she was not allowed to go to school early to play on the playground, but could give no reason why. Her younger sister was in the home at the time of the altercation. This child was in an accelerated reading group and did not have to attend school during the first hour of the morning, which was spent with the slower readers. After the beating, Elizabeth was sent to school.

Elizabeth's teacher related that the child was a contrast to the older brother, who had been in the teacher's class the year before. She added that this contrast was more evident between Elizabeth and the younger child. The teacher was referring to the manner in which the children dressed, their school progress and their social adaptability. It was denied that Elizabeth was mentally retarded or a slow learner. The teacher felt the child was having difficulty in school academic achievement due to an emotional retardation. She indicated that she had no difficulty with the behavior of Elizabeth, and the child was said to be a willing student who would perform the most menial tasks requested. It was stated that Elizabeth went home for lunch every day, but her brother and sister ate in the cafeteria at school. Questioning of the child at a later time revealed that she often prepared her own lunch, usually consisting of cold cereal, although her mother would be home at the time. She said she ate alone on these occasions, as her mother would not come to the kitchen. Most of the noon hour was spent at home in silence, as the mother did not converse with the child.

The teacher related that when she had the older brother in class, the younger sister often brought the lunch money for both children, and would come to the class and give the money for the boy. This had not occurred at all during this school year in Elizabeth's case, but the teacher reported seeing the other two eating at school almost every day. Additionally, Elizabeth was said to have been seen in only two dresses all year, while the little sister was reported to be dressed as if "out of Vogue."

The older brother was interviewed. He was all boy, and as boys are at the age of eleven, was not too impressed with all that was occurring. He said his sister Elizabeth did not eat at school because he and his youngest sister had told their parents not to let her. The reason for this was the poor manners of the child and the fact that

Elizabeth wanted to sit with the other siblings, and this embarassed them. This statement was given in a very matter-of-fact way, as if to indicate a feeling on the part of this boy that he and his younger sister could exert an influence on the parents in relation to the treatment of Elizabeth. He admitted that Elizabeth often ate alone on the rear porch, but gave as the reason her poor table manners. He said that she was denied television, mainly because she would laugh so loud as to disturb he and the younger sister while they were watching a program. After interviewing this child, the feeling of being involved in a story came over all of the adults concerned. It was so drastic a discrimination of a child, and the brother had related the facts of the difference in such an unemotional and unconcerned manner as to cause one to feel it was not really happening.

At the investigator's request, the younger sister was brought into the office. The description of this child's dress was not overdone by the teacher. She was a pretty child, much larger than Elizabeth. Her long black hair had been brushed until it shone. Her clothes were expensive and immaculate. She was a picture, and stood in stark contrast, not only to her sister, but to other children in the school. This child, in a manner revealing her being accustomed to being impressive, reiterated the differences in the treatment received by her brother and herself in relation to Elizabeth. Like the brother, she seemed to display the attitude that all of these differences were all right because of the way Elizabeth behaved. She was questioned regarding the trouble in the home that morning, and not only denied knowledge of any, but denied that she had heard her sister scream. This denial was made in the face of the admission that she was in the kitchen, right next to the porch, at the time the incident occurred. Could it have been that this child was already so calloused toward her sister that the screams of the child would go unnoticed? Or did this girl dislike her sister so much as to lie? The answer to that will be lived, over the years. It will never be known to the investigators, but it may become known to Elizabeth, if she lives to adulthood.

Elizabeth was taken to the public hospital, examined for foster home placement, and then further examined as a possible battered child by the pediatric staff. Photographs of the child's bruises and marks were recorded by a police photographer. Elizabeth was then placed with child welfare services, in protective custody.

Investigators went to the home of the complainant and talked with the victim's grandmother and three of the victim's aunts. They related that the mother was pregnant with Elizabeth when she was discovered to be suffering from tuberculosis. This eventually required the mother's hospitalization for a period of almost two years. Elizabeth was born during this period. She was given to the maternal grandparents. After the mother left the hospital she again became pregnant, and Elizabeth remained with the grandparents until her younger sister was about three years old. At age five Elizabeth returned to her parents, after the death of her grandfather. The grandmother was no longer able to provide the financial needs of the child, and the parents of the child would not contribute to her support in the grandmother's home. It was stated by the sister of the mother, that the latter person blamed her tubercular condition on Elizabeth, feeling the hospitalization would not have been necessary if this child had not been conceived. Allegedly, a rejection of the child occurred, culminating in the present situation. At this time all of the relatives stated their willingness to testify. Additionally, it was stated that their brother, a professional man and living in another community, was anxious to take Elizabeth, to offer the child better conditions of life. He had made this offer to his sister and her husband, but they had turned him down.

The relatives stated the father was suffering from a head injury that occurred to him during the Korean war and resulted in a loss of control over his temper. It was said that this man very often became almost wild with rage and had difficulty controlling himself when under stress. This information was verified by members of the department who had attempted to serve civil papers on the individual in the past and had experienced some of his tirades and temper displays.

The officers went to the victim's home and attempted to interview the mother, after advising her of her constitutional rights. She admitted the officers to the home, which was a nice and well-kept place of abode, in contrast to the surrounding neighborhood. The front room presented a glaring display of the differences between the children. Two pictures, one of the older boy and one of the younger girl, taken in school that year, graced the built-in bookcase. There was no evidence of a photograph of the victim. At the officers request the mother took them onto the service porch where she admitted that she had spanked Elizabeth that morning. In her explanation of the happenings, she indicated that the child often wet her pants, and the day before had done so while playing in the backyard. She was always spanked for this, and so the child hid the underpants in the bottom of the hot water tank near the pilot light in order to dry them and wear them later. Elizabeth's actions were witnessed by her younger sister, who told about the event the following morning while eating breakfast. The mother admittedly lost control and while mad grabbed the first weapon, described by the mother to be a stick, and began striking the child. As Elizabeth began to scream, the mother became more irritated and, by her own statement, did not realize where she was hitting the child.

The hot water tank had the dust shifted in the bottom, as if by a cloth. The weapon was found in the position described by the child. The suspect admitted that was what had been used in the beating. That article was marked for identification and retained by the officers after placing the woman under arrest. She was allowed to phone her husband, and then the suspect was transported to the county jail.

The husband met one of the investigators outside the jail, and for a time it appeared he would be placed in custody due to the disturbance he created. The man, cursing and swearing, threatened the officer's family, threatened to blow up the jail and made threats to the person of the judge, although no one knew who that might be. After finally calming the man down, the officer advised the husband of the procedure to obtain the release of his wife without posting bail. Later, the man was able to arrange for the wife's release on her own recognizance.

At the juvenile court hearing, the child was made a ward of the court and placed in a foster home. This placement occurred after the mother's brother appeared in court and offered to take the child into his home. The mother told the judge that she would rather see the child dead than in the home of the uncle, and the judge abided by her wishes. Thus, the parent was successful in denying her child the chance of being in a home with persons the child knew. Instead, through the mother's efforts, her girl was placed in a foster home, where she would have to adjust to strangers. This seemed to all who witnessed it, the last and final act of inflicting punishment on the child by the parent; and it had been concurred in by the judge himself, the one man charged with the protection of the child.

During a two-day jury trial, the defense was able to convince the jury that the episode was merely the rightful punishment of a child by a parent, and the verdict was acquittal. Nothing else could have been accomplished in the investigation. There was more than enough evidence, the marks were recorded by photograph and medical examination. There was medical testimony. The weapon was introduced in evidence. The admission made by the mother to the officers were presented to the jury. The general treatment of the child was presented through a parade of witnesses, both relatives and school personnel. The victim testified in addition. What more could be done to obtain a conviction? But the jury bought the concept of parental discipline. This case is presented in an effort to reiterate, by example, the difficulty involved in these prosecutions, again urging the efforts of the police in concentrating their action on the protection of the child.

These three cases have been utilized to demonstrate variety, complexity, failure and success in one law enforcement agency's approach to the "battered child syndrome." Together, they are examples of the harm children are exposed to within their own homes, often as a result of the actions of the persons charged with their care. There has been evidence of torture and hideous mistreatment, of the inability to cope with situations that required the adjustment of one party because of the limited age of the other, and of the total rejection of one child because of the imagined harm that child was felt to have brought upon her parent. In Maribelle's case, she was returned to her native country, presumably to live with her mother. Sylvia's death released her from further harm. But Elizabeth has lived to be returned to her family, and there is no reason to assume that the conditions have changed for the child. The discrimination and rejection are still a part of her life, and for the time being she has no where to turn. Only her emancipation from the home through the benefits of age will remove her from the dilemma of existing unwanted. But nothing will remove the emotional damage caused by this deprivation.

The need for society to search out methods of offering more than limited protection to children such as these is apparent. The failure of the disciplines involved to formulate such methods and the legislation to make protection a reality, is also apparent. In the past eight years, much legislation has been enacted to serve the battered child, but it has been superficial and incapable of offering adequate child protection, as well as lacking in its ability to attack the roots of the problem that are just now being isolated. Society has a long way to proceed in the protection of these children. To gain significant advances will require the efforts of the professions, the academic and scientific communities, as well as government and its various services.

Chapter IX

INTERVIEWS AND INTERROGATIONS

ANY discussion of this subject matter in full would amount to an extensive development of one of the most important aspects of police investigation. This is true, even though there have been restrictions placed on law enforcement by court decisions of late. The place in police work of the interview and the interrogation has not been reduced in the face of these restrictions, and the utilization of both techniques remains a significant element of police routine. No investigation can be effectual or complete without good information-seeking practices. The use of verbal communication to obtain this information remains one of the best weapons to which the police have access. Since police investigation is essentially a human experience, it is necessary for the investigator to have a firm foundation in the knowledge and understanding of human behavior. "An understanding of psychology . . . can be of immeasurable assistance to the criminal investigator. It is almost a prerequisite for the interrogator of witnesses and suspects"(1). This is the knowledge needed in order for the investigator to properly evaluate the information received on the basis of an insight into the personality variations of those persons with whom he will come in contact. In order to properly frame questions and analyze the information, a thorough understanding of human behavior is a necessity. This understanding of psychology, of human behavior, is a constant partner of the investigator, and is an absolute essential for the conduct of successful interviews and interrogations.

Within the concept of the law, a person is considered to be responsible for his own actions. Therefore, when a person's actions lead him into conflict with the law, that person is considered to have performed a wrong or illegal act. The law provides that the individual is answerable to society for the wrong performed, and if

194

the circumstances are such as to indicate the responsibility of that person for the wrong act, the performer of that act is liable to punishment. This is the basis of the application of criminal justice in a free society. It has evolved as a result of the influence of the free-will school of philosophical thought that has prevailed upon man since the time of Aristotle, restated by Augustine and Aquinas and perfected by Hagel. The concept, in essence, assumes the will to be a human endowment, a part of human nature, common to all men. Each man is granted the ability to exercise this will in a manner providing a measure of freedom or choice. Thus, a human who has not had the faculty impaired by mental retardation or other mental disorder, utilizes his freedom of will or choice to distinguish between possible human acts. His selection is deemed to be individual and, if free (not accomplished by duress or subterfuge), the individual has acted in keeping with his exercise of free will, and is therefore liable for the outcome or effects of his choice. Such a concept is more complex than the simplified explanation presented here. Free will is not a universally accepted human essential. It is not accepted by many philosophies, but it has been accepted within the evolution of our criminal justice, probably as the result of the Judeo-Christian influence.

As criminal investigators, the police cannot be primarily concerned with the causation of the crime being investigated. That is not the purpose of the investigation. Causality is a complex problem, a many-faceted basis for an act, which may consist of one or an infinite number of factors, and will vary from case to case and individual-to-individual. For the most part, few have been able to isolate actual cause of crime, but instead have been successful in identifying correlating factors that tend to be found common in the backgrounds of those persons committing various types of crime. The police function of investigation is to determine whether a crime has been committed and to identify the perpetrator. The ultimate goal of an investigation is to discover the truth. Crime is a human experience, involving not only the suspect, but the victim and others whose lives will be touched by the act. Since verbal communication is the basic communicative tool of mankind, it is elementary that such a tool be utilized in the course of the investigation of this human experience. Because of the involvement of human nature in the event, the need to have a solid understanding of human behavior is also essential. This means that the investigator must have a background in the psychology of the criminal, and he must also have an effective command of language communicative skill.

Interviews

In the area of criminal investigation, the terms interview and interrogation have different meanings. For many outside the field, there is a misunderstanding of the meaning of interrogation. This is based on the connotation derived from historical and fictional accounts of the interrogative process as employed throughout the centuries in autocratic and totalitarian societies. Therefore, many of the disciplines involved in the protection of the child rely heavily upon interviews, while discounting interrogation due to a punitive concept of that process, usually a result of an exposure to the entertainment media. It should be understood that neither process is an end in itself, but each represents a tool to be utilized by the investigator as a means to the ultimate end of the investigation. As these are just tools, there is no value in formulating a controversy over the use or disuse of the tool. The fact that certain disciplines do not need interrogation does not reduce the value of interrogation, but, rather, points out the difference in the mission and objectives of the discipline involved. For purposes of police investigation, both techniques are essential.

Questioning is a basic function of an investigation. In order to obtain answers, questions must be asked. There is no other technique so basic in investigation. The two types of questioning processes utilized by the police are the interview and the interrogation. In many police manuals and training texts, the emphasis is placed on the interrogation; but for the purposes of this text, the interview will be stressed, as the use of the interview will far exceed the use of the interrogation. Interviews are in order when questioning most victims and witnesses. They are normally persons who are not hostile or, because of a lack of involvement with the commission of the act and the attendant liability, have nothing to hide. The use of the interview in communicating with such persons is usually very productive and, at the same time, can be an effectual part of any police public relations program. Effective interviewing is capable of not only illiciting pertinent information, but it is also a means of developing the positive police image desired by most officers.

Interviewing may be defined as a conversation with a purpose(2). It is a purposeful communication technique. It may involve small talk, but any such verbalization is directed toward the purpose of the interview. Unlike normal conversation, the original reason for the verbal contact with the other person must remain a clearly defined objective in the mind of the interviewer. The purpose will be to obtain information relative to the case under investigation. There can be no other concern, and to this end the conversation must be guided and directed. Interviews are a process of questioning for the purpose of learning facts. These facts are the objectives of the conversation and may be placed under one of three classification:

1. The Accumulation of Information . . . The obtaining of informative matter that will provide the circumstances of the event and corroborate information already gathered.
2. The Identification or Location of Evidence . . . This entails the assistance of the person being interviewed, to supply either the fact of the existence of evidence or the location of that evidence, for the purpose of the collection and preservation of this necessary element of criminal investigation.
3. The Discovery of Witnesses . . . The interview of one person may lead to the identification of a witness unknown to the investigator at the time of the interview.

The interview is usually employed in contacts with the victim or witnesses. In the case of witnesses, these may be persons the investigator has sought-out through the investigative effort, or they may be persons who have come forward to provide information on a voluntary basis. In either situation, the voluntary aspect of the interview must be present. This does not mean that only persons eager to verbalize the events are to be interviewed. There are many reasons why one may not wish to provide information. These reasons do not always involve hostility. Very often they are the result of sincere motivations, or a misunderstanding of the role the witness plays. The reluctance to become involved in a court situation is a valid reason to restrict the conversation. It does not take interrogation to overcome this desire to remain aloof, but it may require interviewing skill and salesmanship. This requires time, and many officers, in haste, create hostility in a person who would become a willing witness if the time were utilized to assist the person to become aware of why involvement should occur. This normal reluctance to be a part of a criminal action should not be interpreted by an officer as hostility until the witness has demonstrated an unwillingness to accept for consideration the reasons the officer presents to overcome a stalemate of apathy.

Officers should become sensitive to the witness, and recognize the motivations tending to keep the individual from appearing cooperative. These can stem from kinship, employment, business, friendship or merely because of a geographical sharing of a neighborhood. These are valid concerns for the witness, and the officer should be cognizant of their effects on the willingness to become involved. By demonstrating a concern for the witness's feelings, the investigator is in a position to alleviate part of the anxiety the person encounters. By continuing the conversation, even in relation to the matter of involvement, the interviewer has kept the interview alive. This is a technique known to a salesman: keep them talking and keep them happy. The same is true in interviews and interrogations. As long as the person is telling the officer "NO," he is still communicating, and the opportunity for dialogue is ever present.

Many witnesses fail to provide the information necessary or desired, due to a lack of understanding on their part as to what is important to the investigator. Few people have many contacts on a personal basis with the police. The interview may be one of the only times that person has ever conversed with an officer. There is an effect on the law-abiding citizen when he is interviewed by the officer. It is a desire to help, and to appear understanding and intelligent at the same time. Many of these people are proud of their assistance. This places them in a position where they are hesitant to state facts they sense the officer will feel unimportant, or to ask clarifying questions they feel will be too elementary.

Thus, many witnesses are interviewed in a state wherein they have a concept of the objectives the officer is seeking that is completely different from the reason for the interview. More often than not, information is withheld on the basis it is not important than for any other reason. An investigator using skillful interviewing techniques will lead the witness to the point of recognition of the importance of a minor detail.

A police interview involves the eliciting of information that the witness has obtained through his senses, by means of effective questioning on the part of the officer(3). The witness has gathered his knowledge of the situation through a sensory experience; the use of his sight, taste, smell, touch or hearing. It has been said that 80 percent of what a person becomes aware of, is presented to him through his sight. It is also known that most individuals will begin to experience a memory loss within one week after the exposure, and, depending on the development of the person's memory, there will be a substantial loss of information within six months. The reliability of the information presented will be of concern to the interviewer, and part of his job will be the verification of the reliability factor. There are many things that can affect reliability, the least of which is veracity. Not only the factors already mentioned, but the physical limitations of the senses employed to gain the information will have an effect. A person with bad eyesight, not wearing his glasses at the time of witnessing an event, may have doubtful credibility as to what he saw, but at the same time he may be making no attempt to mislead the investigator(1). There is the mentality and education background of the individual that must be considered. Persons of low intelligence will have a difficult time in understanding the importance of certain elements of testimony such as hearsay. They may continue to give the officer hearsay accounts after having the concept of hearsay explained. They may be capable of presenting very good information, but be incapable of qualifying as a witness in court. These persons, as with children, may fall victim to leading questions of the officer and respond with information that is false. The desire to assist the officer may cause agreement to police statements or questions that completely mislead the investigator. Such persons must be handled with care, and time must not be restricted. Hasty interviews never are successful.

While some witnesses must be handled with sterness, most respond to a kind and friendly approach, and this tends to bring about the best results in most interview situations. There may be times when the conversation must be redirected, as the witness may wander from the subject, but a congenial attitude on the part of the interviewer will be the most successful approach in general(1). In order to provide this friendly approach, the manner of the interview should be thought of by the witness as informal. The interview is formal, in that it has purpose and needs preparation and skilled techniques. In its application, as the witness is exposed to it, an interview should appear to be a casual conversation. Questions must be formed in the vocabulary of the subject, altering from person-to-person as the demands and backgrounds of the individual vary. The interviewer is not there to impress anyone, he is there to gain information. The use of language resembling a college lecture, with a person of a meager educational background, will not bring about the desired results. The person's lack of understanding of the connotation and meaning of the questions will cause his silence. It will be much easier for him to deny knowledge than to admit he does not understand the questions which are being asked. At the same time, the officer should not utilize first grade conversation when dealing with a witness who has an extensive educational background and a high professional standing. The ability of the interviewer to adapt to the individual being questioned is essential. The interviewer may, in one day, question an illiterate, a PhD. professor of engineering, a prizefighter, an author, a professional criminal recidivist and a member of the clergy(4).

If the information of the witness is the result of a human experience, the interpretation of the meaning of the sensory preceptions will be in light of the experience of the witness. Therefore, the information may be presented to the investigator out of context to its actual meaning or importance, due to the personal and experiental orientation of the individual. As a simplified example, a person with an artistic background may be able to describe color in such a narrowed sense as to cause the investigator to be incapable of perceiving the hue intended. Or a person with limited encounters with dogs may describe as large, an animal that a more experienced person would consider medium or even small. The investigator should be aware of the effect of the person's experience in the evaluation and recounting of the events he witnessed. The converse is also true. The investigator will tend to interpret what is being stated in respect to his experience. It is necessary for the officer to seek clarification from the individual, rather than to accept what has been stated in relation to the personal connotation given the information by the officer.

Locard(5) divided the act of witness experience into stages, to wit: the perception; the observation; the mind-fixation in which bias, fantasy, idea association and personal judgement are influences affecting the finalized memorization of the encounter; and the recounting of the information(1). From this classification it is readily seen that many factors may relate to and affect the finalized version as presented by the witness, including his inability to convey through verbal communication the actual meaning he intends. Interviewing, then, is not an easy task, nor is it a skill readily acquired. It comes from the desire to participate, study and prepare, and is related to the personality of the interviewer, finally perfected through experience. One of the best methods of perfecting the techniques of either interviewing or interrogation is to be present during the course of such procedures when they are being performed by a person of known skill.

The need to prepare for an interview cannot be overemphasized; preparation is an absolute essential. It is necessary to properly orient oneself prior to making contact with the witness, and it is necessary in order to formulate questions that will tend to bring about the objectives of the interview. Many officers are failures interviewing merely because of the lack of preparation for the interview. They approach a witness with only a vague concept of what this witness may have to offer and of what information they themselves desire. The facts of the case are not fresh in their minds, and they do not have a clear concept of circumstances, time elements or crime scenes. The opening question is a fishing expedition, and before the conversation progresses to a beneficial stage, the investigator has been exposed as not knowing what he wants. The witness then becomes more difficult to extract information from, resulting in a frustration on the part of the officer. This will cause the interviewer to become more forceful, thereby driving a wedge between himself and the witness, or to back off, which usually entails the officer giving up, with the resultant loss of information. It is necessary for homework to have been done. The officer should have a concrete plan in mind before making contact with the witness. He should have such a grasp of the case that he can recall the date, day of the week, time and circumstances, as well as formulate a mental picture of the crime scene and the surrounding area. This means that every piece of information given by the witness should readily be assimulated and related to the total context of what the officer already knows. If the witness asks, "What day did this happen?" the officer should know the day of the week, as the date may be meaningless to the witness. The cessation of the interview, while the officer searches for a wallet calendar to determine what day it was, can cause a loss of rapport with the witness or a distraction resulting in the witness losing his train of thought. These problems can only be overcome with adequate preparation prior to initiating the interview.

The place in which the interview is to be conducted is considered important by some authorities, many of whom hold the officer's office to be the most satisfactory interviewing station. This concept is not without merit, as the investigator finds himself on his own ground. But, in making the rounds of many police agencies, most interrogation rooms are found to be woefully inadequate. In addition, many headquarters are so overcrowded that the office of the investigator is either a small and dingy quarter, or he is sharing a desk in a larger office pool. In either instance, the department does not offer proper space and surroundings conducive to meaningful interrogation or interviewing. For purposes of interviewing, anywhere the witness is comfortable will be sufficient. This includes standing under a tree, if the interview is not to be too lengthy. Many productive interviews have been carried on while in the yard of the witness, or while the witness has been performing some task. The home of the person being interviewed is often one of the best places for the conversation. Here, the subject is familiar with the surroundings, is usually at ease and is secure. These factors all lead to a willingness to converse, and allow the witness to feel as if the interview is completely confidential. This is the case when the home is empty, or when others have absented themselves in order to allow the interview to take place in a semblance of privacy. The reader is cautioned not to misinterpret the concept of interviewing in the home, or at other indescriminate locations. This does not mean the subject may be placed in a position where there are numerous distractions, noises or interruptions. Therefore, in the home situation, the other members of the family should allow for privacy or the interview should be conducted elsewhere. There should not be overpowering background noise with which to compete. The witness should not be interviewed in a situation where distractions occur, such as a mother being interviewed with her small children coming in and out, asking for drinks and otherwise becoming involved in interrupting the train of thought. Nor should the witness be interrupted and interviewed when that person is engaged in some task requiring the individual's sole attention. This causes the person to have to spread attention between two unrelated circumstances and will result in a poorly conducted interview. Many investigators have been highly successful interviewing in their car, and on occasions have taken the subject for a ride in the vehicle in order to gain the privacy needed.

There has been some alluding to privacy. This is an important factor in either the interview or the interrogation, but is more critical for purposes of interrogating. In the interview situation, the officer should allow for enough privacy to assist the witness in relating the full details of the information known. This means that other members of the family, friends, employers or employees and others should not be included in the conversation. It may be necessary for the interview to be postponed until a later date or for the interviewer to suggest other arrangements, but no one should be interviewed in the presence of others who will tend to make the witness nervous or reluctant to talk. Nothing is worse than to direct questions to a witness, and have a third party answer. This will happen if the interviewer allows persons not connected with the case to be present. These persons may have been given hearsay information by the witness or others. As questions are directed to the witness, those questions the third party is familiar with will draw responses from him instead of from the witness. There are times when they will enter into an argument with the witness about what the witness has told them in the past. They may state that what is being said now is not the way it has been told. They can become embroiled in a discussion with the interviewer on matters not directly involved in the case at hand. This answering for another is a very common occurrence when conducting an interview of a child in the presence of a parent. For this reason, the parent should be advised prior to the interview of the necessity for the child to answer all questions without prompting or interruption and correction. If the parent will not sit quietly during such an interview, the investigator must make arrangements to interview the child out of the presence of the parent. This is easily arranged by having the interview scheduled for the office of the investigator or some other neutral place, with another police officer or some other official representative of a group or agency present. The extra person in the room allows the parent to feel more comfortable about the manner in which their child is to be interviewed, and at the same time eliminates the parent from the room. These other persons may be a neighbor or adult relative, a school official or a clergyman.

The interview of the young child is a sensitive situation. The officer must establish a rapport with the witness by which the child's normal shyness may be overcome. At the same time, the personality of the investigator should lead the child into the position of desiring to assist, and tell the officer all the child knows. During the course of establishing this security within the child, questions that tend to determine the reliability and qualifications of the child for court testimony may be accomplished. These questions serve as good icebreakers and allow the officer some time to estimate the understanding and personality of the child. It must be remembered that children are like other people, and cannot respond well to all persons they come into contact with. It is possible that for one particular child, the wrong officer is attempting the interview and no responses are forthcoming. If the investigator finds himself met with silence, or very short and meaningless answers, it may be well to have another officer attempt a new interview, after the present one is terminated. It should be stopped when it is noticed the child is not responding to the presence of the officer and the interview is getting nowhere. The subsequent interview should not take place immediately, but should occur at a later date and, if possible, in a different setting. If the child is hard to converse with in these situations, the feasibility of placing the child on the witness stand is lessened. The child witness and the parents of that child must understand the need for the child to recount the story in the presence of strangers. In the event it appears that this child cannot perform such a task, the use of the child as a witness has been ruled out. Questions that will tend to establish the capability of the child to serve as a witness in court are as follows:

1. Personal Questions ... The questioning of the child relating to where the child lives, what the phone number is, what are the names of the parents and the child and whether there are any brothers and sisters. If there are other siblings, the child should be asked their names and ages, if they are older or younger and if they attend school and the questions related to school attendance. The child witness should be able to state the month or date of his birth; either would be sufficient. However, the investigator should not disqualify the child because of the inability to state the year; few young children can.

2. Questions Rating Development and Maturity ... The child should be asked to tell time, whether he can tie shoes or perform other motor control tasks, and general questions regarding the community life as this child is experiencing it, such as the church the child attends, who the minister is and what service is the best liked.

3. Questions Relating to Veracity ... The child should be able to state in his own words, what is meant by "telling the truth." This might be easier for a child, if asked in the reverse, "What does it mean to tell a lie?" It will be necessary for the child to be able to relate some negative to dishonesty and a positive to truth, in order for the child to be administered the oath of a witness. The child witness may not be able to explain truth, but if the child knows that truth is good and to lie is bad, qualification is possible.

4. Questions Establishing a Concept of Time ... It is necessary to demonstrate the child's ability to judge time to some reasonable extent if the matters the child has witnessed are related by time to

the offense. This can be accomplished by asking questions as to the number of days a week the child does not attend school. If answered, the child should name those days. The use of the days the child is not attending is for simplicity. There are only two days involved, and the child has less chance of becoming confused. Yet, such a question will show the child has the ability to know what a week is in relation to time. Asking a child to name the months or the time of year he is not in school will show a realization of time in proportion to a year, as will questions about the seasons. Asking the child to relate the incident in respect to a time of year may be done by discovering if the event happened before or after a birthday, or holiday with which children are familiar such as Christmas, Easter, Halloween and Thanksgiving. Labor Day and other adult-oriented holidays do not impress children. Neither will the birthday of someone else, but their own is a matter of memory and recall. The investigator should choose a holiday close to the incident, and use that as a frame of reference in questioning. Questions relating to the time of day may be approached in the same manner. "Was it before school? Was it nighttime? Were you in bed?" These and other questions — such as those relating to television, various mealtimes, and calling for a recounting of what others were doing — tend to establish at what time during the day an event was witnessed.

The preceding questions can serve to assist in establishing more than just the veracity and witness qualifications of the child. They may also assist in establishing rapport between the child and the officer. It is important for the investigator to be careful not to lead the witness. It is also important not to implant any ideas into the child's mind that he was not aware of prior to the questioning. This is very true during the interviewing of the victim. It is difficult to question a child and try to determine if that youngster has been neglected or mistreated in the home, without making him feel that there is something dreadfully wrong in the home. The officer must be very careful and tactful during such an interview, as it may turn out that nothing is wrong in the home and the child has never been victimized. If that child were left feeling that an allegation toward the parents had been made, there may be far-reaching repercussions. Careful wording and, at times, the use of vague approaches are necessary when dealing with children, in order to keep from implanting unwanted thoughts into their minds. In consideration of leading the witness, there is no excuse for such questions; and for court purposes, with exceptions, the leading question will not be allowed. The interviewer must remember that the young child is very susceptible to suggestion, and the leading of the conversation may cause the child to relate facts that did not occur or which he did not witness. This information would serve no purpose, as it would not stand the test of court presentation. Many officers who find that their witnesses do not hold up when on the witness stand, are experiencing a reflection of their own poor interviewing techniques.

Many types of persons will be encountered in the course of an investigation. Their personalities and inhibitions will be demonstrated in the manner in which they respond to the presence of the officer, and an attempt to interview these various types will reveal the existing differences. The officer is required to recognize these personality and character differences, and he must be able to adapt to each. The shy and nervous person, the introvert, poses a problem. Information must be pulled from him. Usually the answers given will be short, and only reflect the bare essentials of the question asked. It will be necessary to ask separate questions for each detail received. This causes a strain on the interviewer. It also takes considerable time to gain the same information that might be gained from another person in a lesser period. The officer must allow for the extra time and effort if the information is to be obtained in its entirety. It is difficult to obtain full facts from such persons and, as a consequence, their testimony must be viewed as less than reliable. These persons respond best in situations with which they are familiar. The home is a good place to conduct the interview in these cases.

Persons who tend to be quarrelsome or antagonistic present unique problems to the interviewer. Often their information is of an important nature and should not be passed over, but in order to obtain it, the investigator must put up with many discourtesies and abuses. This will tax the restraint of the officer. A flare-up of anger or other negative reaction on the part of the officer is to the satisfaction of the witness. This is what that person is intending and expecting. The investigator who allows himself to respond to the personality of such a person has played into that person's intended behavior pattern. It is necessary to tread lightly, asking cautiously framed questions that will result in overcoming the hostility being portrayed. These persons should be allowed to talk as much as they desire, with the officer steering the conversation back to the point of the interview if the subject matter gets too far afield. They are prone to give false or misleading information, and their answers should be verified by contacts with others.

There is the true hostile witness. This hostility is based on a personal affinity with the suspect and a knowledge of the intent of the interview. These witnesses are hard to deal with. They are on the other side and they do not wish to state anything that will harm the case for their friend or relative. They will lie if necessary and are often prepared to enter court as a witness, with the objective of protecting the suspect. The information received will lack reliability and must be viewed with suspicion; but there are benefits from such contacts. The most obvious is the ability to know prior to entering court, the statements the person will make in favor of the defense. This allows the probation officer or prosecutor an opportunity to prepare for the defense presentation. The information obtained from such interviews may be the key to an understanding of the basis of the total defense. In addition, the hostile witness, in his eagerness to establish the innocence of the suspect or to indicate that the events did not occur, may offer information that will be of an aid to the investigation. As an example, he may relate an incident that the officer was not aware of and, in doing so, also indicate additional and unknown witnesses(1).

In considering information received, it has been found that boys are quite reliable when giving makes of vehicles or reporting events that consisted of motor control actions. They are very alert and their memories are reliable. They can recognize those things with which they have an interest, such as sporting equipment and weapons. They are fair judges of distance, and will be able to provide a judgement of size and age. They will not be as reliable as girls in describing clothes and color. Here, the young girl is quite reliable.

The young adult remains one of the poorest witnesses in relation to reliability, even though the person is also endowed with the best attributes. Physically and mentally mature, their youthfulness provides them with the vitality necessary to perform the task of the witness. But, this group is also idealistic and more emotional than older persons(4). As such they tend to relate happenings from a moralistic and subjective analysis that can alter the information from its true concept. This does not come under the heading of intentional misrepresentation, but rather is a reflection of their efforts to be heard. Additionally, they are very self-oriented during this period of their lives. The young adult is at that period where attempts are being made to transcend into the broader structure of adulthood and society. There are careers to be initiated, courtships and marriages, vocational training, and the need to discover direction. In addition, this group suffers from the frustrations of unanswered questions of living, the burdens of financial adjustments and other personal problems that tend to cause them to be disengaged from the activities within their environment that do not pertain to them. Quite often these factors combine to reduce the attention or involvement that is required to produce a productive witness.

The older person who has neared or reached the age of retirement is a very good and reliable witness in relation to the happenings in the sphere of a now-limited environment. With old age comes some limitations on activities and contacts. Thus, many of the older persons contacted have physical limitations or geographical limitations that will keep them from having witnessed an event, or from having been aware they were seeing an act of an illegal nature. For the most part, they will not come forward and volunteer information, but, if contacted, many will be able to provide important information, especially regarding the happenings in a neighborhood. These people's time is unlimited. They often have little to fully occupy their days, and much time is spent sitting in positions where the life of the neighborhood can be observed. In so doing, they are aware of many events that the younger population do not realize these people see. Their daily rounds are interspersed with conversations and contacts with many of the people living in the area; thus they cultivate a repertoire of information on the activities of the neighborhood. If contacted, they are found to be excellent witnesses in relation to the limitations in which they live(1).

It remains that the best overall witnesses are the mature adults of the age group between thirty and fifty-five. These persons are generally more mature and less emotional than the young adult, but their sphere of contact has not been limited to the extent of their older counterparts. They are less idealistic and are, therefore, prone to present more realistic and objective accounts of the events they have witnessed. As they are concerned with the society about them, as well as with their own concerns, they tend to have a better understanding of the information the interviewer is attempting to gain. This places them in the position of being capable of presenting clear accounts of the happenings with which they have become involved. Unless hampered by relationships with the suspect or the family situation, they give very reliable accounts of what has been witnessed(1).

To gather information requires the recording of that information. This is true in the interview. There must be a recording of the facts that have been given during the course of the contact. If it did not matter, the easiest approach would be to write everything down at the time that it is given; but it does matter. The manner in which information is recorded, and when the information is written down, is very significant in an interview, depending on the witness. With the continued increase of public awareness of crime, law enforcement and the administration of justice, the effect of note-taking upon the witness will become increasingly important. The investigator must be aware of this, and steps must be taken to improve the manner of recording information during the course of an interview. It should be pointed out at this time that the development of equipment, procedures and laws implimenting the use of tape recordings is an area on which law enforcement has not placed enough emphasis. This is because of the court decisions regarding wiretapping, and the general considerations surrounding the rights of the accused. These rights do not apply equally to the witness. The development of legal opinions and the existence of test cases would be beneficial in bringing about a clearer understanding of the legal nature of the recording of the statements of witnesses at the time the witness is talking. The development of inexpensive, small and uncomplicated equipment facilitating clear recordings has been overlooked, as has the formulation of legislation providing for such police action. By the means of sound recordings, the problems of note-taking and report-recording would be eliminated from the interview. Procedures could be developed whereby the officer in the field would tape the interview and in his report merely refer to the filed tape number, thereby recording the fact of the existence of the witness' statement. But, in the absence of such procedures of recording statements of victims and witnesses, the officer is in the position of making notes at the time of the interview, but doing so in a manner as not to alarm or otherwise disrupt the willingness of the witness to render the desired information.

Most persons begin to hesitate and think twice when they notice that the information given is being written down or otherwise recorded. This means that officers cannot get out their notebooks and start writing down information, as this act may cause the witness to become hostile, fearful or overly cautious in the wording of the statement, sometimes altering the meaning. The officer cannot write constantly; therefore, when he does write, the witness knows that was an important point. The interview is to gain information, not give it away. It is to the benefit of the officer not to provide the witness with even the slight knowledge of what the investigator feels is an important point. There is no way to know who will be contacting this witness in relation to this case in the future. The witness should not be in a position of being able to give away any of the thoughts of the investigator. Thus, the very writing of the information in the presence of the witness may be a hazard.

The manner of extracting the notebook and pencil is significant. It should be done in a way that will cause it to be unnoticed. It may be that it can be removed from the pocket during a distraction the witness undergoes, or during a time when the witness is giving a long narrative version of what was seen. At that point the notebook may be removed, held closed in the hand for awhile and opened at a later time when the officer is questioning the person specifically on various points brought out in the narrative that need clarification. In order to prevent the witness from finding out what is considered important, those facts may be written down in relation to an answer to a question that is not important. If the information to be given by the witness is not lengthy, the officer may be in a good position if he does not take notes, but relies on his memory until he leaves the scene of the interview.

The address of the witness can be recorded either as the investigator stops in front of the home, or after leaving the home. The street name can be obtained in the same manner. As most officers will be required to give this information by radio to the police radio operator, it may also be taken from the department's radio log at a later time. This eliminates the need to ask the witness the address. Very often the phone number of the witness may be obtained in the same manner, through the use of a city directory or the telephone book. It may be read off the phone in the witness' home. This may require the officer to memorize the number or to write it down on something as unobtrusive as a matchbook cover, and enter it into the notebook after leaving the premises. By these means the officer does not alarm the witness by asking for this identifying information. It turns out that many people who are willing to talk become sensitive to the fact that addresses and phone numbers are being recorded. They have the same feelings about giving their names. Therefore, in some instances, where the witness is antagonistic or fearful, it is better to gather that information from another source such as a neighbor or a directory.

Every investigator should cultivate a good memory for details and numbers. This is an attribute necessary for the successful investigator. He should be in a position to recall information given to him in an interview in order to restrict the amount of notetaking that must be done in the presence of the witness. If there are two officers, the business of taking notes can be handled better. One will be doing the majority of questioning. The other is able to sit to one side, away from the directed attention of the witness that tends to follow the questioner, and take notes without full recognition by the witness. As an added point, when two officers are involved in the questioning of a person, neither officer should ever answer a question the other officer directs to the person being interviewed or interrogated. This is true even if the question has been asked by the first officer and answered. There are many reasons for the second officer to ask a question over again, including a preliminary base from which to ask an important question. The habit of an officer answering for the witness is as annoying and as damaging to the questioning as when a third party does this.

A talent that is very useful in obtaining information without having to ask questions is the ability to read items that are upside down. Many times this is invaluable, especially in cases where there are registers at counters, or when obtaining information from a file and the person in charge of the file is reading the material to the investigator. By having this ability, the officer can discover information from the file himself, reading from it while it is being held upside down. The names and addresses of witnesses may be obtained from the envelope in the home, as well as the phone number being read when the phone is in the wrong position. It is a talent that does not require too much skill, and can be developed by anyone in their spare time. Most persons are capable of becoming quite proficient at such reading, with a little practice. It is an invaluable aid to an investigator and will be an assist in reducing the number of identifying questions that must be asked in each contact, thereby cutting down the chances of alarming the witness.

With exceptions, when interviewing, the officer should address the person in formal terminology. The old man should not be called "gramps," the clergyman should not be referred to as "padre," but instead, mister and misses are in order. The first name familiarity will find its use, but for the most part it should not be employed. This is true when interviewing persons of a lower social group or minority group, young adults and those who are aged. The officer should keep in mind that disrespect can cause a negative reaction. The witness may be necessary in court, and, as a consequence, the original contact with that person is often not the last. If cooperation is to be expected, the officer must do everything he can from the moment of the first contact to insure the witness' goodwill. The respect shown by means of the formal salutation is worthwhile.

The People Claim Surprise

In neglect and abuse cases, due to the family nature of the offense it is not unusual for a witness or the victim to give one version of the situation, only to get into court and give another version, denying the first. This happens because of the influence of others upon the witness prior to the court action. Often this influence presents to the witness the damage that will occur to the family unit if the action is allowed to proceed; thus many stories are altered or watered-down prior to reaching the witness stand. The changing of a story, of testimony, can be detrimental to the successful outcome of the case. It may cause the presentation of the case to become a benefit to the defense. It may so upset or confuse the prosecutor or person presenting the case, as to cause that person to lose the initiative and equilibrium necessary in such a presentation. This loss alone may be a disaster. It is important for the investigator to remember that a witness who has not changed his story prior to the court action, in the presence of a representative of the law enforcement agency or the person presenting the case, is a person who has caught the people by surprise. As such, the people have the right to claim surprise, and to impeach their own witness by placing the interviewer of that witness on the stand and allowing that person to testify to the information contained in the original version. This will include hearsay, as the testimony of the interviewer may bring out conversations the witness had with third parties. It is a very good tactic, and is usually successful in counteracting the otherwise damaging testimony of the witness, and at the same time presenting information that is necessary to the case. As the investigator on the case, the officer has the responsibility of advising the person presenting the case in court of the existence of the tactic if such a situation should arise. This may be done by passing a note to that person requesting him to claim surprise. Most experienced prosecutors will be cognizant of the move, but some young attorneys may not think about it during the moments of direct examination of a witness. In larger prosecutor's offices, the younger, inexperienced attorneys are often assigned cases of neglect and abuse. Also, in those jurisdictions where the juvenile court presentation is conducted by a probation officer (even when facing an attorney for the defense), that officer is often unaware of the existence of this maneuver.

The rules governing the impeachment of one's own witness will vary from jurisdiction to jurisdiction, but generally the past restrictions in common law have been relaxed. Many experts in jurisprudence now believe all prohibitions from disqualifying one's own witness should be abolished. But, in any case, most courts are now more willing to allow the impeachment to occur if the witness' testimony is inconsistent with previously given statements(6).

Interrogations

No consideration may be given the topic of interrogation without the full understanding of the Miranda decision(7) and its implications and requirments. This entails a presentation of the meaning of "due process," and a discussion of the evolution of this concept in our society, coupled with notice of the court decisions affecting its present application. In contrast to the displays of law enforcement occurring after the historic Miranda decision, this presentation will follow the principle that law enforcement, more than any other group, must be concerned with the rights of the accused as set forth in the U. S. Constitution(7) and restated in the constitutions of the various states. If the law is to be enforced, the enforcers must perform their duties in accordance with the law. If certain rights have been afforded all citizens, including the accused, then the police have the greatest obligation to insure the protection of those rights, not only from outside erosion, but from police misconduct as well.

Otherwise, the police are no different from other groups who contend that obedience to a law is necessary only as long as that law is seen to have a good effect. This contention cannot exist in a free society, as the freedom of that society establishes the means of overcoming bad legislation. The police are bound by the law of the land, the same as other individuals, with the exception that law enforcement exists with an oath to uphold those laws. Therefore, the police must be the advocates of strict adherence to the rights of the accused, and they must insure those rights in the application of enforcement techniques.

In order to view the present in proper prospective, and to understand the fundamental reasons for trends and developments, it is necessary for man to look backward into his past. History serves as mankind's mirror, reflecting the subtle changes that occur during the growth and development of social consciousness. Much of the present awareness of human dignity, rights of man and social order are but the echoes of the soundings of the past.

As civilization dawned, the use of military control over the people was evidenced in direct relation to the monarchical systems of political evolution, with but few exceptions. The Bible presents a documented analysis of the theo-sociological legal evolution; a system that found its way into the middle ages of the Christian era. This concept was a departure from the use of soldiers to enforce civil law. It presented civil law as a part of the theologically determined legal system, held to be divinely inspired. In this system, a civil transgression often was a theological violation also, and the enforcement was controlled, in part, by the religious element of the ruling class. The legal concept of biblical times was to have the chief priests and the law-givers administer the law through the people of the community. The latter made the arrests and brought the accused before the tribunal for trial and sentence, at which time the defendant was placed before the people for the punishment to be enforced. This method was so fully entrenched in Palestine that the Roman conquerors made no effort to infringe upon its application, as it affected the Hebrew people.

Apart from this example, and the Greek attempts at civil control of law, history presents the military control of the populace as the most widely applied method of enforcement in the western world, until the civilizing of the British Isle. For reasons less explained than existing, the people who were to become Englishmen held within themselves a fundamental union with individual freedom that is scarcely understood in its modern American counterpart. This love of personal liberty began to emerge as early as the ninth century. It was modified and improved until it became the basis of freedom, enabling the framers of our Constitution to envision its application in the incredible birth of a nationalistic democracy heretofore unknown to man. This English influence so permeates our legal consciousness, that many of our legal decisions are but restatements of the Englishman's knowledge of individual freedom. The difference in American jurisprudence is that it is practiced without that fundamental ingredient, so subtle and abstract, that developed with the history of England. This elusive quality is best described as the recognition of choice, or the ultimate application of the human faculty of free will. Within this aura of inner consciousness is found a departure of the American system of criminal justice on a misadventure of its own. The English, always foremost in the demand for personal freedom, have been capable of applying justice in an active sense, requiring the individual to answer for the use or misuse of the freedom granted. The English application, whether internal or external, is not as encrusted with misdirected humanitarianism as has been evidenced within the American attempts to insure justice. In the American attempts to administer justice, a social denial of individual fault has emerged, binding our jurists in cords of inertia. In contrast, English history is full of events wherein the individual has freely chosen to repress his rights in order to act in a manner compatible with the best interests of society. The administration of British justice requires the individual to suffer the consequences of his rational act with a detachment from enveloping abstractions which, if considered, would lend themselves to clouded issues and uncertainty of action. The parallel is the American knowledge of the principles of individual freedom. The divergence is the American inability to apply the concept of free will and the recognition of human weakness to the fulfillment of extraneous justice.

Within the recognition of personal freedom, the Constitution was written so as to protect the individual from totalitarian acts on the part of government. Thus this document granted to the citizen certain rights to which he was entitled, and provided that nothing could abridge the freedom he was granted, without due process of law. Included within due process were the rights of the accused. In application, these rights were not extended to bind the states and the agents of the states for almost one hundred years. After the Civil War, with the enactment of the fourteenth amendment the rights of the accused were extended to include the officers of the states. This gave jurisdiction to the federal judicial system to insure that the rights of the citizen were being protected in the application of the laws of the various states. While the federal system held such authority, it was seldom exercised, with the U. S. Supreme Court offering little concern in the manner of the procedures in local courts. One of the first convictions reviewed by the Court relating to the actions of the officers of a state, involved the use of force to obtain a confession. This is the celebrated Brown case of 1936(9). The Court reversed the conviction, which had been based largely on the confessions of the three Negro defendants, on the grounds that the confessions were the result of beatings administered to the suspects for the purpose of eliciting the statements. This means of obtaining the confessions was held to be a violation of due process. The Court acted almost 150 years after the writing of the Constitution, and almost seventy years after the application of the power of review over state judicial actions. Other decisions by the High Court were to follow, beginning with the Chambers decision of 1940(10) and culminating with Miranda, 1966 and Gault, 1967. Of the intervening cases, Spano, 1957(11). Missiah, 1964(12) and Escobedo, 1964(13) present the basic thinking of the Court that culminated in Miranda. These decisions are the most pertinent to police interrogation. They have placed certain restrictions on law enforcement that are intended to insure the protection of the rights of the accused. The major restrictions are the result of the Miranda decision and relate to the admonishment of the accused of his Constitutional rights prior to interrogation or questioning during what the Court termed an "in custody" police interrogation. Just what the Court meant by "in custody" has yet to be clarified, but in practice prosecutors and police officials universally agree that the admonishment should take place whenever the suspicions of the officer focus upon an individual as being suspect in an investigation. This means that as the investigation leads the officer to the place where his attention is focused upon a particular individual as a suspect, that individual should be advised of his rights as an accused person.

This advisement consists of informing the suspect that he does not have to talk with the investigator; his right to remain silent. The accused must be told that any statements or answers to any questions may and will be used against him in a court of law. He must be informed of his right to be represented by counsel, at this time and at any other time during the course of the actions against him; and if he cannot afford legal counsel, he must be informed of his right to have such counsel appointed to serve in his behalf. His understanding must be insured, and he must provide the officer with an intelligent waiver of the right before questioning may proceed. This is the admonishment. Most police agencies have provided their officers with written forms of the admonishment on readily available cards that are carried with the officer and read to the suspect at the time of questioning. This eliminates any failure to completely advise the suspect of his rights, and causes *voire dire* by the defense to be less of a burden upon the officer at the time of presenting testimony.

In practice, therefore, any time a person is contacted, and that person is on the verge of incriminating himself, or the officer's attention has focused upon that person as a suspect, the admonishment must take place. The failure to advise the person of his rights will result in all statements made by the individual afterward to be inadmissible against him in a court of law. Also, any information or physical evidence provided by the individual after the failure to admonish would be inadmissible as evidence. The importance of the advisement of the rights of the accused is undeniable. No officer can afford to attempt to circumvent this requirement preceding the interrogation process.

It should be pointed out that anytime a witness or victim is being interviewed, information may lead to the assumption that the individual is actually a suspect or is on the verge of incriminating himself. This is a time when the officer must stop his present questioning and advise the person of the rights of the accused before proceeding.

It must be reiterated that the rights of the accused are part of the due process provided by the U. S. Constitution. From the decisions identified, the procedure of advising the individual of these rights and obtaining from him a waiver of the rights is necessary before a police interrogation will result in admissible evidence. To do otherwise is to court disaster and will result in the loss of any evidence that was gained(6,7).

The interrogation is a complex subject. There are as many ways to interrogate as there are individuals involved in interrogation. The ability to interrogate requires effort, study, adaptability, imagination, physical energy and a strong desire to become a skilled and competent interrogator(4). The officer must like dealing with people, readily involve himself with their problems and he must possess an understanding of their behavior. There is a need for a good education, for this will add to the broad background of knowledge the interrogator must have. He must be able to converse intelligently about a variety of subjects. He must recognize unusual facts and items when they are disclosed to him. The officer performing meaningful interrogations will be a practitioner of human behavior. He will be able to observe and react to the minute physical changes that are undergone by a suspect during the interrogation. The investigator will have an understanding of attitudes and motive and will have the ability to remain objective throughout. Within the course of the interrogation, he must be able to develop within the suspect a respect for the officer. In some ways this respect has to develop further, into a form of trust.

The use of language must be fully recognized as the vehicle through which the interrogation is conducted. It is imperative for the interrogator to have an above average ability to express himself. Many times he will be required to restate the same concept several different ways. His vocabulary should be extensive. This mastery of words has to be accompanied by logical thinking. The development of the language ability tends to increase the use of logic. The choice of words is important in an interrogation. The officer must know when to use harsh-sounding phrases and when to use more positive terminology. The fluid self-expression of the officer is basic to successful interrogation.

Insight into the meanings of a suspect's thinking, statements and actions will enable the interrogator to be in a position of predicting the direction the suspect is taking during the course of the interrogation. Certainly this calls for background information, basic to interrogation, but it is honed and developed through the experience of interrogating. The best questioners are those persons who have interrogated a variety of people on a variety of offenses. There is no substitute for the experience of interrogation.

Any interrogator must be an actor(4). The officer should be able to perform a role in which he breaks down the reluctance of the suspect to tell incriminating facts about the commission of an illegal act. The role to be played will change during the interrogation, and the investigator is required to recognize when these changes take place and adapt to a new role. This means that interrogation calls for quick thinking, without too much time being taken for deliberation. An interrogation will not allow disruption of thought, conversation and direction. It is a sensitive situation in which a knock on the door or a phone ringing can alter the outcome, with little chance for the regaining of positions previously attained. There is no place for long pauses, during which the interrogator attempts to collect his thoughts. A pause, if it occurs, must be a directed and a meaningful part of the interrogation, intentionally brought on to achieve some purpose.

Interrogation may be defined as systematic questioning in which there is a resistance to answer(2). It is capable of performing many tasks for the investigator. Interrogation can be used to discover a false report of a crime. It is valuable in eliminating suspects, as well as in the discovery of the perpetrator. The discovery of unknown facts of the circumstances of the crime may be accomplished through the interrogative process, as well as the determination of the complete facts regarding the commission of the offense. If there were others involved, this information may be brought out for the first time in the interrogation. It may be an aid in the identification of additional witnesses. The securing of information about other violations in which the suspect may have been involved, is an added product of the interrogation. Its benefits to the police cannot be understated, and the importance of interrogation remains a primary tool of the investigator.

The purpose of an interrogation is to obtain a confession or an admission. A confession is a recognition by an accused person that he is guilty of the crime charge(15). It is the admission of all the circumstances of the crime that are a part of the *corpus delicti,* including intent, and it leaves no room for an inference of innocence(16). An admission is the statement of a fact or description of a circumstance from which guilt may be inferred. It tends to point to guilt, but of itself does not establish guilt(15). A confession, then, will be a statement given voluntarily in which guilt is admitted and the circumstances of the crime are defined, including the intent to have committed the act. It leaves no question of the guilt of the confessor. On the other hand, an admission may be a denial of the crime but an acknowledgement of the suspect's presence at the scene, or a statement that he was the last person with the victim prior to the crime, or the admission of a motive. These admissions may tend to show involvement, but none are enough, in themselves, to establish guilt.

The second objective of an interrogation is to establish the involvement of the suspect in the commission of the crime. This will be accomplished by means of an admission or a confession. There is a situation wherein the suspect denies his involvement and at the same time gives certain facts to establish his innocence. These facts are ones that the investigator already knows are not true, and he is prepared to prove the falsity of the alleged facts in court. This is a negative admission. A negative admission is one in which the denial is based on false information, freely given by the suspect; information easily refuted in court by substantial evidence the officer has in his possession at the time of the interrogation. In and of itself, such a negative admission does not prove guilt, but, coupled with other facts and evidence, a negative admission is capable of becoming damaging to any defense position. For this reason a negative admission should be readily recognized by the interrogator, and such a situation should be utilized to demonstrate the actions of the suspect after the offense, all a part of circumstantial evidence. One of the common negative admissions is a situation in which the suspect is confused over the date and time of the alleged offense and presents an alibi covering a period of no significance to the crime. The investigator allows the suspect to go to elaborate lengths in presenting the alibi. The suspect is then questioned closely regarding his certainty that the alibi relates to the date the suspect says the crime occurred. When the suspect has successfully established his recall of the alibi by association with an unusual event, he is then informed that it will be checked out, but that it really is of no concern, as that is not the date the crime occurred. This places him in the position of either having to devise a new alibi, going through all the detail of the new fact, knowing how ridiculous this is, and also knowing that it is false and cannot be verified; or, he is left without the shield of knowledge of his whereabouts at the time of the offense. The use of such a negative admission is a devastating blow to the confidence of most suspects. It may be shown in court, at a later date, to rebut any alibi.

Not withstanding the purpose of the interrogation, the ultimate objective is to obtain the truth(4). The truth is the final goal of an investigation. This must be the reason for the police effort. It is a requirement of investigation in a free society. The investigator who loses sight of this purpose is no longer performing the investigative function. This places the burden of establishing innocence, as well as guilt, on the investigator. A police officer must be as capable of determining that there was no involvement as he is in identifying and apprehending the perpetrator. This is true in the interrogation. It cannot be said that an interrogation which satisfactorily determines the innocence of a suspect has been in vain. It has performed the most important function the interrogation can perform, it has arrived at the truth.

Preparation for the interrogation is critical. One of the most difficult times in the interrogation will be the opening conversation between the officer and the suspect. The general line of questioning and the opening remarks should be known in advance. The interrogator should have all of the circumstances of the crime in mind before he attempts to conduct the questioning session. He should have as much information about the suspect as possible, including a description of the physical characteristics of the person. Nothing is more hazardous than to begin an interrogation of a person, only to find out he is not the suspect. He may have the same name, but he is not the person to be questioned. This is especially bad when it happens during an interrogation of a person being held in custody. The investigator may tip his hand before the identification is recognized, leaving the third party with information that can be taken back to the other prisoners. Eventually, it will make the rounds of the jail grapevine, and the suspect will be informed. In some of the larger departments, the jail population is such that a mistake is easily made in which the wrong person is brought out for interrogation. The identification of the suspect should always be checked by the interrogator before proceeding.

The interrogator must know the details of the offense if he is to be able to properly interrogate. These details include the crime scene and to compass orientation to the crime scene. This latter is important in overcoming the use of left and right, as these direction indicators are dependent upon which way a person is facing. He should have a knowledge of the suspect's record, and whether the suspect is presently on probation or parole. The date, time and the day of the week the offense occurred should be in the mind of the officer. The story as given by the victim, or as the facts presented themselves during the investigation, should be clearly understood by the interrogator. This background preparation is necessary for the effective interrogation.

A good interrogator will expect both denials and falsifications. It must be understood that the suspect is being interrogated because of his unwillingness to readily admit involvement. The suspect should be allowed to talk, explaining what he wants to, and thus placing himself in the position of involvement in contradiction. There is no one who can lie off the top of his head and repeat the lies over and over without becoming confused. It is difficult to lie continuously and effectively. The interrogator should never allow himself to become upset over the fact that he is being lied to; this must be expected. The suspect will be in the best position when he realizes it is his word against someone else's. But generally, the suspect has no way of knowing exactly how much information the interrogator already knows. It is all right to suggest that the officer has information that does not exist, but it should not be in the form of an irrevocable bluff. An outright bluff may be called by the suspect. If it is, and the officer cannot produce, the interrogation is lost and will never be regained. The suspect has just been convinced to go all the way. The interrogator should not threaten, especially in abuse and neglect cases, as the threats will increase the fear of the suspect about what is going to happen to him; such threats will drive him into a corner from which he cannot come out. There is an element of self-preservation in an interrogation. The suspect has to be allowed to see avenues for admissions or confession. He must be brought to the place where he feels it will serve all concerned, but especially himself, to tell the story. If he can see no way in which this will serve him, he cannot break down the self-preservation instinct. Threats will serve to close off the routes to the confession. Additionally, a threat cannot be backed up with action. If it can, it is not a threat, it is a fact.

The interrogator should attempt to obtain admissions of involvement, such as time and place, or being with the victim at the time of an injury. If the suspect begins to admit facts, the details of the crime should be gone over with him in order to establish a confession. The statement, "I'll say I did it if that's what you want," should never be accepted. It will not be accepted in court. But if the suspect confesses, "I did it," the interrogator should lead the person over the details of the crime and obtain admissions on each point. The suspect should be questioned regarding other offenses that may have been committed, after a confession has been obtained, as the suspect has been softened at this point.

In the interrogation of the neglect or abuse parent, it must be noted that the situation is one of a family nature. This means that the circumstances are emotionally charged. If handled right, this emotional element may be utilized by the interrogator to advantage. What a spouse or the other children are thinking about the suspect is a concern to that person. That person is in a position where he sees himself being separated from all that matters in his life, not just by incarceration, but also through rejection by the family. This means that the suspect can be affected by the emotional approach: questions about what will happen the next time; being reminded he had told himself the last time that it would not happen again, but look what occurred; indications that the interrogator understands the factors that led to his actions leave an impression of empathy; the fact that this conduct cannot be allowed to continue, and that the individual knows this also;

the implementing of the fact that it is all out in the open, everyone knows, including the interrogator and the suspect. Anything that causes the suspect to think and feel will tend to bring the neglect or abuse suspect to the point of admission or confession.

An interrogation is time consuming — physically, and mentally exhausting. The officer should recognize this and attempt to interrogate when the physical and mental capacities are at their best. There should be no restriction on the time that may be given to the interrogation. It is not unusual for an interrogation to last from two to three hours. The only limitation to be placed on the session, in relation to time, regards the physical and mental comfort of the suspect. It is to no avail to obtain a confession from a suspect who has endured hours of hard interrogation. That method will cause the confession to be inadmissible if the length of the interrogation becomes an issue. Common sense should be used in respect to the time of each questioning period. They should not be spaced too closely together. The individual should be allowed toilet facilities. Meals should not be missed because of the interrogation. The suspect must be given an opportunity to eat. Between sessions, the person should be allowed time for proper rest and sleep. Interrogations should not take place at unusual hours unless unavoidable. The interrogator must know when to quit, but his time should not be limited. The comfort that is important is the comfort of the suspect, not the officer. There is such a thing as overinterrogation. This must be judged individually, but when that saturation point has been reached, no further interrogations should take place.

The place of the interrogation is important. It should be conducted in an interrogation room established for that purpose. With few exceptions, the interrogation should take place on police grounds. The suspect should not be interrogated in the home, generally speaking, but instead should be brought to a law enforcement agency or the prosecutor's office. As a rule, police interrogators will be much better at the task than prosecutors. Therefore, the initial interrogations should be conducted by the police, not the district attorney. The latter should be brought into the picture at the time of taking a formal statement.

The interrogation should be recorded by some means if it has been productive. If there are two officers interrogating, they will corroborate each other's accounts of what was said. If the officer's testimony regarding an admission or confession is not believed by a jury, that jury will not believe most recordings of the confession. But, because most prosecutors are in favor of recorded statements, the admission or confession should be recorded. Many departments utilize written statements, but these are not above attack in court. The best recorded statements are either on tape or have been taken down by a shorthand reporter(4).

In light of recent court decisions, many officers feel the interrogation is no longer important, but this is just not true. Many persons, after being advised of their rights are still willing to be questioned. There are effective approaches to enable the investigator to secure the permission of the suspect to be interrogated. It may be that poor interrogators have found an official excuse for not pursuing the interrogation. In the manner by which the admonishment is made, the officer may, consciously or unconsciously, be implanting the idea not to submit. This makes the officer's job easier. He can record in his report that no interrogation was possible, as the suspect invoked his constitutional rights; thus the officer has failed to perform, but has done so in a manner acceptable to his superiors. The facts are that interrogations are an important part of police work and an invaluable investigative tool.

> The interviewing of suspects and witnesses is the most important investigative tool at the disposal of the police(14).

A large proportion of solutions to criminal cases have been the products of interrogation(17). While the restrictions imposed by the Miranda decision are real, they are not more than a restriction. They have not removed the interrogative process from criminal enforcement. By developing techniques of interrogation, the police investigator will insure the productive use of this tool for every occasion on which it can be used.

References

1. Soderman, Harry, and O'Connell, John J.: Modern Criminal

Investigation, 5th ed. Revised by Charles E. O'Hara, New York, Funk, 1962, pp. 27, 38-41.

2. Federal Bureau of Investigation, Law Enforcement Training Course: Interviews and Interrogations, Special Agent Pluckett, Fresno, California, 1958.

3. Liebers, Arthur, and Vollmer, Capt. Carl (N.Y.C.P.D.): The Investigator's Handbook, New York, Arco, 1962, p. 9.

4. Aubry, Arthur, Jr., and Caputo, Rudolph R.: Criminal Interrogation. Springfield, Thomas, 1965, Chapt. 15 and pp. 40-44, 137.

5. Locard, Edmond: French Criminiologist

6. Stuckey, Gilbert B.: Evidence for the Law Enforcement Officer. New York, McGraw, 1968, Chapt. 7 and pp. 92-95.

7. Miranda v. State of Arizona, 384 U. S. 436, 86 S.Ct. 1602, 16 L.Ed. 2d 694, June 13, 1966.

8. U. S. Constitution, Fourth, Fifth, Sixth, and Fourteenth Amendments, With Limited Application of the Eighth Amendment for Law Enforcement Purposes.

9. Brown v Mississippi, 297 U. S. 278, 1936.

10. Chambers v Florida, 309 U. S. 227, 1940.

11. Spano v New York, 360 U. S. 315, 79 S.Ct. 1202, 3 L.Ed. 2d 1265, 1959.

12. Massiah v United States, 377 U. S. 201, 84 S.Ct. 1199, 12 L.Ed. 2d 246, 1964.

13. Escobedo v Illinois, 378 U. S. 478, 488, 84 S.Ct. 1758, 12 L.Ed. 2d 977, 1964.

14. Leonard, V. A., and More, Harry W.: The General Administration of Criminal Justice. Brooklyn, Foundation, 1967, Chapt. 10 and p. 257.

15. Donigan, Robert L., and Fisher, Edward C.: The Evidence Handbook. The Traffic Institute, Evanston, Northwestern U., 1965, p. 33.

16. People v Quinn, 36 Cal, 233, 241, 1963.

17. Barrett, Edward L.: The police practices and the law, from arrest to release or charge. Calif Law Rev, 50:35-44, 1962.

Chapter X

UPGRADING THE JUDICIAL PROCESS

THE term "judicial process," as utilized in this chapter, refers to the totality of the system of administering justice. It includes the police, probation and parole services, prosecutors and defense counsel, judges and court personnel, and the various correctional and treatment services utilized by society in its attempt to salvage persons, bringing them to a level of adequate citizenship.

Generally viewed as the court system, the judicial process is, instead, a complex array of agencies and jurisdictions, with missions that have as objectives precourt investigations as well as missions aimed at the treatment and rehabilitation of the offender occurring after court adjudication. In between is found a complexity of charges and allegations, laws and procedures, adversary contest and judicial review. The system is further confused with the role of the juvenile court, a role that varies greatly from jurisdiction to jurisdiction, and that in some instances is a complex system, established under separate laws and evidencing little resemblance to the normal court process.

To comprehend and understand such a system requires years of exposure to its mechanics, as well as extensive study that is necessary to breech the gap between knowing and understanding. Few laymen have any real comprehension of the system. Many of those persons working within the process do not understand its intricacies. There is an overwhelming tendency to become knowledgeable concerning portions of the process with which one normally comes into contact, ignoring other areas of the administration of justice that are deemed to be of no significance to the individual. This causes many of the persons directly involved in the process to be quite limited in their ability to see clearly the many facets of the system. This limitation causes several problems. First, there are numerous frustrations arising from the lack of understanding of the inherent limitations of the system. Many persons working in law enforcement find they are discouraged with the efforts expended, as those efforts relate to significant successful alteration of a social problem. Secondly, little change in the system can occur unless persons are familiar with the process. Only by understanding the ramifications of the administration of justice can any positive changes occur within the segments of the system. Productive change must be the result of knowledge, thought and consideration. The problem of colloquialism continues to impede progressive change in our judicial process. Third, this limited knowledge and understanding has lead to a lack of leadership existing within the system. Generally, at first glance, leadership is abdicated to the judicial members of the total process. But, within that group, adequate and constructive leadership is most often lacking. It remains, then, that no group or segment of the judicial process is presently assuming the role of leader in an effort to upgrade the system. What changes are made are made within a specific group, exerting little or no effect upon the totality of the process. These changes are internal, instituted for the benefit of that segment to cause its improvement; but the changes seldom are initiated with the thought of assisting the general improvement of the administration of justice, or toward the correlation of this change to changes occurring within other segments of the system.

The judicial process must be seen as a large and complex system made up of numerous parts, each functioning semi-independently of the other and all segments having differing missions, methods and philosophies. The fact that most do not understand the problems and limitations of the others results in the lack of leadership and productive change already mentioned. To know that such leadership and change is needed, one has but to refer to the continued increase in the crime rate of this nation, a rate that has increased about four times as fast as the population increase since 1950(1). In the year 1964 there was a total crime rate increase in the categories of the seven major felonies amounting to 11 percent(1). It is common fact that no major social problem has been adequately controlled through the efforts of the judicial process. There are an estimated four million alcoholics in this country(2). More than a million spouses and children are affected by divorce each year(3). Add to that the homes broken by separation and desertion, of which the amounts are unknown, and the number of persons affected by such family deterioration is staggering. It is impossible to determine the number of drug addicts in this country, but conservative estimates, based on police and hospital files, would indicate one addict per three thousand population(4). It is factual that the major criminal element is the recidivist offender(5,6). Psychiatric treatment of offenders has been viewed as the ultimate in corrections and has enjoyed popularity among correctional personnel, as well as jurists and the general public. Yet there is little empirical evidence to support a justification of this approach as a general treatment method(7,8,9). This is a tool of treatment, not a panacea. It has been successful in specific instances, and this has caused those members of the judicial process who suffer from superficial understanding of the totality of the process to attribute to therapy a success that the facts do not substantiate.

No one working within the judicial process should be satisfied with the administration of justice as it exists today. It is evident that change is needed, but until leaders emerge from the various components of the system, society's efforts to control antisocial behavior and eliminate social problems will continue to be bogged down in the archaic methods of antiquity.

The Judicial Officers

The court system of a free society has several functions, among which are the arbitration of disputes between individuals and the control of the actions of individuals within the society(10). In this discussion of the judicial process, the court's role in controlling society will take precedence, and within that function lies a responsibility often described as awesome. If this control is to be administered within a concept of justice, those persons charged with the court function must maintain the highest concept of that elusive term. It has been held by some authorities that justice defies definition(11), while others have seen it to mean that an individual receives merit or demerit as that individual deserves, under a given set of circumstances(12). It is a term that has been argued for centuries, and the same elusiveness exists in the concepts of justice held by those persons charged with its administration. Thus, the degree by which a judge administers justice will be in correlation to that officer's conceptualization of the term and its connotations. To what degree any jurist could explain justice would vary, depending upon the individual.

Yet to these men has been given almost sole control over the justice that the members of society may expect to receive. What background is brought to such a powerful position? What training is necessary for a person to embark upon a judicial career? How is the position obtained? Is continued training and evaluation necessary as a requisite to retaining tenure? To what extent is review imposed upon the action of the judge? How meaningful is that review? These and numerous other questions should be answered, but literature is disparingly void of any concrete research into such questions.

Part of the reluctance to seek out, by empirical methods, the quality of our judicial officers, is the result of the esteem and prestige attached to that position. Judges for years have held first place among prestigous occupations and continue to do so, causing the possessor of such a position to be held in awe. The idea of a research team studying the questions presented above, tends to be viewed as violating the sacrosanct esteem within which the judicial profession is generally perceived. This reluctance to invade the privacy of the official judicial life has placed those persons under a cloak of protection, eliminating attempts at constructive change based on realistic findings by external disciplines.

At the same time, the internal review of the efforts of the judicial officers is not as complete as it should be. Legal review, for the most part, is a restrictive action, limited to questions of law and undertaken within the confines of the strictest of rules. Thus the appeals court may review a decision of a trial judge as it pertains to the law, but there is little or no review of the discretionary decisions, which by law have been reserved for the trial judge. The basis for the discretionary decision-making of the judge is less known than the basis for police decision-making. The authority attendant to such judicial decisions is much more restrictive than the authority that relates to decisions made by other persons within the judicial process. The power exercised by the judge is subject only to judicial review. This review is performed by other judges whose backgrounds and training have been within the same system that produced the judge whose decision is being reviewed.

The question is not whether the higher courts should review the lower courts, as this is the only reasonable system. The problem is in respect to the basic qualifications of the judges, their training to exercise the power they have been given, and whether continued training to retain tenure has become necessary within the context of a complex society.

Let it be accepted that there is presently only one training ground for a judge, and that is the bench(13). The majority of jurists in this nation are receiving on-the-job training, with little or no supervision. From this base, justice is to be administered. At the same time, most professions and vocations are upgrading requirements of education and training prior to obtaining the position. The legal profession itself has long since abandoned apprenticeship as the primary means of entering the profession and has promoted resident law school matriculation as the foremost means of preparing oneself for membership in the bar.

The cases coming before the courts are more diverse than at any time in history. The issues contain technical, economic and social ramifications requiring the presentation of increasing amounts of expert testimony. The society itself is undergoing change, with problems of such magnitude as to defy solution by the best minds the country can gather. Much of what is occurring in the social evolution of twentieth century America is being adjudicated in court. The decisions of the jurists involved are crucial to the future development of an orderly society. The fact that so many decisions are being overturned, set aside or sent back indicates confusion within the judicial profession. With each review resulting in reversal, the total judicial process is affected by far-reaching ramifications. The judges are placed in positions of indecision, as no judge desires a review and reversal of a case, for too many of these effect his advancement in the field of jurisprudence. This indecision is evidenced in the number of cases and issues that are taken "under advisement" by judges, an action postponing the decision. All of these factors have combined to add to the increase in the backlog of cases now crowding the court calendars; a problem bringing forth warnings from Chief Justice Earl Warren pointing out the need for remedies. Such backlogs reduce the effectiveness of the deterrent effects of swift and sure punishment for offenders(14). Victims are denied the protection and recompense due. Innocent parties may fall victim to the same offender while the suspect is at large awaiting adjudication. Persons accused of crimes who are innocent of involvement are denied quick court findings because of the crowded court conditions. It is not intended to intimate that such crowded court calendars are the sole result of judicial review, but certainly the ramifications of numerous rulings over a short period of time have an effect; and this area of the judicial process should be exposed to scientific research to determine the relationship between the judicial decision, review and reversal, and the court process.

Why not provide for the pretraining of judges? Do years of presenting cases before the court prepare one effectively for assuming the bench? It is quite doubtful there is a meaningful correlation between practicing law and administering judicial decisions. This should be ascertained, and if there is not, then pretraining of judges would be warranted. It is well-known that the most astute legal minds are not found on the bench, but instead are found within the confines of the law schools or as attorneys in private practice. There is no reason why these minds could not devise a curriculum to provide the training necessary to arm the prospective judge with the basic tools for the adequate administration of justice. There is no reason why the decision-making process could not be curriculumized. Society has advanced to the stage where "chance" can be removed from many of the official decisions made in its name and on its behalf. One of the first steps in upgrading the judicial process would be the promotion of the pretraining for judges.

Not only should judges be exposed to training prior to assuming the bench, but continued training and upgrading should be provided as the means of retaining effectiveness on a current basis. The changes within the society are so rapid and complex as to compel all groups in the judicial process to continue training. The reeducation of the jurist is as necessary as the reeducation of the police officer. This society can no longer afford the luxury of training lawyers in a law school utilizing methods that have not been altered since 1850, placing them into practice for several years and then elevating them to the bench; holding that they are then abundantly qualified to render decisions because of a background in law. What about the other ramifications of the case? There is a need for our judges to be better educated in areas of the behavioral sciences and sociology. No longer is a familiarization with generalities sufficient upon which to base decisions. Certainly the judge cannot be expected to be an expert in all areas, but his awareness of the present knowledge of the fields directly affecting his decisions should be evidenced. The only way this will occur is to upgrade law school training, to institute pre-judicial training and to use continued training as a requisite to tenure.

Judges are given the opportunity to hear expert witnesses on a variety of subject matter. This should overcome any lack of knowledge on their part, as does the benefit that has been provided in terms of probation services to the court. These latter services result in recommendations being made to the court, after investigations, to guide the court toward a course of action deemed applicable. The failure of the information of an advisory nature to affect the decisions of judges has become legend, and because of the continued reluctance on the part of judges to be guided by the testimony and recommendations provided, these tools are generally ineffectual in directing the decision-making process of the judicial officer. Therefore, if the judge is not going to effectively utilize the knowledge of others, he should be in a position to have that information as a part of his total knowledge.

Crimes and offenses occur around the clock every day of the year. The rights of the accused are being protected as never before. Suspects are being granted release on bail or by means of their own recognizance, where they often remain after conviction and awaiting appeal. Police detention is being questioned by the courts. The court calendars are becoming crowded. The crime rate is increasing. Juveniles are now being represented by counsel, as are misdemeanor offenders. Attorneys are being tied up in many court situations unheard of ten years ago. Yet, in the face of this tremendous burden of work, and while asserting the right of the accused to a speedy and public trial, our courts are still operating less than eight hours a day, five days per week, less all legal holidays. The system is outdated. Within the context of urban America, courts should operate around the clock, seven days a week. Judges should be working on rotating shifts to handle the intitial processing of cases, removing the right to a jury trial on very minor offenses and allowing for criminal conviction in misdemeanor cases to be accomplished by a two-thirds vote of the jury. Innovations of these types could be utilized to overcome some of the demanding pressures now upon the judicial process. To institute such procedures would require overcoming the resistance of the public, many segments of the judicial process and the judges themselves. But such innovations would assist in dealing with the chaotic situations now facing the courts.

In a speech before the Delinquency Control Institute, Indiana University of Pennsylvania, in June, 1968, George H. Shepard, Training Consultant, Division of Juvenile Delinquency Services, Children's Bureau, Washington, D. C., stated that about 50 percent of the juvenile court judges in the United States have no legal background. This is true, notwithstanding the fact that the juvenile court law is one of the more complicated systems of the judicial process. It is within the framework of such a court system that the underprotected child is offered the protection of society. Of all the judges requiring extensive training, the juvenile court judge demands it the most. In one county, in a jurisdiction placing the highest trial court judges on the juvenile court bench on rotating annual periods, the lack of judicial understanding of the abused child problem has been dramatically displayed.

One judge stated that the underprotected child problem was a situation that would arise no more than two or three times a year. Another judge, exposed to numberous experts working on the problem, returned one underprotected child to the home without so much as obtaining the medical testimony available, only to discover that the child was dead from abuse within five months; this same jurist heard the juvenile court action on the worst case of torture and abuse ever occurring in that jurisdiction and removed the child from the home. Later, within six months, the same judge heard the adult prosecution of the mother and the brothers involved in the torturing of the child. The case was heard without a jury, placing the burden of deciding guilt or innocence upon the judge. After exposure to the case, the testimony and the evidence in both the juvenile court and the adult court actions, the judge still took the matter under advisement before reaching a verdict. Nothing more could be added. He had heard the story twice, yet he was incapable of rendering a decision without a week in which to decide.

A third judge ascended the bench and approached all underprotected child cases coming before the juvenile court with the requisite that before he would afford the child the protection necessary, a definite establishment of a direct act perpetrated on the child by the parent must first have been shown. As this is often impossible in such cases, for one year many petitions were denied in court, finally culminating in the reluctance of the probation representatives to file such actions.

Another judge serving on the juvenile court bench had occasion to preside over the predetention hearing on a child who was hospitalized as the result of a beating administered by the mother. The mother had admitted the offense and the attack had been witnessed by the child's stepfather. The woman was in jail, charged with abuse, and she had been arraigned by another court and held in lieu of bail.

The law required her presence at the hearing in the juvenile court, a hearing to determine if there was enough cause to retain a hold on the child pending a juvenile court action. Without hearing anymore than the allegation read in the petition, the judge dismissed the action and released the woman from jail, causing a later dismissal of charges against her by the prosecutor's office. At the very time the judge was taking that action the investigating officers were placing the other siblings in protective custody, after the investigation revealed they had also suffered abuse at the hands of the mother. The original victim in this case, as well as several of her brothers and sisters, has since become an active delinquent in the community. This jurist's actions took place in a jurisdiction that had the benefit of active experts on the problem of the underprotected child.

If these actions occur in situations where the judges have legal training and are considered to be judicial experts, what is the situation in those jurisdictions where the juvenile court judge needs no special or legal training? Obviously, these conditions must be altered. The provisions for the effective training of judicial officers must become a consideration of the leaders of the judicial process.

The Prosecutor and Defense Counsel

It has become necessary for the law schools to reconsider their curriculum and their methods of instruction. The case-law approach for the development of lawyers is no longer sufficient to meet the needs of the legal profession in dealing with the complexities of modern urban social existence. The law student needs an exposure to the concepts of the behavioral and social sciences. There is a need for an awareness of the pattern of our changing society, for a recognition of altering customs and moral cognizance and for an understanding of the existence of numerous cultures that do not always blend into the expected pattern of social tradition. The lawyer must be prepared to deal with human weakness, recognizing the signs of maladjustment and frustration, and he must be knowledgeable concerning the assistance society is capable of offering. These abilities are obtainable through academic preparation, and this preparation should be provided.

The prosecuting attorney holds a unique and important position in the judicial process. The prosecutor retains a broad degree of latitude in deciding whether to seek the prosecution of a case(12). In this area of the performance of his role, the prosecutor is relatively free from external, official control. As an elected official, he may come under some political pressure in specific cases, but, generally speaking, the decision to prosecute rests almost entirely with his office(11). Because the effectiveness of the district attorney is measured in terms of rate of conviction, the decision to prosecute is often based upon the recognized opportunity to convict(11), although he is ethically bound to the duty not to convict, but to see that justice is done(15), the prosecutor is often found to be in the position of compromising the issue. In order to insure the successful outcome of the case, the district attorney will bargain with the defense, accepting a plea to a lessor or different charge rather than to persue a prosecution that is in doubt. By this means, the ends of justice are served. The suspect stands convicted, the prosecutor has been successful in relation to the conviction rate and the defense attorney has performed his task, that of representing his client, obtaining the best results in a poor situation.

This should not be seen as unethical or shocking, for the legal profession is one that serves "compromise" more than any other element. Attorneys are trained to provide for the reconciliation of parties to a matter in order that each is capable of gaining some degree of satisfaction in the issue. This is the major portion of the practice of law. More cases are settled between counsel or in the judges chambers than are decided in open court. The attorney is, in effect, a "compromise broker."

The fact that most laymen understand the court situation to be as it appears in fiction is in stark contrast to the findings of researchers in studies regarding prosecutions and convictions. One investigator, studying federal court cases in the period from 1960 to 1963, discovered that 86 percent of the convictions were the result of guilty pleas(16). Another study revealed that over 90 percent of the convictions in felony cases in one county were the result of guilty pleas, and, of this group, almost one third had originally pleaded not guilty(17). For most persons engaged in the judicial process, these facts are reality.

The low monetary remuneration of the position of prosecutor in many jurisdictions causes it to be filled with young, aspiring attorneys; or in the major jurisdictions, where the salary range is much greater, the office is often used as a stepping stone toward higher aspirations. This reduces the length of tenure in many instances, resulting in changing policy and procedure as well as staff membership with each new prosecutor. These changes have both direct and indirect effects on the administration of justice in that jurisdiction. From the police to the courts and correctional services, alterations must be made to conform to the change in prosecutor services; and the judicial process feels the reverberations throughout.

The staff assistants to the prosecutor are normally young, inexperienced attorneys just out of law school. They seek these positions to gain needed courtroom experience before embarking into private practice. Thus, many well prepared cases are lost in court due to the inexperience of the prosecution staff. At the same time, this inexperience is utilized by the defense attorney in his efforts to seek reduction of charges or otherwise bid for better situations for his client.

This system favors the defendant. It brings added confusion and frustration to an already perplexed judicial process. Such a system has a direct bearing on the protection of children, both in jurisdictions where the prosecutor presents cases in juvenile court and in those areas where that task is performed by the probation arm of the court. A young and inexperienced attorney acting as prosecutor is hard put to understand the ramifications of the underprotected child case. He has difficulty adjusting to the role in juvenile court, which is less than advisory in nature and is in behalf of the child. His main objective is prosecution and conviction of an offender, and, due to such a background, he may lose sight of the objectives of the juvenile court action. By concentrating on the parents as offenders, the protection of the child assumes a secondary position, even in the juvenile court presentation. On the other hand, if the jurisdiction does not utilize the prosecutor's staff in juvenile court, that officer is left with little connotation of the importance of the overall problem society is attempting to rectify. Thus, many prosecutors view the child protection case as merely another criminal act, approaching the adult segment of the case in a traditional manner. In so doing, the case is exposed to the same dickering for considerations as other criminal cases. Often, in allowing the suspect to plead guilty to a lessor or different charge, the offense is disguised in the record. As an example, a father who has hit his six-month-old son in the face with a fist has been charged with the specific act of child abuse. But such a charge carries a heavier penalty than the charge of battery. The suspect is allowed to plea to battery. The effect on the offender's record is to hide the meaning of the original act.

Anyone noting that the man had been convicted of battery will assume that the situation involved the striking of another adult, possibly with provocation. Unless the actual investigation report is obtained, the fact that the suspect was guilty of beating his own infant will be hidden in a cloud of legal maneuvering.

The prosecutor is often unaware of the familial and social ramifications of cases involving underprotected children. His response to the act may be one of shocked outrage such as might be displayed by a rookie patrolman; certainly inconsistent with the office. The need for a thorough understanding of the etiology of the "battered child syndrome," the manifestations of neglect and abuse and the objectives of society in cases of the underprotected child is crucial to the significant efforts of the judicial process in combating the problem. Not only must the prosecutor have this knowledge, but he must also involve himself in local, state and national efforts; providing the leadership necessary to the formulation of adequate statues and legal procedures sufficient to cope with the phenomenon.

Increasingly, the use of defense counsel in juvenile court is evidenced. This will continue in light of recent and pending decisions of the U. S. Supreme Court. Many children are now represented by counsel during the juvenile court hearing, and in many cases of neglect or abuse the parents are represented. This representation is generally approached by the defense as just that; defense. This means that the child is being defended from the very protection he needs.

Few defense counsels are primarily interested in criminal law. The most lucrative legal practice is in the area of civil or corporate law. The true criminal attorney is a rarity, and only exists in the larger metropolitan areas. Normally, defense is provided from one of three sources: the public defender; the private attorney hired by the individual, usually because of a legal-business association; and the private attorney appointed by the court for a specific issue. Of these, only the public defender is explicitly interested in criminal defense — the others take the case because they must. Their interest is not honed toward criminal or juvenile court situations so as to allow them a sophisticated comprehension of the attempts of society to protect the child and reunite the family.

The approach is one of a traditional adversary role, often resulting in a frustration of efforts for the adequate protection of the child.

It may be stated that such an outcome indicates there was no cause for the action originally, and that society was in error. But, the inner workings of the legal process are such as to lend themselves easily to a successful defense of a situation when the truth opposes such success. This is apparent in those jurisdictions where the juvenile court case is presented by a probation officer or some official other than an attorney, who must face an experienced practicing lawyer who is acting for the defense. The nonattorney, in trying to present a case, is at an insurmountable disadvantage, quite often resulting in the loss of the issue. In those areas where the law provides for the prosecutor to present the case in juvenile court, the presence of a defense attorney will have a significant effect on the outcome. First, the prosecutor does not wish to take time from the crowded criminal calendar and indulge in an exhaustive case presentation in juvenile court. This requires time to prepare answers for the issues the defense will raise, as well as the necessity for presenting a more extensive case than would be required if the defense were not present. More witnesses must be called, and each must undergo direct and cross-examination. This means that the case will be a time-consuming presentation. The juvenile court itself does not wish the matter to be extended. A suggestion from the defense that a settlement can be reached, eliminating the need for the action, will certainly be given consideration. Secondly, the prosecutor is not interested in juvenile court actions in general, and tends to view the protection of the child by seeking dependent court wardship as akin to social work, and not in the scope of the prosecutor's traditional role. For these reasons, as well as the general reasons related to the emphasis on the rights of the individual, many cases of underprotected children are subjected to traditional court adversary procedures.

In order to overcome these disabilities, the legal profession should strive to insure the understanding of the problem and to focus attention upon the needs of the child. By this means, both the prosecutor and the defense could work together in protecting the rights of the individual, while at the same time protecting the child from those elements of his environment endangering his safety. This understanding can be brought about through the efforts of the various bar associations and other legal organizations, the law schools and the numerous legal publications received by most attorneys. Emphasis should be placed on the needs of the child, and there should be a redirection of the effort of the individual attorney, which now is aimed at securing a successful position as the outcome to a contest.

The Probation and Social Services

Probation serves as the arm of the court. In juvenile matters this service includes precourt investigations, often the court presentation, and post adjudication supervision. The role of the probation officer in juvenile matters far exceeds the adult probation role because of the active participation of that service in the case throughout its legal processing. The same is true in some jurisdictions regarding the social services in considering dependent child cases coming before the court. Both the probation and the social services have important roles in matters involving the underprotected child, depending upon the jurisdiction. In some areas probation does the precourt investigation, but cases of abused or neglected children are assigned to the social service for supervision after the juvenile court action. In other areas the probation department handles all facets of the case. In still other situations the two services may only enter the case after the court adjudication, on a supervisory basis. In any event, it is extremely important that such services have a solid foundation in the totality of the underprotected child.

There must be a realization of the objectives involved in the actions taken, and local policy and procedures in these cases should be the result of that realization. These policies and procedures should be developed carefully, and such rules should be subject to constant review. Alterations as needed should be directed toward a better attainment of the protection of children. Such rules and regulations cannot be allowed to impede services, and the personnel involved must be aware of the tendency to allow agency regulations to become so entrenched as to take precedence over the action role the agency is attempting to perform. The bureaucratic dangers inherent in these agencies must be recognized, and steps should be taken to remedy any situation of internal administration which may lead to a child being placed in jeopardy.

The workers coming into probation and social services are often not the recipients of professional training in the field. They are generally college graduates, but many times their academic work has been in other fields. The regular schools of social work and criminology are including work in the area of the underprotected child, so the graduate thus prepared comes into the field with a basic understanding of the problem. But, as the majority of workers hold degrees in other areas, the need for in-service training is apparent. Very little of this training is taking place at the present time on a formal level. What training is occurring within these departments is in relation to the performance of the task and is the result of worker-supervisor contact. To what extent this training is effective would relate to the individuals involved, but no such training can adequately substitute for the necessary formal training.

Since there are many workshops, institutes, seminars, extension courses, night courses and regular college instruction courses occurring within short distances of most areas in this country on a continuing basis, it would be to the benefit of those departments to have their personnel obtain such educational background. In addition, most institutions of higher learning are in a position to provide instruction to the department at a convenient location, with the instruction geared to the needs of the individual agency. Depending upon the unit of instruction and the jurisdiction, there are federal and state funds available to assist in procuring needed training.

As a word of caution, it should be noted that the knowledge and understanding now available in the area of the underprotected child is of recent origin. Therefore, those persons taking degrees in social and probation services eight years ago would have received little or no instruction enabling them to meet the demands of this problem at present. This should be a consideration in the selection of workers and supervisors who are to deal directly with such cases, and efforts should be made to upgrade these persons through formal training.

The personnel employed in these services are often working in close proximity, if not harmony, with the juvenile court. This places the probation officer and social worker in a unique position to influence the judge's conceptualization of the problem. Many judges would welcome the assistance offered, but it is withheld out of timidity. Those dedicated and skilled workers who are knowledgeable in the facts of the underprotected child have no reason to remain shy in the presence of the judge, especially in those opportunities for informal contact in chambers or elsewhere. This may be the only time the judge has been apprised of any meaningful information about neglect or abuse. The author, who has been involved in numerous panels and seminars on this problem, has yet to witness a judge present, except in the position of a learned expert. As noted earlier in this chapter, judges do not, as a rule, enter into continuing education or reeducation.

One of the major errors committed by most service agencies in relation to the underprotected child is the assignment of one person or a small staff to the administration of the cases. This leaves the other workers in the position of viewing that person or group as specialists, causing a lack of concern to infiltrate the majority of the department. This lack of interest reduces the motivation for learning the techniques of dealing with such cases. Many times the assigned personnel are ill, on vacation or have left the department, causing another worker to have to perform functions with which the latter is not familiar. In order to overcome this functional void, all department members who may come in contact with the problem should receive orientation and training.

These services should provide the leadership for the development of auxiliary services that may be utilized by the juvenile court in its decision-making role and its role of supervision. Since probation and social services are working closely with the children and the families over long periods of time, the needed supportive, diagnostic and treatment services are better recognized by these workers than by any others. Each worker who has supervised such a case has recognized areas of need for which the community was lacking service. These services will never be thoroughly provided until attention has been brought to the matter. Psychological evaluations and work-ups, with attendant treatment recommendations, have long been recognized as a need that remains unfilled in most areas. Supportive assistance to family situations are just now being introduced. These include nutritional and child-care orientation, shopping and economic guidance, home caretaker assistance, correlation of educational services and many others. Much of the neglect now experienced could be overcome by such services. Most of these have been identified by probation and social workers involved in these cases. They are common topics of discussion when these persons indulge in critical but informal analysis of limitations. It must be from the rank of these services that leadership will be demonstrated at the local and state levels whereby the necessary tools for the juvenile court's productive intervention will exist.

The Police

Many of the problems encountered by the police have been discussed in preceding chapters. This portion will be restricted to several areas not previously entered into in depth. The first area of consideration will be police training. In recent years the emphasis on education and training as the major means of upgrading police services has received dramatic attention. This has been evidenced by concern and assistance from the federal to the local level. Today, police training efforts are of significant proportions throughout the country(18). The increase in these efforts are of credit to the dedication and foresight of police leadership. In the area of police administration and general procedures this upgrading through education and training has had a tremendous impact on the modernization of police service.

This same intense involvement has not been demonstrated in the area of the underprotected child. Most juvenile enforcement training has been in the area of the delinquent offender and juvenile procedures. Little attention has been given the dependent child situation. These juvenile enforcement efforts have been limited, in general, to those officers specializing in that area of police service. Line officers of supervision and administrative rank have not availed themselves of the educational and training programs offered in juvenile work. Administratively, juvenile knowledge has been brought to those positions by persons with experience working in juvenile bureaus during earlier periods of service. Top police administrators are woefully lacking in an understanding of the problem of the underprotected child. There are no productive in-service training programs covering this aspect of the police function. Many officers assigned to juvenile specialization are inept in their handling of abuse and neglect cases. Those juvenile units serving as a part of detective divisions are under the administrative command of detective chiefs who view a departure from traditional police procedure with suspicion. As this is the general alignment of a juvenile unit, the majority of these officers are working under policies and procedures that are inadequate in dealing with the problem.

The situation among patrolmen is worse. Their knowledge of juvenile enforcement is usually limited because of their reliance upon the specialist. They are exposed to many cases of underprotected children, and their inability to proceed is due to the failure of the department to include knowledgeable training in this area, within the scope of the general training provided.

In agencies rotating officers through the juvenile assignment, the ability to gain the experience necessary to develop a sophistication regarding these cases is lost. The assignment of a major portion of underprotected child cases to female officers has brought about a "woman's work" connotation, thereby reducing the desire of male officers to interest themselves in the handling of such cases. Admittedly, female officers are excellent in dealing with these cases, but this excellence is mainly confined to the early mechanics of the case. There is no reason to restrict investigative assignment of neglect and abuse cases to policewomen. The need for a thorough and tedious investigation requires the services of extremely competent investigators. Since his experience is usually broader, the male officer, by and large, will be the best investigator. The rotating of these officers precludes their specialization, and the last area of police work in which specialization occurs is the area of underprotected children.

Institutions offering courses in law enforcement programs should include the underprotected child in the basic curriculum. At present, there are few programs that include such instruction.

The same must be said regarding police training programs. The instructional emphasis is on a familiarization with juvenile enforcement in general. Time limitations often result in underprotected child situations being overlooked altogether.

The necessary police leadership within the community relating to neglected and abused children will not be forthcoming until police administrators become attuned to the problem. Investigative officers and specialists have neither the time nor the position necessary to become involved effectually on the community level. The administrator, through police associations and organizations, is in the position to influence legislation; but this will not occur until the police are aware of the needed directions such legislation should follow.

The ability to work with other agencies and disciplines involved in the protection of children will remain the burden of the individual officer until the police administrator sees clearly the interrelationship that must exist. Until that time, the police, on an official basis, will continue to approach the problem in a traditional way, isolated from the efforts of others and performing the task of the protection of these children in a perfunctory manner.

References

1. Uniform Crime Reports, 1959. U. S. Department of Justice, Federal Bureau of Investigation, 1960-1963.
2. Ginsburg, S.W.: The neuroses. Mental Health in the United States, Ann Amer Acad Polit Soc Sci, 286:55-64, 1953.
3. Health, Education, and Welfare Trends. U. S. Department of Health, Educations, and Welfare, 1960.
4. Ausubel, D.P.: Controversial issues in the management of drug addiction: Legalization, ambulatory treatment and the British system. Ment Hy, 44:535-544, 1960.
5. Sutherland, Edwin H., and Cressey, Donald R.: Principles of Criminology, 7th ed. Philadelphia, Lippincott, pp. 541-546.
6. Crime and Delinquency in California, 1965. State of California, Bureau of Criminal Statistics, Sacramento, 1966, p. 136.
7. Adamson, LaMay, and Dunham, H. Warren: Clinical treatment of male delinquent: A case study effort and result. Amer Sociolo Rev, 21:312-320, 1956.

8. Second Annual Report, Intensive Treatment Program. California State Department of Corrections, Sacramento, 1958.

9. Adams, Stuart: The PICO Project. In Johnson, H., Savitz, L. and Wolfgang, M.E. (Eds.): The Sociology of Punishment and Correction. New York, Wiley, 1962, pp. 213-224.

10. Bellow, Gary: Prevention through the judicial process. In Amos, W.E. and Wellford, C.F. (Eds.): Delinquency Prevention — Theory and Practice. Englewood Cliffs, Prentice-Hall, 1967, p. 208.

11. Leonard, V.A. and More, Harry W.: The General Administration of Criminal Justice. Brooklyn, Foundation, 1967, pp. 242, 253.

12. Germann, A.C.; Day, Frank D., and Gallati, Robert R.J.: Introduction to Law Enforcement. Springfield, Thomas, 1967, pp. 21, 158.

13. The Earl Warren Center at the University of California, Berkeley, provides training for new judges, as well as up-dating sessions for tenured jurists.

14. Municipal Police Administration, 5th ed. Chicago, Int. City Manager's Assoc., 1961, p. 33.

15. The Canons of Ethics of the American Bar Association; Canon 5.

16. Skolnick, Jerome H.: Justice Without Trail. New York, Wiley, 1966. pp. 12-15.

17. See: The Law Enforcement Assistance Act of 1965: The Challenge of Crime in a Free Society; Report of the President's Commission on Law Enforcement and the Administration of Justice, 1967; The Safe Streets Act, 1968; and The California Commission on Police Officers Standard Training.

18. See listings of educations institutions offering programs in Criminology, Law Enforcement, or Police Science:
Leonard, V.A.: The Police and the Twentieth Century. Brooklyn, Foundation, 1964, Appendix B, pp. 145-146.
Germann, A.C.; Day, Frank D., and Gallati, Robert R.J., op. cit., Appendix D, pp. 335-358.

Chapter XI

A COMMUNITY ACTION

THE material in this chapter is not intended to be interpreted as a finalized approach to the problem of the underprotected child, but rather it is a presentation of the attempts of one community to meet the needs of children. It is being presented to allow the reader the opportunity to evaluate some of the shortcomings encountered by those participating, while at the same time identifying the strengths inherent in the approach. It must be noted that the approach is interdisciplinary, and this method is not universally accepted. There are many with expertise who oppose such methodology for various reasons; however, the fundamental design of an interdisciplinary approach to a community problem is sound, on the basis that the problem involves more than one discipline. Therefore, if the problem is community and multidimensional in nature, there is nothing inconsistent with a community and interdisciplinary attempt to cope with that problem. The breakdown occurs not from the unification of the disciplines, but from the fact that the various services and professions are opposed to unification.

It is hoped that the serious reader will be able to determine the factors upon which this community action was established, as well as being able to recognize the areas of conflict and dysfunction. The first and most important matter is the identification of the problem of the underprotected children as being a community concern. If it is not such, then it is not multidimensional, and the approach described in this chapter is admittedly in error. But, if this is a social problem, with many ramifications, often leading into all segments of community service, then the interdisciplinary approach is valid. It became the concensus of those practitioners involved that each had a role to play in the protection of the children of the community. Furthermore, these professionals felt strongly that a unification of actions was necessary to insure the successful protection of the child and the eventual development of adequate control techniques; in this respect the Fresno County Battered Child Committee is unique. It is a story of desires and aspirations, of successes and failures and of frustrations and compensations. It is a story that should be told.

Prior to 1963, Fresno County, California was like the majority of jurisdictions throughout the United States in its approach to the problem of the underprotected child. Centrally located in the vast San Joaquin Valley of California, this county of four hundred thousand people is a major agricultural center. Having as its county seat the largest community between Sacramento and Los Angeles, Fresno County maintains numerous services on the local, county and state levels. Consequently, numerous community resources are available, and many of these perform various roles in situations of neglect and abuse. The major problem was a lack of recognition of the existence or role of any other agency except the one within which a person was employed. There was no coordination of services and little liason between agencies. This was especially true in respect to children's services.

To compound the problem, there was little recognition of the true manifestations of neglect and abuse, with each case being handled according to the policy of the agency involved and the subjective analysis of its representative. There was no definition of the problem of the underprotected child, no long term objectives, and the procedures that did exist were individual and not universally known.

The medical profession had never demonstrated any interest in the problem, and the need for that profession's involvement was not being met. Leadership was sorely needed but was not forthcoming. There were individuals who recognized the limitations of coping with child protection under the existing pattern of agency participation, but there were no voices capable of arousing the community.

Early in 1963, the leadership void was filled in the person of William Ziering, M.D., who became the Chief of Pediatrics at the Fresno General Hospital. Dr. Ziering was not only interested in the abused child problem, but he was exceptionally well-informed. Shortly after his arrival in the community he chaired a seminar on the "Battered Child Syndrome," sponsored by the Fresno General Hospital. Practitioners with expertise were gathered from the local area as well as from out of the area. These persons represented the services most fully involved in the problem(1).

More than two hundred professionals attended the seminar on April 5, 1963. They represented a diversity of community services, including: welfare services; probation and parole; the superior court, as well as the municipal and justice courts; the medical profession and various paramedical services; public health; law enforcement; mental hygiene services and private psychological services; the schools; and city and county administrative offices. The objectives of the seminar were twofold: first, to present the problem in such a manner as to instill the need for action; and secondly, to develop a climate within the community for the reception of a community action. The first objective was well met, but the second one was harder to come by than had been anticipated.

Some broad recommendations came out of the seminar, but none offered any clear-cut approach or demonstrated any immediate solutions. A panel of leadership from the local scene was appointed to meet subsequent to the seminar to develop a course of action. For reasons never fully identified, this group never met. Due to this default, Dr. Ziering organized and chaired the Fresno County Battered Child Committee. This group consisted of agency representatives from the hospital, welfare, probation, public health and law enforcement. Additionally, there were associate or advisory members from such institutions as the schools, the medical society, various private service agencies, mental health and the local state college(2). The committee began meeting as needed, usually biweekly. Meetings were held during the noon hour at the Fresno General Hospital; thus, the membership were donating their time.

The committee directed its attention to the protection of battered children, and determined that the prosecution of suspected parties would be incidental to this concern. The attainment of the objective of child protection compelled the committee to support the immediate separation of the child from the damaging environment, at least in the more severe cases. It was recognized that this solution was at best but a partial answer; yet the high morbidity rate demanded this precaution until adequate alternatives could be worked out to insure the safety of the victim.

As the Committee expended effort, it uncovered other needs; and objectives were formulated that would lead to the reduction of the many facets of the problem. One of the main concerns was early recognition of the problem. To implement this, the alerting of the general public as well as key agency personnel and other practitioners became a prime objective. This meant assistance from the committee to define respective responsibilities; promote cooperation; encourage reporting of known or suspected cases; case reviews, from initiation to disposition; and the development of community services into effectual rehabilitative resources.

This also meant that educational emphasis would have to be shared between internal and external effort. The representative agencies had many personnel who were not knowledgeable regarding the problem, but who were performing tasks relative to it. The dissemination of information to those persons was to become an on-going task, but, unfortunately, one that was never fully implemented. There seemed to be a breakdown in the communication of this need at the committee level. The membership, while in general agreement with the need, seemed to resent an imaginary infringement in the individual agency training program. Although the subject was brought before the group on numerous occasions throughout the years, few agencies ever responded to meeting the need of agency training of personnel on a full scale. Instead, the members would either relate the problems involved in getting the employees together, or would indicate that such training was being performed. In reality, little of what was taking place within the committee was being effectually communicated within the individual agency.

This caused a specific occurrence to become evident: each member of the committee was developing an expertise concerning the "battered child syndrome." As "experts," these persons were being recognized within their agency as advisors in such cases. The difficulty leading from this individualized information monopolization was that personnel who should have been equipped to handle their own cases were coming to the committee member within the agency for answers to problems the worker should have known. Instead of this being a means of training, it became a means of establishing one's own expertise. Furthermore, the realization that someone was present who was capable of handling the matter with dispatch led to more and more cases being allocated to that committee member. This increased the individual's specialist role, and at the same time decreased the ability and the interest of other workers to involve themselves in these cases. It is apparent that one of the largest areas of failure has been in-service training in the representative agencies of the committee.

The committee became quite successful in educating the public and other agencies and practitioners. The formation of a speaking panel of the members from the five participating agencies greatly enhanced this end of the program. This panel was eventually to present programs to the Fresno County Medical Society, the California State Juvenile Officers Association, the Northern California Pediatrics Association, as well as numerous civic, educational and service groups within the community. In addition, many of the members had occasion, singly or in small numbers, to be included with other groups in panel seminars throughout the western United States as well as in the Fresno area. These services are still being performed; and as some members have left the local scene, the information and lessons resulting from committee participation have been carried to locations distant from the source.

The Central Index

It rapidly became evident to the committee that to insure the protection of the child, an efficient method of information exchange was necessary. This awareness developed through contact with cases. The parents or caretakers of the abused child were found to forfeit their normal pattern of seeking care for themselves or their children when confronted with an injury they had inflicted or caused to happen. Consequently, the committee found, as others had in different areas of the country, that people involved in these cases tended to seek assistance from quarters where they were not known. It became imperative to establish a clearinghouse for information on such cases. Through this means the various physicians, hospitals and agencies would be able to amass information that could be pooled for both investigative and casework purposes. The concept of an early exchange of information on suspected child-abuse cases would be best suited to a central repository. The central index concept was born to counter the parent who, wishing to avoid detection, would take the child victim from one doctor or emergency room to another, negating the opportunity for the development of a continuous record of repeated trauma.

It became necessary for the committee to differentiate between unwise and excessive discipline and willful, repeated assault. The totality within which the case would be processed depended upon such a judgment. The prognosis of the victim's safety and well-being was also dependent upon such a differentation. But to arrive at this conclusion required every available piece of information, and adequate and necessary information would best be acquired by means of a central information file. Not only would the criterion of early exchange of information be satisfied by this system, but also the initiation of case evaluation would be facilitated. Therefore, the committee determined that for a child to be truly protected, that protection would have to be assured by the accumulation of all relevant data from every possible source. By this means, willfully inflicted repeated trauma could be distinguished from a disciplinary problem. Through this source, the foundation for community action to protect the child would be available.

With the assistance of a private pediatric practitioner and the resources of the county medical society, the initial system was devised for a countywide central index to be located at the Fresno General Hospital in the office of the chief of pediatrics. Two doctors began to orient the medical profession within the community to the procedures to be followed.

The index was a functioning reality. Upon receipt of information regarding a case, the chief of pediatrics made contact with the five representative agencies and determined from each the information within their files. Added to this was the medical evaluation, whether performed privately or at a hospital. The pediatrics chief then notified the proper agency of the need to inititate action, and by the time of that notification, the index had already cleared the records of the participating agencies, condensed the medical evaluation of the victim's present condition, and contained a professional analysis of the case by Dr. Ziering. Also, the Index had relayed the same information to the juvenile court to alert that jurisdiction to the matter. Additionally, the index caused follow-up to occur.

The more extreme cases were not only forwarded to the agency with the responsibility to take action, but they were also brought before the whole committee for case evaluation. These evaluations would continue to occur as the procedural action was being carried out.

The establishment of the system was considered to be the most singularly important contribution of the Battered Child Committee, and early implementation of the index became vital. By the summer of 1963, the central index was operable, and during that year every patient with suspected inflicted trauma coming to the attention of the Fresno General Hospital was admitted to that hospital. Within twenty-four hours a complete written medical report with a medical evaluation was forwarded to law enforcement, probation and the juvenile court.

Law enforcement would commence an investigation, placing a "hold" on the victim in the hospital. Upon completion of the investigation by the jurisdiction responsible, an evaluation of the findings was made, with the intent to protect the child as the paramount issue. This usually called for a referral to the probation authorities, requesting petitions to be filed in the juvenile court. If the evidence warranted, a simultaneous action was initiated by law enforcement through the prosecutor's office, seeking criminal action. It was a secondary act, and one that remained within the realm of law enforcement participation, independent of committee objectives or the objective of child protection.

The probation department would evaluate the petition request and the supporting information and, if warranted, the matter would be scheduled for juvenile court. By the time the court action took place, the probation staff had additional information summarized. They had interviewed witnesses, prepared subpoenas and were ready for the presentation of the case to the court. During this period the child welfare services were supervising the case, and if the child were capable of being released from the hospital, adequate home care was provided. This was usually by placement in one of the foster homes licensed for that purpose.

The juvenile court hearing consisted of testimony and other evidence tending to establish that the home environment of the victim was detrimental to the child's health or safety. Seldom was there an attempt to identify the perpetrator, but, instead, emphasis was placed on the fact that the medical history given by the parents was not supported by the nature of the injuries or other factual circumstances. Upon the adjudication of the court the child was generally placed in a foster home, with both child welfare and probation services involved in supervising the child, the parents or both. It should be noted that the jurisdiction of the juvenile court does not extend to the adult parent figures, but, nonetheless, the probation staff would have systematic contact with the parents, and this amounted to supervision, although informal. The fact remains that the court was kept current on the happenings within the totality of the case.

The central index functioned well from the Fresno General Hospital setting for about one year. In the spring of 1964, Hazel H. Weidman, PhD, was retained by the Fresno County Board of Supervisors under a California State Department of Public Health grant, to study the committee and community services, and to develop a central index. Dr. Weidman discovered several problems within the committee structure and procedure. First, the composition of the committee needed redefinition, as it had grown to the place where it was unwieldly. Secondly, there was the unsolved problem of the legal status of the committee, which had been operating on a quasi-legal basis since its inception. Members were developing a growing concern as to their right to proceed into areas of need without official sanction.

Dr. Weidman assisted in the resolution of the composition of the committee by dividing the membership for purposes of performance. This researcher envisioned three levels of membership, and eventually this structure was implemented. On the first level, the basic working committee, composed of the representatives of the five participating agencies, would become responsible for attaining the immediate goal of establishing interagency procedures for processing cases. To deal with advising the basic committee on procedural implementation, a second level of associate members was formed. Some of these represented new agencies, while others were from the agencies already on the basic committee. The reason for this apparent overlapping of membership, was the enormity of the problem. It was a fact that no one person could adequately represent the total agency, because the problem was so varied as to require insights from areas of an agency's functions with which the basic committee member was not fully familiar. From various sources within the community, including professional groups and allied public as well as private agencies, the researcher drew a consultant group whose purpose was to advise and assist the committee in the development of long-range community planning. Thus, when the system became firm enough to incorporate schools, other hospitals and private services, there would be existing on the committee a representative measure of that portion of the community. This group would already be involved, it would have been exposed to the basic ramifications of the problem and it would serve as a nucleus from which to expand services throughout the area.

The second problem, that of legal status for the committee, had never been legally resolved. At the same time, the committee had been functioning with the tacit approval of the heads of the various departments and agencies involved. Still, there remained an uncertainty of status that tended to reduce the willingness for innovation. Naturally, innovative conceptualization is important in developing new procedures and policies for dealing with a recently identified problem. The scope of the problem, coupled with the breadth of the attempt to meet it on a community-wide level, had uncovered areas of needed attention that had now begun to lay heavily upon the membership. This lack of security was being demonstrated within the committee and could be recognized by their failure to move ahead with operative proposals after lengthy and exhaustive discussion. Dr. Weidman made the initial steps toward bringing about the development of legal status, but her efforts became bogged down when another problem was encountered that related to the central index. Consequently, the researcher was able only to identify the need for the legal status. The implementation of that status was to come after her departure.

In the development of the central index on a permanent basis, conflict arose between the researcher and the committee. Part of the conflict was the result of the time limitation for the purposes of the survey, a period of three months. It also appeared due to a philosphical misunderstanding between Dr. Weidman and the membership. The researcher was interested in presenting a system that would be conceptually correct. It entailed the development of an index that would, in effect, have control functions within its structure. In many respects, her concept of the index was that of a guiding unit, with control and direction functions extending to the agencies. Through such an index the case would be reported, information collected and exchanged, the course of action decided through the extension of the committee action, and an evaluation procedure undertaken to determine that the protection of the child had taken place.

The membership was found to be approaching the same need from a more practical point of view. Each member realized the lack of legal status of the committee and at the same time knew the limitations of his own agency, as well as the laws relating to various facets of information exchange. The researcher's concept of the index was seen by the membership to be the creation of a "super agency," with power over the existing agencies. Knowledge of a legal conflict arising from the existing statutes, and the concern over the individual agencies' chief administrators condensending to the establishment of an index with control power, caused the members to oppose the concept. The committee visualized an investigative tool as the role of the index. This concept would establish an index to serve as a central repository of information which could be made available for the utilization of the participating agencies. But, that is all it would perform. There would be no requirement for agency response, nor would there be a built-in evaluation system. This concept set forth the agencies' desire to have readily available information, but to experience no loss of control over agency action. The conflict was never to be resolved during the tenure of the researcher, and before the effort was completed, some personality clashes were evidenced.

In retrospect, it may be found that a degree of correctness was inherent in Dr. Weidman's approach to the index, but, more importantly, the behavioral lessons involved are worthy of consideration. The researcher came into a colloquial area with some preconceptions, one of which was that the practitioners comprising the committee would share her beliefs in the establishment of a directing index. In addition, the researcher failed to appreciate the limitations placed on the various agencies by the existing laws, which often were only remotely related to the "battered child syndrome." The committee used these laws to demonstrate the lack of feasibility of the proposed system. The constant refusal of the membership to accept the conceptualization became more and more a frustration to its proponent, with the ensuing consequence of a magnified insistence that the membership to come to terms. The conflict was brought out in the researcher's final report to the board of supervisors(3); not directly, but indirectly, through her interpretation of the intent of various members of the committee. Because of the personalities becoming embroiled in the conflict, the committee has never made use of the final report. Many items of information that may have been beneficial have been left unattended within the pages of the report.

Grave concern was evident among the department heads of the various agencies that dealt with confidential information, and certain committee members were anxious regarding the legal basis for the centralization of confidential information and its eventual exchange. Dr. Weidman saw the laws of confidentiality as being obstacles to the development of programs for the protection of children. There were committee members who were in agreement, but they also realized the difficulty in changing state legislation.

In an effort to address the problem of confidentiality, the committee had to cope with sections 118 and 827 of the California Welfare and Institutions Code, which placed legal restrictions on the release of information deemed to be confidential. These agencies could not release or exchange information with large segments of the community. In order to make an index operative, it was necessary for the restricted information to be included. The committee went to the city and county attorneys for legal opinions. The result was a shift in housing the index. Within both of the restrictive sections, the agencies concerned could legally release information to a law enforcement agency. It was the opinion of the community's legal advisors that moving the index to a law enforcement location would provide the ability to ease the legal restrictions regarding the release of confidential information. The index had the problem of first protecting agencies in order to protect children.

The traditional law enforcement services, already burdened with immense records systems, would not agree to the inclusion of the index. By default, the probation department agreed to accept the index and to incorporate it into an already existing central juvenile index. On the surface, this adoption may appear to be satisfactory; however, several weaknesses were to develop. First, it necessitated a move of the index from the medical setting at the Fresno General Hospital. This was at cross purposes, as the abused child problem is one of a basic medical nature. The role of the medical services in the identification of the victim is so crucial, that such a move away from the basic resource is a lessening of the effectiveness of evaluation of information. Secondly, within the established central juvenile index, the new index would be little more than a different colored card. As only one or two persons were assigned by the probation service to operate the new index, others in that agency were not cognizant of the information. Additionally, many persons within that agency cleared the main file system or utilized it in varying degrees. This constant use of the file allowed for a greater chance of filing error, reducing the effectiveness of the abused child index. In the event the worker assigned to the special index was not present when a report came in, the information was delayed or, in some cases, was never distributed. The original request-for-information form was often not forwarded to the participating agencies. When it was, there was a question on the part of those agencies as to how to complete the form. The request-for-information form, as well as the form to return information, was the same form used for the general index. This caused confusion at both the housing agency and the participating agencies. Over the years, it has been discovered that the participating agencies do not send information to the index on a regular basis unless this information is requested. Consequently, the main purpose of the index, that of accumulating information, has not been well met. This weakness could have been overcome by adequate in-service training of personnel; but with the lack of such training, and the shift in personnel comprising a given agency, the importance of the index and its function has been lost. Ultimately, Dr. Weidman's realization of the need for a built-in index control was correct. Within four years after the establishment of the index, its functioning has become questionable.

Legal Status

By November, 1964, the central index was operating at the probation department. Plans were instituted through the county administrative office to initiate procedures leading to legal status for the index and for the committee. Progression was slow, but persistence on the part of the committee was rewarded in April, 1965. All but one of the participating members, and several associate members, were present before the Fresno County Board of Supervisors when official, legal sanction was given to the index and the committee.

It had been a long move from the seminar in April, 1963, to this date in 1965. Much had transpired, both positive and negative. The group had accomplished several important tasks, including the establishment of the first countywide abused child resource. Additionally, through the efforts of the committee, many groups and organizations had been presented formal and informal training sessions on the problem of the underprotected child, local procedures for processing cases and the intent and mechanics of the index.

The chairmanship of the committee had changed in October, 1964 from Dr. Ziering to the author. The committee had been subdivided into three working subcommittees: the case study committee, the education and training committee and the legislative committee. By this time each agency had developed and presented to the main body their own working procedures in battered child cases. The task of the case study committee was to screen and present to the committee serious cases requiring complex solutions. Planning training and educational programs, as well as locating various groups to be recipients of committee presentations on the problem, was the objective of the education and training committee. During this period much legislation was being offered on the state level relating to abused children. The legislative committee had the responsibility of identifying the various bills, obtaining copies of each, analyzing the bills and reporting to the committee. Further, the legislative group was charged with following the progression of each bill. The committee had decided not to lobby or recommend, but to explain, instead, the effects of the various proposals to those groups and organizations that would be interested in such legislation.

The Committee Slows Down

In October, 1965 the chairmanship changed again. It was decided not to hold meetings until needed. Arbitrarily, the next meeting was set for early in 1966. There was nothing urgent at that time, and for reasons known only to the chairman, no further meetings were called. In the fall of 1966 Dr. Ziering contacted the chairman, as did the author, urging a meeting. But no meetings were forthcoming. It was not until the spring of 1967 that a meeting was finally held, and at that time a new chairman was elected. His first meeting was in September, 1967. This meeting was well-attended. The task of reviving the representatives had not been overwhelming.

During the time the committee was inactive, certain manifestations occurred with the developed system. Several key committee personnel were altered in their agency positions and one member left his employment, but entered another field that allowed for his continued representation. The change of personnel within agencies caused a breakdown in abused child procedures.

This was the effect of limited agency training of personnel, so that when a key committee member was no longer performing a particular task within the agency, there developed a void in that area. Thus, by the spring of 1967 the index itself was not working and, in effect, was nonexistent. This was readily noticed by the number of cases identified by the hospital staff that were not coming to the attention of the index or the other agencies.

Much new legislation had been introduced on the state level during that same period. Only Dr. Ziering was keeping up with these legislative attempts, and at the same time trying to be of some assistance in the formulation of more effective laws. The person who was to become the chairman in 1967 was, at the time, the state president of a large and influential professional group. This member was contacted by Dr. Ziering in an attempt to have some of the pending legislation brought before that organization's legislative committee for study, but the inactivity had taken its toll and no action was evident. The breakdown of the agencies' working relationships, as well as individual member participation, was dramatic. These factors, coupled with an alarming increase in the number of cases identified during the spring of 1967, led Dr. Ziering to exert his influence to reactivate the committee. Until its reconvening the fall of 1967, the situation in the county had regressed to the pre-1963 state. This points up the need for continued group participation if efforts of the group are to continue to function. Nothing takes the place of involvement. With the decrease and ultimate cessation of committee meetings, the membership ceased relating to committee objectives. They were still performing their agencies' functions, but were doing so independent of the interagency goals that had previously been evident. The answer, then, was the reconvening of the committee.

Recent Effectiveness

With the reactivation of the committee, one fact stood out dramatically: the central index had ceased to function. A decision was made for two committee members to seek out a solution. It was decided to investigate the possibility of moving the index back to the Fresno General Hospital. The law affecting confidentiality of records had not changed, but there was one method by which the index could be moved and still remain within the requirements of law enforcement housing. By placing the index under the administrative responsibility of the district attorney, the law enforcement requirement would be met. If, after accepting the index, the district attorney placed it at the hospital under the supervision of Dr. Ziering, the original concept of the index could be a reality.

Dr. Ziering was more than willing to accept the index under these conditions. The matter would have to be agreed to by the district attorney. That official had participated on the committee at various stages and he was presently an advisory member. Dr. Ziering and the author contacted William Daly, Fresno County District Attorney, in April, 1968. The situation was explained and the solution was presented for his consideration. In May Mr. Daly contacted the committee and advised the group that he would accept the index if it were to be moved. This decision was one of the most important advancements for the protection of children that had ever occurred in Fresno County. It was a completely unselfish act on the part of Mr. Daly. He was accepting the administrative responsibility for a function that would be performed by the Fresno General Hospital staff, over whom Mr. Daly had no administrative control. The district attorney's decision reflected his awareness of the importance of child protection; and it was a tremendous vote of confidence directed to the integrity and competency of the chief of pediatrics.

In the real world there are always problems. This situation proved to be no different; this would not be a story that would progress smoothly. The day the district attorney's decision was received, information was also received that Dr. Ziering was planning on leaving county service to enter private practice. This information was verified at the last committee meeting in May. The doctor was leaving effective July, 1968. As no person had been named to replace the doctor, the committee decided not to act on the district attorney's offer until a replacement was actively in the position of chief of pediatrics. At another meeting, subsequent to Dr. Ziering's leaving the area, the committee reaffirmed its original position; and, as no successor had been named, the possibility of moving the index back to the general hospital location was shelved.

It is too bad that one person is so important in certain situations, but it is also true that a leadership personality will leave voids when removed from the scene. This is what happened with Dr. Ziering's resignation. He had been the heart of the committee and Fresno County's attempts to protect abused children through an interdisciplinary approach. In more areas than just the index his leaving was felt. But in relation to the change of the index, the departure was dramatic, as it caused effectual consideration of the move to cease. Furthermore, the time interval between the resignation and any tenure of a new physician would negate the probability of instituting the plan. Naturally, the district attorney's offer was dependent upon Dr. Ziering, and in effect made to him. The personnel change actually released the district attorney from the obligation.

The central index remains at the Fresno County Probation Department. Since the reactivation of the committee the index is functioning better than during the period when the committee was not operating. Even so, because of the manner in which it was conceived, it cannot function in its present location as effectively as it would have at the general hospital. At the present time, the move of the index is still being considered, but as yet no replacement has been named at the hospital. The final decision will be made by the district attorney and the new chief of pediatrics.

The committee continues to meet, and the membership just recently addressed the necessity of the continuation of the activities of the group. They overwhelmingly agreed to the need for the work of the committee to continue. The committee is again attempting to have the individual agency procedures updated. There is a new emphasis being placed on agency personnel training and education. On a continuing basis the group is reviewing cases in an attempt to determine better procedures and to locate weaknesses in existing programs.

As yet, the effectiveness of the committee to develop meaningful community programs and services beyond those established has been very slow. It should be recognized that many of the internal problems must first be reconciled before effective community work can take place. Many members are aware of the need for research on the local scene in attempting to support existing conclusions regarding the abused child problem. Such research could become a reality through the use of the various graduate students in related programs at the local four-year institution. In order for this to occur, the committee will have to establish liaison with the college community. As yet, this has not happened, but the recognition of the existence of this resource may bring about needed research in the future.

An Analysis of the Committee

There is no doubt that the group has made an impact on the Fresno area. The work of this group has been effective in many ways, but most assuredly in bringing about a better relationship between the representatives of various agencies. Additionally, the group has brought the "battered child syndrome" to the attention of a vast segment of the community. It has shown people in many areas the need for vigilance. It has influenced the medical profession as well as the juvenile court. Children are being protected better than in the past. The committee has made many errors, and in some instances it has been ineffective, but the community would have remained archaic without its efforts.

Some of the problems encountered by the committee are worth reviewing. One of the major areas of problems was the existence of varying philosophies. Issues such as the definition of the problem, establishment of procedures and the delineation of agency responsibilities were focal points in which the philosophical differences of the group were experienced as grave concerns, often with bad effects on the basic objectives of the committee.

Another problem area was the unofficial status of the committee that gave rise to cautious movement, and in some instances provided an excuse for inertia. Many members were reluctant to become innovative out of fear of agency conflict. This apprehension resulted in some motions that were presented for consideration never being acted upon. Thus, when disciplinary considerations were not the issue, agency considerations were. At first the membership displayed a tactful regard for each other, but as principles were pursued in depth, cleavage appeared. More criticism became evident, and the members were found to be quite sensitive to such criticism. The defense of an individual's, or his agency's, position became more time-consuming. As it became evident that the undertaking was larger than some had imagined, completion of pertinent business could not be accomplished during the alloted time. The formation of subcommittees was to have been an answer to the time problem, but as these subgroups were seldom functional, the chairman and several others began to do all the necessary work between meetings. Other members lost continuity with what was taking place, and this tended to increase the breakdown of meaningful membership participation.

After the establishment of the index at the probation department, information was available from the index to the participating agencies only. This was not satisfactory to other groups such as the medical profession. The fact that some areas of the community could only report to the index and could receive no feedback from it undoubtedly affected the willingness of these groups to report at all.

Some of the alternatives to these problems will be summarized to assist others contemplating similar actions. First, the statement of responsibilities and procedures that each agency presented to the committee should have been the result of a committee within that particular agency, rather than reflecting the concepts of one person. This would have increased the validity of the procedures and would have negated the constant change of procedures as encountered by this group. It would have eliminated subjective interpretation of an agency's procedures, and it would have then been possible to develop machinery to provide for the continuation of the updating of procedures within each individual agency.

Second, the establishment of effective orientation through agency in-service training of all personnel involved in the agency's role could have easily been effected through the proper utilization of the committee's educational panel. This panel was never utilized on an agency level.

Third, the early receipt of official recognition should have been sought. This would have appraised agency administrators of the functions of the committee, and such an action would have reduced the anxiety of the membership when taking action. Official recognition at an early period was vital to the membership, as well as a means of involving the agency administrators in supporting actions of the committee.

Fourth, the elimination of personality cults should have been planned. As it was, when certain members changed assignments or left their positions, they also left the committee. In each instance the function of the committee was disrupted, as no provisions existed for orderly assimilation of replacements. It was possible to attend several meetings without introduction or orientation. No organization should be allowed to develop around a few personalities without whom the ability to function may be curtailed.

Several lessons stand out. One was the inability to attempt official action from an unofficial base over a long period of time. The result of such an attempt was a lack of control, allowing the actions of the group to become dysfunctional in certain areas and at certain times. This lack of function was displayed by the failure of the subcommittees to be responsive to the needs of the group. In turn, this overburdened a few members. Agendas were developed that were too cumbersome for effective consideration during regular meetings. The lack of official status gave rise to a continuation of the independent philosophies of each agency incumbering the work of the committee. The personalities involved were able to assert their own positions without regard for the totality of the situation. Even after sanction was granted, the members remained wary of their status, limiting committee response. Leadership responsibilities cannot be abdicated and still retain vitality.

Administrators must remain alert to the needs of the community, and when there are staff members willing to donate their time and effort to dealing with a recognized need, the administrators should support and motivate the activities of the group. Administrative leadership has been strikingly absent on the part of the heads of the participating agencies. Department heads should become more involved in such activity.

Groups such as the Fresno County Battered Child Committee could be effective tools in dealing with community problems. They could assist each agency in better attainment of agency goals. But, administrative support is needed, as well as innovative desire. This calls for the lessening of philosophical restrictions, the increase of cooperation and coordination, and the knowledge on the part of the agency representative that his administrator is backing him as well as overseeing the work of the group to insure that administrative guidelines are retained and goals are met.

The road chosen by the members of the committee has been long and difficult. It is a journey in effort that is far from over. The need for the committee remains and its goals are yet to be reached. Progress, no matter how painfully slow and deliberate, has been forthcoming. The committee still meets, and its insight into the problem grows with each meeting. Recognition of the work of the committee cannot be summed up, as it is intangible; but an editorial from the Fresno Bee, dated December 27, 1963 gave credit to a community action:

> The incomprehensible, but all too common case of the parent who injures his child in a fit of temper . . . and does it again and again . . . is being detected more quickly in Fresno because of the work of the battered child committee.
>
> The committee serves as a clearinghouse in which public agencies can compile a central index of known and suspected cases of child abuse. It is the sort of concerted action which sounds simple, but is not. All too often public agencies lack either the time or the inclination to compare notes.
>
> In the case of the battered child committee, the pediatricians who took the lead in bringing the agencies together report excellent cooperation.
>
> All concerned with this enterprise deserve the community's thanks. Because they cared, lives may be saved.

References

1. Ziering, William H.: Unpublished seminar. The Battered Child — A Community Challenge. Fresno, July 26, 1963, p. 1. Seminar speakers included Dr. Horst Weinberg, Chairman, Department of Pediatrics; Dr. William H. Ziering, Chief of Pediatrics, and Dr. Merritt C. Warren, Resident in Pediatrics, Fresno General Hospital; Dr. John L. Guinn, Radiologist, and Mrs. Helen Boardman, Director of Social Services,

Children's Hospital of Los Angeles; Miss Marie Emmal, Executive Director, Child Guidance Clinic, Valley Children's Hospital; Det. Sgt. C. J. Flammang, Juvenile Division, Fresno County Sheriff's Department; and Dr. J. J. Bocian, Radiologist, Fresno Community Hospital.

2. Composition of membership in the original Fresno County Battered Child Committee consisted of: Dr. William Ziering, Chairman; Mr. Ernest Viau, Assistant County Probation Officer, Probation Department; Mrs. Margaret Stumpf, Supervisor of Children's Services, Department of Public Welfare; Miss Elaine Fineran, Director of Public Health Nursing, Department of Public Health; Lt. E. G. Haley and Sgt. C. J. Flammang, Fresno County Sheriff's Department; Dr. Richard Houghton, Chief Pediatrics Resident, Fresno General Hospital; Mr. Jack Berry, Director, Infant of Prague Adoption Society; Dr. Dorothy Pollack, Director, Family Counseling Services; Dr. Jack Scott, Representative, Fresno County Medical Society; Dr. Mary Hayes, Acting Director of Public Health; and Dr. O. J. Tocchio, Department of Criminology, Fresno State College.

3. Weidman, Hazel Hitson: Unpublished report to the Board of Supervisors and the California Department of Public Health on the Results of a Three Months Study Focusing Upon Increased Protection to Physically Abused Children, June 1, 1964.

Chapter XII

THE FUTURE

AN attempt has been made to present the police role in dealing with the problem of the underprotected child, indicating the etiology of the various manifestations of childhood dangers. Both neglect and abuse have been explored in relation to the role of the police. Law enforcement objectives have been established, with presentation of a basic rationale. Police procedures in differing situations have been augmented with discussions of existing inadequacies. Present knowledge of the problem has been probed, with a focus on police needs, in order to increase understanding. A review of the overall system of judicial procedure as it pertains to child protection indicates the existence of needs that are not being met. Some thoughts about the future are seemingly in order. As these are pursued, there may be new and different concepts on what the reader may have been exposed to within the traditional conceptualization of law enforcement services. Other concepts will transcend the police field and intrude into areas of several disciplines. In some instances innovation may appear, with the accompanying effects of criticism, an element of reaction to proposals for change. It is apparent to many that our present approach is not significantly coping with children who are being placed in jeopardy early in their existence. To conclude this effort without recommending new avenues for consideration would be a disservice to the victims still lacking protection. It is incumbent upon all concerned to endeavor to bring about meaningful legislation and procedures for meeting the demands of the underprotected child; to this end, the following concepts are presented.

Awareness and Involvement

It is vitally important that the practitioners of the various disciplines become knowledgeable concerning the problem of underprotected children, and these persons must then relate the problem to the general public. By doing so, those with direct roles in the protection of children will not only instill the importance of public awareness and participation, but will also have the sophistication and depth of understanding whereby their own areas of endeavor will become more fully involved in the development of methods and procedures to increase the effective protection of children. In order for children to be protected, two criteria must be met: the ability to identify the case, and the means of quickly reporting the incident. Neither will occur until the official representatives of society are cognizant of the problem and have established easy access for the reporting of the cases.

The public will never report fully, but reporting activity could be increased if the public was adequately informed. This is a process to be undertaken by an informed professional, but a few practitioners crusading for the protection of children is not the answer. What is needed is a well-balanced understanding of the problem existing within all segments of the professional community. Thus the sentiments of one discipline will be echoed by others. The public will become convinced of the existence and the nature of the problem. The willingness to report will increase in proportion to the belief in the necessity to report. Through the development of effective reporting procedures, easily understood and with simplified mechanics, the willingness to report will be transformed into the reality of reporting. The professionals must increase their own understanding in order for them to act without the diversity of opinion that now exists. A united and organized group of informed practitioners cannot be excluded as the basic need for bringing about adequate child protection.

This awareness and involvement on the part of the members of the various disciplines cannot be left to chance. There should develop a methodical approach to the education and training of the practitioners. This dispensing of knowledge should begin with in-service personnel. The various agencies have the nucleus within their present staffs for training officers. In some instances the agency, with the support of other groups or institutions, could arrange to sponsor workshops or seminars. Such activities could include one or two outside experts, complemented by local persons with knowledge of the problem from the standpoint of the particular area. There are funds available for educational activities to take place in order to answer a community need. Both agencies and educational institutions are able to seek these monies.

Staff personnel can be encouraged to inform themselves of the nature of the problem, and the agency should include within its library the current information that does exist. Local community libraries should be encouraged to include books and journals that present the problem for professional as well as public consumption. Most of the agencies involved are in the position to do limited research into their contacts with neglect and abuse cases. This provides statistical information that can be correlated with more widespread studies. This type of study has been very successful on the hospital level as a follow-up in cases of known abused children.

Opportunites to publicize the efforts of the agency or the community to the general public should be grasped, for in this manner the public becomes aware of the citizen's role in the protection of children. This is most certainly true regarding the reporting of the offense; but beyond that stage there is the need for public support for the development of resources and the institution of procedures to be used in the overall handling of the case. Thus social and counseling services, foster homes, homemaker aid and numerous other means of assisting the disoriented family unit may be included or increased within the community through successful public contact. Additionally, every agency is concerned with its image. The very fact that the agency is represented before the public as being involved in a community problem will gain favor for that agency or profession.

Professional knowledge must be increased, and that places a burden upon the training and preparatory institutions to include adequate training in child neglect and abuse on the preservice level. It is a fact that only recently has there been given to this problem the attention that it warrants. Therefore, educational institutions are still lacking in this needed curriculum. Such courses should be developed and included as a part of the background received during the period of professional study. With the inclusion of this material, the incidence of interest to do graduate research in the field should increase. In turn, the knowledge on the subject of underprotected children will expand, and with that knowledge improved methodology for coping with the problem will develop.

It is not enough for the professionals to be aware of the problem; there must be professional involvement to accompany the knowledge. As has been pointed out, this involvement should be in the community as a practitioner, within the agency as a training resource, in the area of public awareness and support, and in the education of the professional on the preservice level; this is the involvement that is needed. It can only come about through recognition that each discipline with a role in the protection of children views that role as a part of the totality of the professional experience, and not just isolated handling of individual situations. The underprotected child must be seen as a professional responsibility.

Cooperative Understanding

One item that has been lacking in most efforts to achieve stability in dealing with a social problem has been the inability of various disciplines to reduce parochialism. The desire to resist change in policy and procedure is strongly inbedded within most administrative organizations. The mission of the organization often becomes the defense of tried and true methods rather than the goal of service. As organizations function through the utilization of disciplines and specialties, the agencies themselves tend to become disciplinary. This in turn causes an inward focus, with a corresponding lack of insight into the totality of the problem under attack. Personnel become negativistic toward innovation, and many are quick to point out why a certain course of action cannot be successful. Often, the reason centers within the objecting discipline, but is stated by that source to exist within another area or agency. This can be seen in the use of the old argument regarding lack of funds. But, as most practitioners are well aware, not all innovations require excessive expenditure. The fear of infringement upon the role of the discipline or organization is often the cause of the resistance.

How many times have conferences dwindled into a mire of self-protecting statements of various disciplinary approaches? The attending representatives utilize their time and energy not in seeking new solutions, but in presenting and defending their positions. They come with their philosophy, pay lip service to cooperative measures and leave with the conviction that they were correct. Between certain disciplines there has existed animosity, and the occasion to speak will be accompanied by an almost automatic "tuning out."

Understanding does not come easy. Old beliefs and myths must be first overcome in order to make room for new ideas. Each practitioner must prepare this objectivity for himself. The intention to "listen" is a personal act. Through the desire to hear, the ability to hear will be made evident. There is no argument with the fact that the system is not perfect. With that realization, the desire for improvement should be recognized. And improvement can only come about through the active participation of the various disciplines. This participation should be accompanied by cooperative understanding. The ability to see the limitations of the other agency, the knowledge of the problems of administration, the recognition of the lack of resources and facilities; and the awareness of the need for the development of new approaches must all permeate the disciplinary participation.

Since the problem of the underprotected child has not received the attention it should within any given specialty, it has often been considered an isolated part of the disciplinary mission. It has been something to deal with on an individual-case basis, with poorly defined criteria for role determination. Through the cooperative understanding and participation of the various fields, definitions, roles and procedures can be worked out leading to the adequate protection of children in our society. The disagreements over roles and methods cannot continue, as the energy necessary for problem solution is directed toward problem support. If there are disciplines with advanced insight, let this knowledge be shared; and such specialties should render assistance to other fields in order to bring about clarification of direction. Leadership must develop within the professions to guide those areas of the community that lag behind. This leadership should strive to construct a climate of innovative participation.

Conferences and workshops, with expertise and well-planned agendas are needed to foster full participation. It is important that these be attended by all of the groups and specialties with a role to play. It must be recognized that some groups are necessarily only planners. They have little direct activity with the actual cases but are capable of lending assistance at the planning stage. Their counsel should be sought, and they should be included in any developmental participation. Such groups are public and hospital administrators, legal advisors and legislators. In some instances psychiatry might be included in an advisory capacity. Personnel administrators should be apprised regarding the backgrounds and the specialties desired in order to staff agencies with properly trained personnel. The local medical society should be in attendance. Other medical services may be found to be of importance, and consideration should be given to their inclusion. As an example, the author has yet to see a dentist involved in recognizable participation at any meeting on the abused child, but such persons are in contact with numerous neglected and battered children. Some vision should be evident in developing the participants. It is quite easy to include only those groups with readily defined roles, overlooking much of the community in the process.

The educators dealing with the elementary school child, including the staff services of the school system, should be consultants or participants. But educational services should not be limited to that level. Institutions of higher learning and professional preparatory staffs should be included as consultants. Here is a two-way street. Not only will the community gain the insight and knowledge that these persons may offer, but, in turn, the institutions will be given the opportunity to appraise the value of introducing subject matter regarding the underprotected child into their curriculum. This is important, because the development of curriculum tends to be related to the recognition of professional need. In addition, research, which is so necessary for innovation, will follow the establishment of such curriculum content.

Early meetings of this nature cannot be left to dangle. The

planners should take into account the limited perspective many disciplines have toward the underprotected child problem, with many seeing it as only incidental to their traditional mission. It is necessary to prepare for future involvement and participation before the meeting. Whether it is a workshop, seminar or conference, plans for the continuation of coordinated involvement are essential. Without such planning, the meeting will have been only for the purpose of the dissemination of information. Obviously, there are other media for carrying out informational services. The bringing together of persons with expertise and professional backgrounds should not be on an occasion of limited purpose. The full utilization of their time and energy should be the objective. Adequate planning will facilitate the continued effort of the practitioners toward innovative participation.

A word must be directed toward the police. In this discussion, the main theme has been innovation through cooperative understanding. The police services should be included in any community endeavor toward the protection of children. For police participation to be productive, several factors must preexist. First, the police must recognize their role in child protection in the fullest sense. It cannot be a mere task that law enforcement performs as another duty, being placed upon the police through default. The police role will have to be viewed in its true light, as an intregal part of the police function. Second, the police administrator should have an interest in bringing his agency into the area of full community service. To do so he must be willing to lend the authority of his office to the community planning that precedes actual community effort. In some instances this may mean only his approval for departmental participation. In other cases it may be necessary for the chief to present himself at planning meetings. The means by which he may give approval are varied, but the approval is not. It must be clear and understood not only by the community, but also by the internal agency which he controls. This latter approval is important because of the traditional line-staff administrative relationship existing in police service. The police representative must know where he stands with his agency's administration before participation begins. The police administrator will not be able to give such approval unless he has done his homework. It is incumbent upon the chief to understand the problem of the underprotected child and to develop relating policy with his staff prior to police community involvement.

Third, the assignment of participating personnel is crucial. The officer chosen to represent the department must be capable of assimilating information presented in conceptualized form. Participants from other disciplines often make presentations of complex ideas. In some instances these ideas are quite abstract, or are based on knowledge to which the officer has not been exposed. Policemen are used to dealing with facts, but these facts are realities and can be categorized. They are not used to encountering vague conceptions or abstract ideas. Officers tend to follow the law, and give import to words in their common usage. All of these factors work against the officer participant. Many times, the statements of others will be misconstrued, or meanings will be accepted to be as commonly used, where actually the use was germane only to a given discipline. The police officer will desire concrete proposals, but innovative planning does not lend itself to ready answers, nor do the other disciplines work with ready answers. The officer may report negatively on what has occurred, due to his lack of understanding. The police representative should be chosen with care. If possible, the officer should have a college background. If this is not feasible, patience and insight coupled with a good vocabulary will be adequate substitutes. Above all the officer should have an understanding of the nature of the underprotected child and he must be interested in participation on the community level.

Fourth, the police should not rotate this assignment. It is important that the police representative have a constant representation to insure continuity of the activities of the group. If necessary, more than one officer should be assigned to attend.

Fifth, those disciplines with which the police have traditionally had bad relations should be encountered with an open mind. The realization of the existence of differing philosophies will tend to overcome past suspicions. It is understood that for this to work, it must occur from both directions. That other disciplines are prone to be suspicious of the police should also be considered. However, cooperation must begin somewhere, and it will be to the credit of the police if they initiate it.

Finally, the officer should recognize his own expertise. This should be an awareness and not a conscious thought. In the presence of other specialties, represented by persons possessing advanced degrees and other worthy credentials, the officer may tend to be unsure of his own position. This need not be, as a competent and technically correct police officer is the backbone of a free society. He possesses skills and experience that others only see through limited and impersonal vision. The officer's expertise is found in his skill, his experience and his devotion to duty.

Immediate Concerns

There are some areas of concern that should come under immediate consideration. One of the first relates to the involvement of the medical profession. It has already been pointed out that the key to the protection of the abused child is the participation of the medical practitioner. This is also true in some cases of neglect. Assistance is needed from the medical resource in the education of the public and participating services. No other profession is as capable of reaching the mainstream of the community. The public will listen to the doctor. This country has developed an abiding faith in the medical practitioner, and the physician stands as the best source of community education in the protection of children.

Beyond that role, the direct participation of the medical profession in the cases to be alleviated is necessary to secure protection. Because of the nature of the problem, the medical profession is involved. The adequate protection of abused children requires active medical participation. Because many doctors do not desire to participate or do not have the time to give to such a role, other solutions must be found to insure participation. One such solution would be the establishment of a trauma committee within the local medical societies. This committee could be comprised of various medical specialties necessary to the diagnosis and treatment of the "battered child syndrome." The doctors could serve on a rotating basis, possibly one year at a time. Any physician or paramedical person suspecting inflicted trauma would refer the case to the committee for evaluation. After the medical evaluation the committee could report an identified abused child to the proper authorities by means of the executive office of the medical society. The work of the local committee could be augmented by a similar committee from the state association, comprised of renowned specialists. This group would serve as consultants to the local committee. It could lend itself to supporting the findings of the local group in cases where such support were needed. By this means the liability factors would be reduced. The trauma committee would act in totality and, backed by the state committee, there would be no fear of effective reprisal.

The findings of the committee would give to the agency or court processing the case, adequate tangible evidence of abuse. Thus both the child and the parent would be protected. Individual doctors would no longer be requested to stand alone; the burden would be shared by the medical society. The rotation of service on the committee would preclude any one physician from having to serve for long periods. Reporting of cases would be from physician to physician. The committee would serve as a consulting group to the original doctor. Any reporting to authorities would not be handled by physicians but, rather, by the executive officer of the medical society. Time in court would be reduced, as lawyers would be hesitant to attempt to contest the medical findings of a full trauma committee, possibly supplemented by a state committee. The medical participation in the protection of children would become an effective and efficient reality, insuring equality for all concerned.

Hospitals and emergency institutions, in cooperation with physicians, medical examiners and coroners, should institute procedures to insure full-bodied X-ray surveys of all children under a given age (suggested to be three years) who are injured or killed through trauma other than automobile accidents. This would insure that children receiving inflicted trauma and falling within the category of the battered child syndrome would be subject to detection at the time of emergency treatment at an institution. It would further insure the identification of such children who are "dead on arrival" at emergency rooms or in doctors offices. At the present time, only the more sophisticated institutions and staffs are performing this rudimentary diagnostic service. It should be expanded to become as routine a procedure as a complete blood count.

Medical examiners and coroners should make sure that all suspected cases of abuse coming under their jurisdiction receive the same skeletal survey. Beyond this, there is one important finding that would be of great assistance to investigations following a death. That factor is body weight taken at the time the body is received and before embalming. For some reason, body length is measured, but the weight is often not a part of the information of record. This is needed in subsequent investigations that might indicate neglect in the home. This would be in cases where action is necessary because of the manner in which other children are receiving care, or to substantiate findings that the deceased was being neglected prior to the death.

Procedures such as those outlined should be given precedence, with only one area receiving higher priority. That would be the establishment of adequate reporting procedures and a central index in the event that such does not exist within either a state or locale. A statewide central repository of information is necessary, and one should exist within each state. However, due to limitations placed on such state receiving centers, the information may be quite limited if not supplemented on the local level. Since the underprotected child is a community problem, the community should insure the reporting of its own cases. Participating agencies and services will vary from area to area, and the need for local adaptation is thus apparent. Without local indexes, the information at the state level will be cursory in depth, and in most cases will not reflect the true picture of the problem within the state. This is due to the limitations relative to who is to report, and when reports are to be made. These limitations come as a result of attempting to legislate a civic and moral responsibility for the whole state. Therefore, only limited groups or professions are indicated as required to report. This becomes a built-in excuse for those not mentioned in the legislation. In addition, such reporting devices are incumbent on one agency or source from a local area reporting into the state system what has occurred in the community. The control on local reporting to the state is often weak; thus many cases fail to be reported to the state level and remain buried in an agency file. Local reporting tends to be broader and better publicized, with the additional factor of being available for public reporting. The local device, if properly established, could be the control and clearinghouse for state reporting. This would increase the ability of the state level to receive and house information that more nearly duplicates what is being reported throughout the state.

The Interdisciplinary Approach

The following proposal is intended for those who are in positions where they are influencing legislative activity within the state. It is an approach based on innovation, and an optimistic conception of the sincerity of those who are concerned with the protection of children. The concepts involved are neither new nor the result of one person's effort; rather, they encompass the thoughts and experiences of many. In some jurisdictions, part of what is proposed has been tried or may already be in effect. In other areas, the thoughts treated here will be foreign.

No writing that is critical of an existing system should be limited to downgrading, and that has not been the intent of the concepts presented in this book. Instead, certain weakness in many areas of public and professional services have been identified; not to condemn, but to point out the need for innovative alternatives. The alternatives and proposals presented so far, have not been presumed to be total answers or solutions to the complex problems faced by those involved. At best they are but thoughts that need expanding by those who have the ability to discern, innovate and actuate. The following proposal is offered in the same spirit. It is a proposition for consideration. It needs expansion. It needs smoothing and refining. It is an idea in the rough.

The use of protective services has loomed into the picture of child protection off and on throughout the years. It has been tried in many areas with varying degrees of success. It is a concept that has one meaning to some and a completely different meaning to others. To many, it has never been presented. To others, they feel they own it outright. But the concept of protective services offers more hope to the protection of children than any other we now know.

Basically, protective services is a social work concept. Much of its early history relates to attempts to assist welfare recipients to adjust or reestablish themselves. Some of the misconceptions surrounding the service are the result of this earlier usage.

The proposal is one of protective services, but not in its traditional application. In the newness of this approach is envisioned the coordination and expediting of the total commitment of the community toward the protection of its children. Protective services, in this context, is seen as the community response to the needs of children. Because it is a community response to a community need, it must be a response of totality. It is new, it is different and it has the potential for adequate protection.

This manner of protective service would involve the creation of a new agency. It would be administratively under the head of a member of the social welfare discipline, obviously with an advanced degree and considerable experience. Its services would not be related to financial assets, but eligibility would be based on family or individual need for protection. Therefore, not only would the indigent population be served, but the total community could avail itself of the service as well. As in other established services, financial charges could be based on the ability to pay. This would mean that the basic cost of the service would have to come from public monies. Some of this would be available from federal participation, part from the state and part through local support.

The agency would be staffed with caseworkers to perform the basic function of case identification, definition of eligibility and casework techniques. These workers would be augmented by casework technicians. These latter persons would be assistants with training beyond that of clerical help, and whose duties would include interviewing and assuming the more routine tasks now applied to casework. The caseworker would be freed to perform the more difficult efforts related to family assistance. There would also be specialized social work personnel such as medical social workers, psychiatric social workers and adoptions and child welfare workers. The basic core of the personnel would be the caseworkers.

Attached to the staff would be clinical psychological service, with psychiatric service available on a consulting basis. The psychological staff would exist for the purpose of performing diagnostic examinations, making recommendations to the agency and the courts relating to further service, and assisting the caseworkers and other personnel in the activity of case follow-up. The cases identified for treatment would be referred to those mental health services already in existence.

While the major portion of the cases would be handled on a voluntary basis, there could be occasions when the family would resist attempts to intervene. For this reason there would be a law enforcement unit attached to protective services. This unit would be a part of the agency, and the personnel would be subject to the administrative policy of the agency administrator. The group would be small in number, probably never surpassing 5 percent of the total agency personnel.

The unit's task would be to act as liaison with traditional law enforcement agencies, the various legal services, the probation department, parole and the courts. Records of the agency of a law enforcement nature would be established and maintained by the unit. Unit personnel would have the function of assisting caseworkers in aggravated cases and coordinating traditional police activities in cases involving police investigations.

These persons would be drawn from the ranks of police juvenile officers, meeting requirements for the position of protective services law enforcement liaison officer as established by the state.

In the performance of their duties relative to the protection of children, these officers would have police powers.

By instituting such a service, the community would be providing all the basic tools for protecting children under one roof. Society could intervene on a voluntary basis in cases of family disorientation. Case work techniques could be employed to assist the family in revitalizing itself. The agency would have the power of referral, and problems that could be handled by existing agencies could be referred for proper action. In some instances the need might be financial as well as protective. In such a case, the traditional welfare service could be called upon to assist from the financial aspect, with protective services retaining case control. In educational matters, the school's staff could be utilized to assist in overcoming the deficit, but control would be maintained by the protective service agency. The same is true of homemaker care, public health service, legal service and mental health. Police activities in relation to the protection of children could be coordinated through the law enforcement liaison unit, but with protective services retaining case control.

Both the adults and the children involved could be served by the one group with a coordinated effort that would reduce the number of children that are displaced from the home for protection. Persons now hesitant to report to a law enforcement agency would be more inclined to report to a protective service agency. The agency could maintain the central index files relating to underprotected children on the local level. The ability to educate the community regarding the problem and the services offered would result in increased recognition and reporting of incidents. The central responsibility and control afforded protection cases would reduce the existing confusion relating to roles and procedures. The availability of psychological resources for diagnostic evaluations would result in better action based on proper evaluation and recommendations. Many cases would be effectively handled without official action, but the hard core cases requiring "forced feeding" could be dealt with through the law enforcement unit.

Such an agency could offer the totality of service that is needed to cope with the complexities of neglect and abuse. The ability to work with the whole family, the total participants, would increase the protection of children. The universal recognition of the role and mission of the protective service unit would increase the incidence of case identification and would place the responsibility of protection with one agency, although from an interdisciplinary approach. It would be an active agency and at the same time a coordinating agency, assisting in the effective utilization of community resources. Through its law enforcement unit it would have the capability of being involved in the initial investigation of acute cases, and the direction of the case toward the goal of protection could be a reality.

It would not be necessary to establish such agencies in every county of a state. In areas where the population did not warrant the service, a regional service could be established, serving several counties. All that would be mandatory is that the service be available to all areas of the state, with service in some areas being more concentrated than in others. Such a proposal should be given consideration. It should be researched and planned for; and it should be tried on a pilot basis in several areas within the state before being finalized.

Underprotected children have been with society for a long time in varying forms. Neglect and abuse of our children has just recently received the attention it deserves. The proposal for a new concept of protective services may hold the possibility of adequate child protection. Evidence indicates that the present system is not effective. Some method of innovation must be worked out to identify and reduce incidents of the underprotection of children. This proposal would lead to greater success.

A New Court

Consideration should be given to the establishment of a new court for the purpose of ajudicating cases of neglect and abuse. Such a court would have to meet certain criteria. It should be constructed to function under constitutional tests. This could be accomplished through the formation of a legal committee comprised of a representative of the state's supreme court, the judicial council if there is one within the state, the attorney general's office, and several legal scholars and active jurists. Attention should be given to providing the court with a significant level of jurisdiction, comparable to a higher trial court. Tenure of the judicial officer should afford the opportunity to become experienced in dependent child cases. Appointment should be to this bench only, eliminating rotation during tenure. Preference should be given to those persons with previous juvenile court experience.

The court should be in an informal setting, without the adversary system. This could be accomplished by having attorneys representing the interests of either the child or the parent act as friends of the court, or in a similar capacity. In contrast to the present juvenile court system, the interests of the child must be safeguarded, and the means to do so should be a part of the court.

This court would hear all cases involving dependent children, including neglect and abuse. It could also be given jurisdiction over custody matters resulting from divorce actions, as well as adoption proceedings. These latter concepts would be for the legal committee to determine. The jurisdiction of the court should extend to the parents or guardians and should not be limited to the child. By this means the court would be able to order necessary remedial assistance for the adult figures that would encourage the rapid reorganization of the family unit, resulting in the early return of a separated child. In instances where the child was not removed, the court could insure compliance with orders regarding home care and parental cooperation with caseworkers and others officially involved in the case.

The system should allow for the fullest amount of relevant and material evidence to be admissible. These rules should extend to family history and other social data that would allow the greatest information to come before the court. This would insure the judge receiving all available information upon which to base his decision.

Regional or district courts could be established, in the event one county's caseload did not warrant the maintenance of such a court. This would reduce costs and retain a proper balance of cases.

Court actions would be initiated by petition, with the petitioner going through the probation department. In the event there was a protective service unit, it could also file petitions. By means of precourt investigations and precourt meetings of counsel for the child and the parents, the facts supporting the best interests of the child could be brought out and compromise alternatives identified. The object of the court action would be to insure the safety of the child while supporting the integrity of the home. Thus in the majority of instances it would be hoped that alternatives could be found that would provide for the child remaining in his own environment. Help for the parents could be initiated and secured under court order. This would eliminate the difficulty experienced at the present time, wherein the juvenile court has no jurisdiction to order the parents to submit to any remedial family assistance.

In summary, the virtues of such a court would be its informal and nonadversary nature, its unique jurisdiction over both the child and the adult, and the development of liberalized evidence rules insuring the supply of adequate information to the court in keeping with constitutional protections.

Summary

This chapter has attempted to set forth some direction for the future in order to bring society closer to adequate child protection. Much of the improvement yet to come will be the result of professional involvement and interdisciplinary cooperation. Several factors that need immediate attention have been described, including the establishment of both state and local repositories of information on these cases; the use of full-bodied x-ray surveys in accident cases involving children under three years, with the exception of automobile accidents; and the addition of body weight as a matter of coroner record.

The devlopment of a fully armed protective service, capable of performing the role of child protection within the community and staffed with an interdisciplinary representation, has been proposed as the most hopeful opportunity to deal with the problem. And finally, the suggestion for a specialized court, utilizing specialized procedures to deal with a specialized problem affecting a special group. The remaining recommendation is for all concerned to demonstrate an interest in legislation dealing with the underprotected child; and for each to cause his legislators to wirte, initiate or support only those laws that will be significant in the improvement of an inadequate system.

BIBLIOGRAPHY

Books

Adams, Stuart: The PICO Project: In Johnson, N., Savitz, L., and Wolgans, M. S. (Eds.): The Sociology of Punishment and Correction. New York, Wiley, 1962.

Allen, Anne, and Morton, Arthur: This is Your Child: The Story of the National Society for the Prevention of Cruelty to Children. London, Routledge and Kegan, Paul, 1951.

Amos, William E., and Willford, Charles F. (Eds.): Delinquency Prevention — Theory and Practice. Englewood Cliffs, Prentice-Hall, 1967.

Armstrong, Barbara: California Family Law. San Francisco, Bancroft, 1953, vols I, II.

Aubry, Arthur, Jr., and Caputo, Rudolph R.: Criminal Interrogation. Springfield, Ill., Thomas, 1965.

Becker, Howard S.: Outsiders: Studies in the Sociology of Deviance. New York, Macmillan, 1963.

Cavan, Ruth: Juvenile Delinquency. Philadelphia, Lippincott, 1962.

Chesser, Eustace: Cruelty to Children. New York, Philosophical Lib. 1952.

DeFrancis, Vincent: Child Abuse — Preview of a Nationwide Survey. Denver, Amer. Humane Assoc. Chil. Div. May, 1963.

Donigan, Robert L., and Fisher, Edward C.: The Evidence Handbook. Evanston, Northwestern, 1965.

Eldefonso, Edward: Law Enforcement and the Youthful Offender. New York, Wiley, 1967.

Fontana, Vincent J.: The Maltreated Child. Springfield, Thomas, 1964.

Germann, A. C., Day, Frank D., and Gallati, Robert R. J.: Introduction to Law Enforcement. Springfield, Thomas, 1967.

Gibbons, Don C.: Society, Crime and Criminal Careers — An Introduction to Criminology. Englewood Cliffs, Prentice-Hall, 1968.

Goldman, Nathan: The Differential Selection of Juvenile Offenders for Court Appearance. New York, Nat. Council Crime Delinq. 1963.

Glueck, Sheldon and Eleanor: Unraveling Juvenile Delinquency. Cambridge, Harvard, 1950.

Helfer, Ray E., and Kempe, C. Henry: The Battered Child Syndrome. Chicago, U. of Chicago, 1968.

Housden, Leslie G.: The Prevention of Cruelty to Children. New York, Philosophical Lib. 1956.

Kaplan, Louis: Foundations of Human Behavior. New York, Harper, 1965.

Keeney, J. P., and Pursuit, D. G.: Police Work With Juveniles. 2nd ed. Springfield, Thomas, 1959.

Kvaraceus, William C., and Ulrich, William E., in collaboration With John H. McCormick, Jr. and Helen J. Keily: Delinquent Behavior: Principles and Practices. Washington, Nat. Ed. Assoc. 1959.

Leonard, V. A.: The Police of the Twentieth Century. Brooklyn, Foundation, 1964.

Leonard, V. A., and More, Harry W.: The General Administration of Criminal Justice. Brooklyn, Foundation, 1967.

Lierbers, Arthur, and Vollmer, Capt. Carl (N.Y.C.P.D.): The Investigator's Handbook. New York, Arco, 1962.

McCord, William, and Joan: Origins of Crime. New York, Columbia, 1959.

Municipal Police Administration: Chicago, Int. City Manager's Assoc., 1961.

Myren, Richard A., and Swanson, Lynn D.: Police Work With Children. U.S. Department of Health, Education, and Welfare, Children's Bureau, 1962.

Rein, Martin: Child Protective Services in Massachusetts. Florence Heller Graduate School for Advanced Studies in Social Welfare, Waltham, Brandeis U., 1963.

Riese, Herta: Heal the Hurt Child. Chicago, U. of Chicago P., 1962.

Skolnick, Jermone H.: Justice Without Trial. New York, Wiley, 1966.

Soderman, Harry, and O'Connell, John J.: Modern Criminal Investigation, 5th ed., rev. by Charles E. O'Hara. New York, Funk, 1962.

Stuckey, Gilbert B.: Evidence for the Law Enforcement Officer. New York, McGraw, 1968.

Sutherland, Edwin H., and Cressey, Donald R.: Principles of Criminology, 7th ed., Philadelphia, Lippincott, 1966.

Periodicals and Other Writings

Adelson, Lester: Slaughter of the innocents — A study of forty-six homicides in which the victims were children, New Eng J Med, 264:1345-1349, 1961.

Andrews, J. P.: The battered baby syndrome. Illinois Med J 122:494, 1962.

Bain, Katherine: The physically abused child. Pediatrics, 31:895-897, 1963.

Bakwin, Harry: Multiple skeletal lesions in young children due to trauma. J Ped 49:7-16, 1956.

Barta, M. A., Jr., and Smith, Nathan J.: Willful trauma to young children. Clin Ped, Oct. 2, 1963.

Battered children and abusive parents. Roche Med Image, 10(No. 4) Aug. 1968.

Boardman, Helen E.: a project to rescue children from inflicted injuries. Soc Work, 7:43-51, 1962.

Braun, J. G.; Braun, E. J., and Simonds, C.: The mistreated child. Calif. Med, 90, Aug. 1963.

Bryant, Harold E., et al., Physical abuse of children: An agency study. Child Welfare, March 1963.

Caffey, J.: Multiple fractures in the long bones of infants suffering from chronic subdural hematoma. Amer J Roentgen, 56:163-173, 1946.

Caplan, G.: Concepts of Mental Health and Consultation: Their Application in Public Health Social Work. U.S. Department of Health, Education, and Welfare, Children's Bureau, 1959.

Child Welfare Services: U.S. Department of Health, Education, and Welfare, Children's Bureau, 1962.

Class, Norris E.: Neglect, social deviance, and community action. Nat Prob Parole Assoc J, 6:17-23, 1960.

Coles, Robert: Terror-struck children. New Rep May 30, 1964.

Connell, John R., Jr.: The devil's battered children: The increasing incidents of willful injuries to children, J Kansas Med Soc, 64:385-391, 1963.

Curtis, G. C.: Violence breeds violence — perhaps. Amer J Psychiat, 120:386-387, 1963.

David, Lester: The shocking price of parental anger. Good Housekeeping, March 1964.

DeFrancis, Vincent: Parents who abuse children. PTA Mag, 58:16-18, 1963.

Delsordo, James D.: protective casework for abused children. Children, 10:213-218, 1963.

Dodge, R. R.: Medical implications of the physical abuse of children, protecting the battered child. Amer Humane Assoc. 1962.

Dominic, Sister M.: Religion and the juvenile delinquent. Amer Catholic Sociol Rev, SV, Oct. 1954.

Earl, Howard G.: 10,000 children battered and starved. Hundred die. Today's Health, Sept. 1965.

Elmer, Elizabeth: Abused children seen in hospitals. Soc Work, 5:98-102, 1960.

Erwin, Donald T.: The battered child syndrome. Med leg Bull, 130:1-10, 1964.

Fairburn, A. C., and Hunt, A. C.: Caffey's 'third syndrome' — A critical evaluation. Med Sci Law, 4:123-126, 1964.

Ferguson, William H.: Battered child syndrome. Attorney General's opinion regarding the reporting of such occurrences. J Kansas Med Soc, 65:67-69, 1964.

Fisher, S. H.: Skeletal manifestations of parent-induced trauma in infants and children. Southern Med J, 51:956-960, 1958.

Flammang, C. J.: The abused child—What we are doing. Sheriff's Rev, 1965.

Flato, Charles: Parents who beat children. Sat Eve Post, 235:30-35, 1962.

Fontana, Vincent J.; Donovan, Denis, and Wong, Raymond J: The maltreatment syndrome in children, New Engl J Med, 269:1389-1394, 1963.

Gil, David G.: First steps in a nationwide study of child abuse. Reprint Series No. 20, Reprinted from The Social Work Practice, 1966; Waltham, Brandeis U., 1966.

Gil, David G.: Nationwide Study of Legally Reported Physical Abuse of Children. No. 15 Papers in Social Welfare, Waltham, Brandeis U., May 1968.

Gil, David G., and Noble, John H.: Public knowledge. Attitudes and Opinions About Physical Child Abuse in the United States, No. 14 Papers in Social Welfare, Waltham, Brandeis U., Sept. 1967.

Gill, Thomas D.: The legal nature of neglect. Nat Prob Parole Assoc J, 6:1-18, Jan. 1960.

Harper, Fowler V.: The physician, the battered child, and the law. Pediatrics, 31:899-902, 1963.

Health, Education, and Welfare Trends. U.S. Department of Health, Education, and Welfare, 1960.

Homicide by starvation—The nutritional varient of the battered child. JAMA, 186:104-106, 1963.

Jacobziner, Harold: Rescuing the battered child. Amer J Nurs, 64:2-17, 1964.

Kaplan, Morris: Deaths of young studied by city. New York Times, May 5, 1962.

Kempe, C. Henry, et al.: The battered child syndrome. JAMA, 181:17-24, 1962.

Kvaraceus, William C.: Delinquent behavior and church attendance. Sociol Soc Res, SSVIII, March-April 1944.

Leserman, Sidney: There's a murder in my waiting room. Med Economics, 41:62-71, 1964.

McCort, J., et al.: Visceral injuries in battered children. Radiology, 82:424-428, 1964.

Miller, Donald S.: Fractures among children. Minn Med, 42:1209-1213, 1959; 42:1414-1425, 1959.

Mintz, A. A.: Battered child syndrome. Texas Med, 80:107-108, 1964.

Morris, Marian G., and Gould, Robert W.: Role reversal: A necessary concept in dealing with the battered child syndrome, Amer J Orthopsychiat, 33:298-299, 1963.

Myren, Richard A., and Swanson, Lynn D.: Police Work With Children. U.S. Department of Health, Education, and Welfare, Children's Bureau, 1962.

National Study Service (Final Report): Planning for the Protection and Care of Neglected Children in California. Sacramento, State Social Welfare Board and Calif. Delinq. Prev. Comm., August 1965.

O'Doherty, N. J.: Subdural hematoma in battered babies. Develop Med Child Neurol, 6:192-193, 1964.

Oettinger, Katherine B.: Protecting children from abuse. Parents, 39:11-12, 1964.

Pfundt, T. R.: The problem of the battered child. Post Grad Med, 35:426-431, 1964.

Piliavin, Irwing and Briar, Scott: Police Encounters With Juveniles. Survey Research Center and Center for the Study of Law and Society, Berkeley, U. of Calif., 1964.

Platou, R. V.: Battering. Bull Tulane Med Fac, 23:157-165, 1964.

Protective Services for Children. Report of the Assembly Interim Committee on Social Welfare. Sacramento, Assembly of the State of Calif., Jan. 1967.

Reinhart, J. B., et al.: The abused child: Mandatory reporting legislation. JAMA, 188:358-362, 1964.

Report of meeting on, Physical Abuse of Infants and Young Children. Basic provisions of needed state legislation, U. S. Department of Health, Education, and Welfare, Children's Bureau, May 25, 1962.

Rubin, Jean: The need for intervention. Pub Welfare, July 1966.

Schloesser, Patricia T.: The abused child. Bull Menninger Clin, 28:260-268, 1964.

Schmideberg, M.: Tolerance in upbringing and its abuses. Int J Soc Psychiat, 5:123-130, 1959.

Schrotel, S. R.: Responsibilities of physicians in suspected cases of brutality. Cincinnati J Med, 42:406-407, 1961.

Silver, Henry K., and Kempe, C. Henry: The problem of parental criminal neglect and severe physical abuse of children. Amer J Dis Child, 98:528, 1959.

Silverman, F. N.: The roentgenographic manifestations of unrecognized skeletal trauma in infants. Amer J Roentgen, 69:413-427, 1953.

Swanson, Lynn D.: Role of the police in the protection of children from neglect and abuse. Fed Prob, 25:43-48, 1961.

Tentative Summary of Child Abuse Reports Received From States Between January 1, 1967 and December 31, 1967. The Florence Heller Graduate School for Advanced Studies in Social Welfare, Nationwide Epidemiologic Study of Child Abuse (Children's Bureau Grant No. H-83, Waltham, Brandeis U. 1968.

Toby, Jackson: The differential impact of family organization. Amer Soc Rev, 22, No. 5, 1957.

Wooley, P. V., Jr.: The pediatricians and the young child subjected to repeated physical abuse. J Ped, 62:628-630, 1963.

CALIFORNIA STATE LAWS
FOR THE PROTECTION OF CHILDREN

THE PENAL CODE OF CALIFORNIA
PART I. CRIMES AND PUNISHMENTS

Title VIII. Crimes Against the Person

Chapter 9. Assault and Battery

Section 240. Assault defined. An assault is an unlawful attempt, coupled with a present ability, to commit a violent injury on the person of another.

Section 242. Battery defined. A battery is any willful and unlawful use of force or violence upon the person of another.

Title IX. Crimes Against the Person and Against
Public Decency and Good Morals

Chapter 2. Abandonment and Neglect of Children

Section 272. *Contributing to delinquency of a minor.* Penalty. Every person who commits any act or omits the performance of any duty, which act or omission causes or tends to cause or encourage any person under the age of 21 years to come within the provisions of Sections 600, 601, or 602 of the Welfare and Institutions Code or which act or omission contributes thereto, or any person who, by any act or omission, or by threats, commands, or persuasion, induces or endeavors to induce any person under the age of 21 years or any ward or dependent child of the juvenile court to fail or refuse to conform to a lawful order of the juvenile court, or to do or to perform any act or to follow any course of conduct or to so live as would cause or manifestly tend to cause any such person to become or to remain a person within the provisions of Sections 600, 601, or 602 of the Welfare and Institutions Code, is guilty of a misdemeanor and upon conviction thereof shall be punished by a fine not exceeding one thousand dollars ($1,000), or by imprisonment in the county jail for not more than one year, or by both such fine and imprisonment in a county jail, or may be released on probation for a period not exceeding five years. The district attorney shall prosecute all violations charged under this section.--Stats. 1961, Chap. 1616.

Section 273a. *Willful abuse or injury to person or health of child.*

(1) Any person who, under circumstances or conditions likely to produce great bodily harm or death, willfully causes or permits any child to suffer, or inflicts thereon unjustifiable physical pain or mental suffering, or having the care or custody of any child, willfully causes or permits the person or health of such child to be injured, or willfully causes or permits such child to be placed in such situation that its person or health is endangered, is punishable by imprisonment in the county jail not exceeding one year, or in the state prison for not less than one year nor more than ten years.

(2) Any person who, under circumstances or conditions other than those likely to produce great bodily harm or death, willfully causes or permits any child to suffer, or inflicts thereon unjustifiable physical pain or mental suffering, or having the care or custody of any child, willfully causes or permits the person or health of such child to be injured, or willfully causes or permits such child to be placed in such situation that its person or health may be endangered, is guilty of a misdemeanor.--Stats. 1965, Chap. 697.

Section 273d. *Corporal Injury to Wife or Child.* Punishment. Any husband who willfully inflicts upon his wife corporal injury resulting in a traumatic condition, or any person who willfully inflicts upon any child any cruel or inhuman corporal punishment or injury resulting in a traumatic condition is guilty of a felony, and upon conviction thereof shall be punished by imprisonment in the state prison for not more than ten years or in the county jail for not more than one year.--Stats. 1965, Chap. 1271

Section 273g. *Immoral practices in presence of children.* Any person who in the presence of any child indulges in any degrading, lewd, immoral or vicious habits or practices, or who is habitually drunk in the presence of any child in his care, custody or control, is guilty of a misdemeanor.--1907.

Title XV. Miscellaneous Crimes

Chapter 2. Other and Miscellaneous Offenses

Section 650½. *Injuring person or property of another.* A person who willfully and wrongfully commits any act which seriously injures the person or property of another . . . . is guilty of a misdemeanor.--1921.

PART IV. PREVENTION OF CRIMES AND APPREHENSION OF CRIMINALS

Title I. Investigation and Control of Crimes and Criminals

Chapter 2. Article 2. Reports of Injuries by Hospitals

Section 11160. *Wounds and injuries to be reported by hospital.* Every person, firm or corporation conducting any hospital or pharmacy in the state, or the managing agent thereof, or the person managing or in charge of such hospital or pharmacy, or in charge of any ward or part of such hospital to which any person suffering from any wound or other injury inflicted by his own act or by the act of another by means of a knife, gun, pistol, or other deadly weapon, or in cases where injuries have been inflicted upon any person in violation of any penal law of this state shall come or be brought, shall report the same immediately, both by telephone and in writing, to the chief of police, city marshal, town marshal or other head of the police department of any city, city and county, town or municipal corporation of this state, or to the sheriff, if such hospital or pharmacy is located outside the incorporated limits of a city, town or other municipal corporation. The report shall state the name of the injured person, if known, his whereabouts and the character and extent of his injuries. Stats. 1953, Chap. 34.

Section 11161. *Wounds or injuries to be reported by physician.* Every physician or surgeon who has under his charge or care any person suffering from any wound or injury inflicted in the manner specified in Section 11160 shall make a report of the kind specified in this article to the appropriate officers named in Section 11160. Stats. 1953, Chap. 34.

Section 11161.5 *Reports of injuries to minors.* In any case in which a minor is brought to a physician and surgeon, dentist, resident, intern, or chiropractor, for prognosis, examination or treatment, or is under his charge or care, and it appears to the physician and surgeon, dentist, resident, intern, chiropractor, or religious practitioner from observation of the minor that the minor has physical injury or injuries which appear to have been inflicted upon him by other than accidental means by any person, he shall report such fact by telephone and in writing to the head of the police department, the sheriff or the district attorney. The report shall state, if known, the name of the minor, his whereabouts and the character and extent of the injuries.

No physician and surgeon, dentist, resident, intern, chiropractor, or religious practitioner shall incur any civil or criminal liability as a result of making any report authorized by this section.

Copies of all written reports received by the head of a city police department, sheriff or district attorney shall be forwarded to the state bureau of criminal identification and investigation. If the records of the bureau of criminal identification and investigation maintained pursuant to Section 1110 reveal any reports of suspected infliction of physical injury upon the same minor or upon any other minor in the same family by other than accidental means, or if the records reveal any arrest or conviction in other localities for a violation of Section 273a inflicted upon the same minor or any other minor in the same family, or if the records reveal any other pertinent information with respect to the same minor or any other minor in the same family; the city police, sheriff or district attorney shall be immediately notified of the fact.

Reports and other pertinent information received from the bureau shall be made available to any licensed physician and surgeon, dentist, resident, intern, chiropractor, religious practitioner, or probation department, and to any agency offering child protective services--Added Stats. 1965, Chap. 1171.

Section 11162. *Violation: Penalty.* Any person, firm or corporation violating any provision of this article is guilty of a misdemeanor and is punishable by imprisonment in the county jail not exceeding six months or by a fine not exceeding five hundred dollars ($500), or by both.--Stats. 1953, Chap. 34.

WELFARE AND INSTITUTION'S CODE AND
LAWS RELATING TO SOCIAL WELFARE
DIVISION 2. CHILDREN

Part I. Delinquents and Wards of the Juvenile Court

Article 5. Jurisdiction

Section 600. *Who is in the jurisdiction of the court defined.* Any person under the age of twenty-one years who comes within any of the following descriptions is within the jurisdiction of the juvenile court which may adjudge such person to be a dependent child of the court:

(a) Who is in need of proper and effective parental care or control and has no parent or guardian, or has no parent or guardian willing to exercise or capable of exercising such care or control, or has no parent or guardian actually exercising such care or control.

(b) Who is destitute, or who is not provided with the necessities of life, or who is not provided with a home or suitable place or abode, or whose home is an unfit place for him by reason of neglect, cruelty, or depravity or either of his parents, or his guardian or other person in whose custody or care he is.

(c) Who is physically dangerous to the public because of a mental or physical deficiency, disorder or abnormality.--Stats. 1965, Chap. 535.

DIVISION 9. STATE PROTECTIVE SERVICES FOR CHILDREN
Part 4

Chapter 5

Section 16500. The state, through the state department of social welfare and county welfare departments, shall establish and support a public system of statewide child protective services to be developed as rapidly as possible and to be available in each county of the state. All counties or combinations of counties shall establish specialized units of protective services for children.

Section 16501. As used in this chapter, child protective services shall include casework and related services designed to forestall or reduce the need for action by law enforcement agencies, probation departments and courts, and to render these services in behalf of children who are without parents, proper guardianship, or custody, or who are being neglected or whose general welfare is being damaged by the conduct of parents, guardians, or custodians, whether willfully or otherwise.

A child protective services program shall receive any referral or complaint from a public or private agency or from any person having reasonable cause to know that the welfare of a child is endangered, and shall take such actions as are considered necessary to protect the child and correct the situation, including but not limited to:

(A) Social services to children, parent, parents, or guardian.

(b) Financial assistance as may be required, within the scope of this code.

(c) Alternate care of the child if care outside the home is required, such as institutional care, foster care, and day care.

(d) Referral to law enforcement agency for investigation.

Section 16502. The child protective services authorized by this chapter shall be established in any county or combination of counties when a plan which includes financing of such services has been certified by the department. Such certified plan of child protective services shall then be operated in accordance with standards and regulations established by the department, subject to all the provisions of this code relating to the supervision of public social services by the department.

Section 16502.5. As used in this chapter, "child protective services" means public social services which supplement, or substitute for, parental care and supervision for the purpose of preventing or remedying, or assisting in the solution of problems which may result in, the neglect, abuse, exploitation, or delinquency of children, protecting and caring for homeless, dependent, or neglected children, protecting and promoting the welfare of children of working mothers, and otherwise protecting and promoting the welfare of children, including the strengthening of their own homes where possible or, where needed, the provision of adequate care of children away from their homes in foster family homes or day-care or other childcare facilities.

Section 16503. As used in this chapter, "the department" means the State Department of Social Welfare.

Section 16504. Protective services shall be extended to every child in need of protection, regardless of family income.

Section 16505. The services offered to families under this program shall be voluntary.

Section 16506. This chapter shall not be construed to give the department or county welfare departments any law enforcement powers.

Nothing in this chapter shall not be construed in such a manner as to give the department any law enforcement powers, nor to change or interfere with the responsibility of law enforcement, probation officers and departments to take direct action on behalf of children as provided in Article 6 (commencing with Section 625) of Chapter 2 of Part 1 and Article 7 (commencing with Section 650), of Chapter 2 of Part 1 of Division 2. Nor shall this part in any way relieve persons administering and working in child protective services programs from the obligation resting on all citizens to report crimes to duly authorized law enforcement agencies. Further it is the purpose of this part to supplement and not supplant existing services for children by the addition of state protective services for children, and nothing herein shall be construed as changing in any way the responsibility of probation officers and departments for initiating juvenile court proceedings as set forth in Article 7 (commencing with Section 650), of Chapter 2 of Part 1 of Division 2, nor other duties and responsibilities assigned to them by law.

Section 16507. The department shall report annually to the Legislature on the operation and progress of the protective services program.

Section 16508. Notwithstanding any other provision of this chapter, no child who in good faith is under treatment solely by spiritual means through prayer in accordance with the tenets and practices of a recognized church or religious denomination by a duly accredited practitioner thereof shall, for that reason alone, be considered to have been neglected within the purview of this chapter.

Section 16509. Anyone participating in good faith in the making of a report pursuant to this chapter shall have immunity from any liability, civil or criminal, that might otherwise be incurred or imposed. Any such participant shall have the same immunity with respect to participation in any judicial proceeding resulting from such report.

Section 16510. Services for children who qualify as actual or potential recipients of public assistance under aid to families with dependent children shall be financed as a regular part of the administration of that program.

Section 16511. Services for children not qualifying under Section 16510 shall be financed from federal funds allocated to the state for child welfare services pursuant to Part B of Title 4 of the Social Security Act. The department may limit the allocation of child welfare service funds in the following manner: (1) If Congress does not increase the appropriation for child welfare service funds the department may then limit the allocation specifically for protective services to the same proportion of the federal grant as obtained for the 1967-68 fiscal year. (2) If and during such times as the federal government increases the allocation of child welfare services to the state, all of the increased funds resulting from this action shall be devoted to providing protective services for children who do not qualify for service under Section 16510; provided, however, the department shall be permitted to allocate sufficient funds to the development of other aspects of child welfare services in order that the state remain eligible to receive funds pursuant to Part B of Title 4 of the Social Security Act.

Sec. 2. Nothing in this act shall preclude the Legislature from adopting other priorities for the use of child welfare service funds as may be set forth in the Budget Act.

EMERGENCY HOMEMAKER SERVICE

For many years the welfare department has provided placement in emergency homes for children picked up by law enforcement for protective care and supervision. However, it has become increasingly difficult to recruit and keep enough emergency homes to serve this purpose and we have at times been unable to provide emergency placement for children.

For this reason, effective July 15, 1968, the welfare department will provide emergency homemaker services in those instances in which law enforcement officers deem it appropriate and preferable to removing children from their homes temporarily. This service could hopefully be used in some situations in which children have been left alone unsupervised and protection must be provided until the parents are located and a decision made regarding the action to be taken. Another instance might be one in which the only parent in the home is or should be jailed for a short time, and there are no relatives to supervise the children.

These situations could occur during the day or at night, and of course the final decision might be removal of the children and foster home placement. However, the homemaker service could prevent abrupt removal and/or removal of children during the night and would allow some time to prepare the children and to arrange for their placement. This would be less frightening and less damaging to the children and could avoid the disruption for children who would be returned home within a very short period of time. It would at the same time alleviate some of the problem around lack of space in emergency homes.

At the present time three homemakers will be available. Because this is a new program and we do not know what the demands will be, the service will be limited to the metropolitan area of Fresno at this time.

Procedures

1. Law enforcement officers called to investigate situations involving children left alone, etc. will make the decision as to whether or not emergency homemaker could be utilized.
2. If an emergency homemaker is to be requested, the officer will contact the child welfare representative to confirm that a homemaker is available at that time and give the necessary information for assignment.
3. The officer will then obtain an order from the juvenile court judge ordering the placement of a homemaker in the home (printed forms to be provided by the department of public welfare). The judge has requested that the order be brought to his home for his signature nights, week ends and holidays. If the judge is not available, the juvenile court referee will sign the order. If he, too, should be unavailable, the order will be signed by any one of the other superior court judges.
4. An officer will meet the homemaker when she arrives at the home, and will leave with her a copy of the order authorizing her presence and care of the children.
5. Officer will check the neighborhood periodically during the night while the homemaker is on duty. If the parents return, the homemaker will advise them of her position and assignment for protection of the children, but will refer all other questions to the officer. If the parents return the officer might decide to dismiss the homemaker and leave the children in the care of the parents. If there is no phone in the home, the officer checking the situation would need to arrange to have a taxi called for the homemaker's departure.
6. The officers will need to keep the department of public welfare informed of the follow-up, disposition of matter, release of or continued need of homemaker, etc.

INDEX